W9-BRD-126

Lies We Live By

Lies We Live By

Defeating Double-Talk and Deception in Advertising, Politics, and the Media

CARL HAUSMAN

Routledge
New York   London

Published in 2000 by
Routledge
29 West 35th Street
New York, NY 10001

Published in Great Britain by
Routledge
11 New Fetter Lane
London EC4P 4EE

Copyright © 2000 by Routledge

Printed in the United States of America on acid-free paper.

All rights reserved. No part of this book may be
reprinted or reproduced or utilized in any form or by
any electronic, mechanical, or other means, now
known or hereafter invented, including photocopying
and recording, or in any information storage or
retrieval system, without permission in writing from
the publisher.

10 9 8 7 6 5 4 3 2 1

Library of Congress Cataloging-in-Publication Data

Hausman, Carl, 1953–
    Lies we live by : defeating double-talk and deception in
advertising, politics, and the media / Carl Hausman.
        p. cm.
    Includes bibliographical references and index.
    ISBN 0-415-92280-1 (hc)
    1. Decetion. 2. Truthfulness and falsehood. I. Title.
BF637.D42 H68 2000
177'.3—dc21   99-049263

Contents!

Acknowledgments!

Many people contributed ideas and inspiration to this book, although I confidently state that all mistakes are mine alone.

Thanks first to my editor, Melissa Rosati, who helped conceive the idea, and to the editorial and production staff at Routledge who turned this into a book.

Among those who helped provide ideas for the book are Mike Ludlum, Steve Flanders, Toni Libro, Bill Burrows, Henry Schulte, Philip Benoit, Richard Petrow, and Sherry Hausman.

A word of thanks must go to the authors whose work has helped me form a more complete view of the world as one built with words and images: Neil Postman, Kathleen Hall Jamieson, Darrell Huff, Arthur R. Miller, and Daniel Boorstin.

Finally, my gratitude goes to Nina Graybill, whom I nominate as the World's Best Agent; she combines legal and business acumen with superhuman patience when dealing with the World's Most Difficult Client.

Lies We Live By
Is Destined to Be the Number 1 Bestseller by Carl Hausman!*

*Sorry, I just lied to you. But I also told the truth, and that illustrates the problem. You thought I meant "the number one bestseller" on the *New York Times* list, didn't you? Sorry . . . I meant that the book will be the number one bestselling book written by Carl Hausman. And frankly, the income from my previous books is not something Alan Greenspan considers when plotting the course of the economy. In any event, if I'm wrong about my projected sales figures, blame destiny. You can't blame me, because my proclamation is so broad and inflated that I really can't be held to any specific meaning.

Welcome to the world of double-talk, fine print, verbal loopholes, phony statistics, and other half-truths that have become coin of the realm in commerce and government. *Lies We Live By* exposes these outrages of everyday life—*your* everyday life. Make no mistake about it, you have been mugged by manipulation if you have:

- Felt safer on the streets of your hometown because police officials mutated the definition of a "crime" so that they could lower the "crime rate."
- Signed up for a credit card where hidden charges are buried in the fine print.

- Paid tuition to a college that inflates its average SAT scores by not counting certain groups of students with low scores.
- Visited an auto showroom after seeing an ad for a"zero down" lease, when all sorts of up-front charges were cloaked in fine print or jabbered incomprehensibly in the closing micro-seconds of a radio commercial.
- Voted for a politician who mischaracterizes his opponent's record by deliberately misleading you with juxtaposed visual images.
- Shopped at a store that imaginatively uses an asterisk to mod-ify the meaning of its claim that "all" merchandise is on sale.

These and other tactics are detailed in the three sections of this book.

The first part of *Lies We Live By* provides a crash course in how to hoodwink with half-truths, fallacious arguments, veiled facts, misleading graphics, and tortured statistics. I have divided these strategies into basic techniques that are easily remembered, decoded, and, eventually, short-circuited.

The second part of the book, beginning with chapter 4, is a rogues gallery of institutions and businesses that flagrantly and repeatedly mutate and mutilate the truth. We'll demonstrate, for example, the industry-specific methods used by credit card com-panies, government agencies, auto salespeople, colleges, advertis-ers, and politicians.

The third part is a guide for would-be guerrillas in the war for information integrity. I provide ten checklists for decoding propa-ganda, interacting with the news, and figuring out the intent behind a message. I also show how to complain and where to seek redress when you think someone is hoodwinking you with half-truths.

Of course, not everyone lies. But it's my belief that today's climate of spin, fine print, and verbal chicanery is profoundly corrosive to the quality of our lives and to what passes for national discourse. Honest communicators are put at a competitive disadvantage. And in the long run we have ceded—by default—our commercial and civic conversations to professional dissemblers.

Your first reaction to my claim that we're being inundated by half-truths might be, "So what else is new?" And you have a point: persuasion has been a fact of life since Eve convinced Adam to change his dietary habits, and much of the arsenal of persuasion was forged by tricksters. Rhetoric, the art and science of persua-sion, originated in ancient Greece and Rome, and it was a practical necessity because, in most cases, you had to represent yourself in court. There were some Greeks known as Sophists who were pretty good at rhetoric, so skilled in fact, that Plato accused them of trickery, of using hollow words to make an empty case. Plato's smear stuck, but word roots in our modern language retain a clue to the ambivalence we hold for tricky persuasiveness. On one hand, someone who is knowledgeable and expressive is *sophisticated*, but someone who earns vacuous debating points is guilty of *sophistry*.

Rhetoric was the core of education throughout the Middle Ages, but before there was a system of mass media persuasion could only be carried out by personal contact or a movement that rallied around a powerful symbol. Organized religion used both methods, and proselytes put some thought into methods of spreading their message effectively. The modern term "propaganda" comes from a Latin phrase meaning "congregation for propagation of the faith."

But when the printing press was perfected in the late 1400s everything changed. Anyone who could afford the price of hiring a printer could propagate a message, and many of the first uses of the press were blatantly commercial and more than a little misleading. For example, Christopher Columbus printed brochures describing the glut of gold in the New World and circulated them in advance of his fund-raising trips throughout Europe. Columbus was pretty elastic with the truth, but the rulers of Spain—desperately in hock because of their wasteful wars—fell for the sales pitch and sent Columbus to the New World, hoping he would return with boatloads of gold and spices.

We've been suckers for half-truths ever since. The first ad printed in the United States was published in the *Boston News-Letter* in 1704 and was an ad for a patent medicine of dubious value. The American Revolution was inspired in part by pamphlets and polemics that were at times overheated and one-sided—but incredibly widely read. One hundred thousand copies of Thomas Paine's *Common Sense* were printed in 1776—one for every twenty-five colonists.

You could make a case that the Civil War was sparked in part by an inflammatory book that took some liberties with factuality, *Uncle Tom's Cabin*. None other than Abraham Lincoln credited the book with playing a part in the war. He once patted the novel's author, Harriet Beecher Stowe, on the head and proclaimed, "So you're the little woman who started this big war." (Luckily for Lincoln, he did not have to deal with the National Organization for Women or cable talk show hosts.)

After the Civil War, the media industry mushroomed. At the same time, there was an explosion in commerce. As a result advertising and public relations both emerged as thriving industries. The details are recounted elsewhere in this book, but the essential point is that the late 1800s were a particularly rotten time in our history, with industry grinding the common man in its gears and commerce descending into a buyer-beware free-for-all.

The muckraking media, along with politicians like Theodore Roosevelt, led a revolt. Investigative magazines ran features on the crooked dealings of John D. Rockefeller and on products such as lead-based mascara, which made women's eyelashes look beautiful but, unfortunately, also made women go blind. Government attacked abusive businesses and passed a variety of legislation, including antitrust laws and the Pure Food and Drug Act of 1906.

Business interests fought back using the very press that had attacked them. Corporate leaders hired ex-reporters to generate favorable stories and put favorable spin on bad news. The "public relations" industry, or PR industry as it has come to be known, began manufacturing news, staging events that had no real substance but which attracted media coverage.

4 Politicians, never ones to shirk from stealing a good idea, soon adopted PR as their own. This wasn't an entirely new phenomenon. As far back as 1833, Andrew Jackson hired a former newspaperman to spruce up his plebeian image and convince the public he was good enough to hobnob with aristocrats. But in the twentieth century, the government used PR systematically to help wage war. World War I and World War II saw massive and sophisticated public relations efforts. During World War II, Franklin Roosevelt mastered the finer points of cultivating the press, holding regular press conferences with a small coterie of reporters, whom he would cut off at the knees if they behaved badly. Roosevelt used the press to test public opinion. He invented the concept of leaking an unattributed story to test public reaction. If reaction was unfavorable, he would disavow the story. The "trial balloon" remains a popular and effective tactic today.

World War II diverted attention from the development of television, but after the war research once again focused on this new device. Within a decade, TV was well on its way to becoming the most pervasive of all media. Advertising dollars began to shift to television. Politicians became almost completely beholden to the medium, an example of what media critic Neil Postman calls the "ecological" change brought about by technology and media. What Postman meant was that the whole system changed. By the 1960s we didn't have an American political system *plus* television, we had a *completely different* system. In the same way that destruction of mosquitoes creates an ecological change in the environment by starving the fish who feed on the mosquitoes and, in turn, starving the bears who feed on the fish, media change everything ecologically in unexpected ways, ways we often cannot see unless we step back and view them from a distance.

All of this bears directly on where we are today. We live in a media-driven society fueled by consumption which, in turn, is fueled by advertising. Our decisions—about what to buy, whom to vote for—are shaped, in large part, by an ecological system of persuasion. Persuasion has grown into a serious and sophisticated business and has interwoven itself into the fabric of society—so much so that we're sometimes not quite sure what's "real" and what's "made up." When a presidential candidate visits a flag factory, wraps himself in the flag, and says, "flag sales are doing well, and America is doing well," did something really *happen*? It made the news, but again, did something really *happen*?

Even though we're infinitely more sophisticated technologically today than we were a hundred years ago, there's still something of the sophist in us. It's hard to pass up the chance to tell a compelling half-truth or to stage a convincing pseudo-event.

This book tells the whole story behind half-truths. It examines the nature of information and the difference between what we know and what we think we know. As such, it is more than a consumer manual. While the book looks at the specific techniques used to persuade and sometimes to hoodwink, it also deals with what we might call "information literacy," the ability to cope with the avalanche of out-of-context and often misleading fact and factoids that assaults us every day.

Chapter One

Term Warfare

How to Lie with Words

 When Bill Clinton was asked in 1992 if he'd ever smoked marijuana, he told reporters that he had never broken the laws of his country. That sounded like "no," but of course it wasn't. When the press finally decoded the evasion, Clinton admitted that he'd smoked marijuana in England, although he (ahem) never inhaled.

That was the tee shot for a Master's Tournament of presidential wordplay. Over the next seven years, Clinton responded to allegations of an affair with a denial of the *duration* of the affair, making that denial sound like a denial of the affair itself, and secured his place in history by inventing a definition of the mechanics of sexual relations that we'll mercifully skip here.

During roughly the same period, evasive wordplay seemed to become the method of choice for a variety of people who had a vested interest in clouding the truth. In general, advertising, public relations, and political communication in the late 1990s have deteriorated to a blur of mouse type and stilted wordings constructed to pry open loopholes. Perhaps the 1990s will be known as the decade of doublespeak. Or maybe the fact that a president was impeached partly on the basis of prevarication will mark 1999 as the year the backlash took hold.

Interestingly, those of us in the business of decoding chisel-speak and propaganda feel vindicated! (And even, dare I say, *useful*.) The victims we used to corner at cocktail parties and pummel glassy-eyed with our theories about the mechanics of language now seek us out. How, they wonder, can a long-distance company get away with burying hidden charges in a slag-heap of tricky wording? Why, they lament, do the claims of our elected leaders so often dissolve into muddy puddles of prevarication?

The answer is that we've trained liars to exploit us by rewarding them with our money, or our votes, or both. The industries of influence—honest, dishonest, and in the gray area—are huge, and when we make decisions we're up against a well-financed army of persuaders.

Liars climbing up the learning curve discovered that we've become too time-starved to untangle complex claims, and so accustomed to being lied to that we reflexively roll over and expose our bellies when confronted with misleading information. That's the bad news.

The good news is that, like the anchorman in *Network*, we're mad as hell and we won't take it any more. Look around: People are fed up with tricky tacked-on fees that double their car-rental bill, or 10-10 telephone numbers that use evasive language to hide the fact that, in all but a very specific set of conditions, their rates are among the highest in the Wild West of telecommunications. We're exasperated by credit card companies that bury expensive interest rate changes in the fine print, stores that claim big discounts derived from "suggested" prices that no one ever really pays, hotel chains that offer attractive weekend packages "from" $40 a night, but offer that price only in one hotel, in a small city, where very few travelers would want to go, and merchandisers who imply their products are American-made when, in fact, they are not.

I have even better news. *Decoding half-truths is easy.* All you have to do is learn how the chiselers do it and adjust your defense accordingly, in much the same way you install a deadbolt after a reformed burglar shows you how to slip a cheap lock with a credit card.

I've attempted to separate the techniques of lying into three categories: lying with words, lying with numbers, and lying with images. Each category has about a half-dozen techniques. While there are many other variations on each theme, I'm going to keep my set of terms simple because a complex collection would be too cumbersome to be of practical use. While these categories are my own inventions, note that they do reflect techniques identified in the formal study of propaganda, logic, and critical thought.

Words are tricky devices because a) they carry bulky baggage, and b) English is a sloppy language. The first point relates to the fact that a word carries a literal meaning and an implied meaning. The words "liberal" and "conservative" are perfect examples, because they often lose all meaning when someone uses them to describe someone else—turning the words into weapons. When a political candidate sneers that his opponent is a "liberal," we're not sure exactly what it means but we know it's not good (especially if it's accompanied by a modifier like "card-carrying"). And when someone calls someone else a "conservative," what he usually is insinuating is that that person is a "neanderthal." In this way, words convey simple, but misleading, meanings and when directed at uncritical readers or listeners their effect is very powerful. Our side is made up of "freedom fighters." Their side consists of "terrorists."

Words can sound sinister and be used to bolster a point even when there is no literal meaning attached to them. When I was in elementary school during the height of the Cold War our teacher read us stories about the terrors of communism. One particularly vivid passage detailed how political dissidents were taken to party headquarters to face God-knows-what in "closed cars." Because I was already a difficult person, I asked my teacher what a "closed car" was. With the windows closed? With the *doors* closed? Don't most drivers keep the *doors* closed when they drive? My teacher was annoyed and more than a little flummoxed. She told the class she didn't know exactly what the reference meant, but that I should have sense enough to know that it's something *bad*.

As for English being a sloppy language, consider Hamlet's needling of Ophelia:

H: Lady, shall I lie in your lap?
O: No, my lord.
H: I mean my head upon your lap?
O: Ay, my lord.
H: Do you think I meant country matters?
O: I think nothing my lord.
H: That's a fair thought to lie between
   maid's legs.

Puns, wordplay, and double-entendres exploit the elastic meanings and relationships between English words. Shakespearean wordplay would be meaningless in some other languages. But what's good for sarcasm is bad for accuracy, and the same elasticity that allows for puns also opens the door to obfuscation.

With those points in mind, let's look at how language can be used to mislead.

Technique #1: The Tortured Definition

The strategy used here is to get around telling the truth by *redefining one of the words that determines the truth*. Torturing a definition is a powerful strategy because people usually don't check all the premises on which you've based your argument, and if they do—and you're caught—you can always claim honesty because the results actually do follow from your mutated definition.

That is precisely the strategy Bill Clinton followed in redefining that particular act we are not going to talk about. But since this is a family-oriented book, I will illustrate the tortured definition with a Macy's ad. Macy's has a habit of imaginatively redefining key words in its newspaper ads. You'll notice in figure 1.1 that the big type trumpets savings of "20–50% OFF ALL* JEWELRY." I trust you did not miss the distinction between ALL and ALL*. In the fine print we learn that ALL* jewelry means everything except "best values, watches, fashion jewelry, bonus dollars off sale prices."

Another ad offers (in the big type) "20% off merchandise STOREWIDE." But check out the fine print in figure 1.2! The definition of storewide is considerably narrowed in the mousetype. The offer excludes entire departments, including designer cosmetics, fragrances, handbags, furniture, and women's shoes; entire lines of clothing collections, such as Levi's; and complete categories of merchandise, including watches and fashion jewelry. No doubt about it, that's a pretty confusing ad. But I'm sure that there was no intent to mislead here and that Macy's is completely HONEST*

*if you define being honest as running an ad that excludes a hell of a lot of stuff in the fine print.

My personal favorite in the tortured definition category is the imaginative signs posted by some gas stations on Long Island offering gas for $1.06 a gallon. When motorists attracted by the bargain pull in and ask for the attendant to fill the tank with "regular" they get a more expensive gas. The $1.06 stuff is called "economy" or some other made-up name that you don't get unless you ask for it

10

LAST 2 DAYS! DIAMOND 20%-50% OFF ALL* JEWELRY

SALE

SAVINGS OFF REG. PRICES. *DOES NOT INCLUDE BEST VALUES, WATCHES, FASHION JEWELRY, INC JEWELRY, BONUS DOLLARS OFF SALE PRICES; REFLECTED IN PRICES SHOWN. DOES NOT APPLY TO BEST VALUES, SUPER BUYS, PRICE BREAKS, FASHION JEWELRY, WATCHES, STERLING SILVER AND 18K GOLD OVER STERLING.

BONUS DOLLARS OFF THROUGHOUT OUR JEWELRY DEPARTMENT

Figure 1.1: Macy's ad touting "20–50% OFF ALL* JEWELRY."

Figure 1.2: Macy's ad claiming "20% off merchandise
STOREWIDE."

12

and, of course, nobody does. (The Nassau county legislature
recently passed a bill outlawing this practice.)

Torturing a definition is a vastly useful technique, and we'll
examine its application in many of the industry-specific chapters in
the second part of this book. (Wait until you find out how stores
define "American-made.")

Technique #2: Reduction to the Ridiculous

To use this technique, *oversimplify an issue to the point of absurdity and then point out the absurdity of the resulting oversimplifi-
cation.* With this strategy you can completely mischaracterize an

action or opposing point of view, while still claiming a basis in fact. Moreover, you can pull this off while making yourself appear analytical.

New Jersey Senator Frank Lautenberg used a classic reduction strategy against his 1994 election opponent, State Assembly Speaker Chuck Haytayan. Briefly, the story is this: Haytayan, along with many others in the assembly, voted for construction of a $28.6 million underground parking garage at the Trenton, New Jersey, State House. The garage was built to provide parking for state lawmakers, the press, and members of the public who visit the State House and the adjacent library and museum. The complex also included some office space and a generating plant.

To make a long story short—and that's the problem with the whole truth, it tends to be the long version of events—Lautenberg took the cost of the garage and dividing it by the number of parking spaces came up with the figure of $26,000. Lautenberg then used that figure to imply that Haytayan had gratuitously built himself a $26,000 parking space. TV ads showed a head shot of Haytayan with the caption "Politics as usual," and another caption, "$26 thousand for a parking space."

Reduction strategies are particularly useful in politics because they provide a shorthand, bumper-sticker recounting of events, and take a grain of out-of-context truth and puff it into a dune of duplicity. Did your opponent vote against any bill that contained a provision that could be viewed as beneficial to children? If so, characterize your opponent as anti-child. In a particularly ironic juxtaposition based on this strategy, Bill Clinton characterized Bob Dole as being against the elderly because Dole voted against Medicare. The annoyingly detailed long version was that Dole *did* initially vote against Medicare because his party was advocating a competing, but basically similar plan, called Eldercare. When Medicare won the battle of the plans and worked its way into conference committee, Dole voted for it. But the damage had been done.

13

Technique 3: The Evil-Twin Word Substitution

In this technique, *you confuse people with a similar-sounding word.* You either benefit directly from the confusion or use the technique to mischaracterize someone else's position.

Evil-Twin name deceptions are effective because we are so inundated with names of people and organizations that they all sound pretty much alike. One enterprising reptile in California exploits this factor with over 200 sound-alike charities registered under his name. He gives them names similar to legitimate charities. When callers who don't know the precise name of the real charity call directory assistance looking for the telephone number, they are often directed to the bogus sound-alike and are squeezed for donations when they call.

Even organizations as moral and high-minded as tobacco companies are not above using the Evil-Twin technique. Big Tobacco recently bankrolled a series of ads opposing a proposed per-pack sales tax on cigarettes. The commercials featured furrowed-browed actors, earnest and troubled, clucking about the proposed "tax on working people." Obviously, one way to interpret that phrase is that the tax is a tax on people who work for a living, a reading that makes marginal sense at best, given that many smokers are unemployed because they can't crawl out of their iron lungs or unhook their life-support systems. But I'm sure the intent of the commercial is to confuse the viewer into believing that the measure is a "tax on working," or an *income tax*, that most hated of all levies.

Believe it or not, even trial lawyers sometimes stretch the truth with an Evil-Twin substitution. One group of liability lawyers gave themselves a high-sounding name that smacked of concerned citizens investigating auto safety. The group staged its own safety tests of a car that conveniently acted in a very unsafe manner when videotaped, and then distributed the tapes to television networks. They then used the network-aired tapes in court when they sued the manufacturer.

Technique #4: The Incognito If

This is probably the most versatile of all verbal deception methods because it can be used to obfuscate the truth in virtually any circumstance. All you need do is *forget to mention one contingency in the sale, agreement, or offer*. If you're caught, you can argue—with some justification—that no ad or offer can reveal every detail. In fact, you can even mention the Incognito If, but entomb it in esoteric contract language, or simply shovel some fine print on top of it.

Incognito Ifs serve the primary function of luring suckers into the tent where the high-pressure sales tactics begin. For example, while on an undercover reporting assignment, I attended a sales pitch for condo time-shares. The initial come-on was this: I had "won" (lucky me) a "free" trip to Europe. All I had to do was attend a "brief orientation to the time-share concept."

The following Incognito Ifs were hidden in the offer:

- While I actually could get a free plane ride to Europe, I had to stay at—and pay full rate for—one of the time-share company's absurdly overpriced hotels.
- I had to provide the time-share company with three time periods over the next year during which I could take a one-week vacation. They would not let me pick one in advance; I had to be prepared to accept one at the last moment.

Given the above conditions it would have been difficult for me to take advantage of my "prize" and expect to do any better than if I'd funded my own last-minute trip to Europe. But for the time-share company, the mission was accomplished: the suckers, myself among them, were lured into the tent, because in order to "win" the contest, you had to endure the entire day's hard-sell. (We only learned of the Incognito Ifs attached to the prize at the end of the session, which incidentally was akin to something inflicted on prisoners of war. We weren't allowed to break for lunch, and the salesman was reluctant to let us out of the room, even when my wife feigned the onset of a diabetic coma.)   ★15★

Here's an Incognito If technique for getting car buyers into the tent. Can you spot the opportunities for slipping an Incognito If into this commercial aired by Nissan?

> They tell me that if I buy the Camry or the Accord, they're gonna give me a hundred dollars. . . . So what's the catch. . . . There's no catch! Just test drive a Nissan Stanza first. No sweat, easiest hundred I ever made, right?

This was part of an ad campaign called the Nissan Challenge, and the real challenge was collecting your hundred dollars. The Federal Trade Commission put a stop to the campaign, pointing out that in order to collect the money, the consumer had to:

a) purchase the Accord or Camry
b) take delivery of it within a week
c) submit proof of the purchase to Nissan within a week

d) *not* buy the Accord or the Camry on the same day as the test drive.[1]

Technique #5: Logical Leapfrog

The study of logic is complex and rigorous, which of course is why no one ever studies it. But at the heart of almost all analyses of misleading pseudo-logic is a concept that's easy to grasp: the phony cause-effect relationship. Repeat after me: *Just because Event A followed event B, this does not necessarily mean that Event A caused Event B.* By the same token: *Just because Event A and Event B are somehow statistically linked, it does not necessarily mean that one causes the other.*

For example, I once covered a local politician's crusade against adult bookstores. I flagged as illogical a statement by the politician that went something like this:

> There had been three rapes in the city last month. Three men arrested in the separate cases had also admitted to frequenting an adult bookstore. If we close the adult bookstore we will reduce rape.

16 Maybe there is a cause-and-effect relationship between adult bookstores and rape; but to infer a cause-and-effect relationship based on happenstance is illogical. (The politician took umbrage at my observation and gave me a taste of Reduction to the Ridiculous when he accused me of "being in favor" of adult bookstores and came damn close to implying that I was a supporter of rape as well.) A more likely assumption is that rapists have a predilection for visiting adult bookstores. That's not the same thing as cause and effect. It's also possible that the events were purely coincidental.

Sometimes there are underlying linkages that seem tantalizingly like cause and effect and, therefore, appear persuasive on the surface. Opponents of capital punishment often point out that murder rates are highest in states with the death penalty, which is true. That *sounds* a lot like saying that capital punishment is not only ineffective, but also contributes to murder. But you might argue that people in states with capital punishment support it in *reaction* to the high murder rates. There's a Latin name for this fallacy: *Post hoc, ergo propter hoc.* This means *after this, therefore because of this* in English, which of course doesn't sound nearly as impressive. Genuine cause-effect relationships certainly do exist, but they're not easy to prove. Cause-effect arguments are also used in statistical pseudo-reasoning, the subject of the next chapter.

But before moving on, let me point out that there are several other ways to use words to evade logic. Testimonials, for example, are often inherently illogical. The presence of a celebrity usually does nothing to bolster a claim, but we're a sucker for celebrity testimonials. Witness the ultimate absurdity of an actor making pseudo-medical claims after informing us that he's not a doctor, but plays one on TV.

A testimonial can rightly be called a propaganda technique, meaning (my definition) the promotion of a point of view using one-sided, illogical, and hollow arguments. Another variety of propaganda is name-calling, a technique used successfully in many political campaigns.

George Bush slyly mated name-calling with the Evil-Twin Word Substitution technique when campaigning against Michael Dukakis in 1988. Bush called Dukakis a "card-carrying member of the ACLU." The term "card-carrying" was an obvious holdover from McCarthy days when "card-carrying communists" were in season. Whether or not voters remembered the precise derivation of the term, they knew it connoted something sinister.

Such insinuations are possible because the English language is very elastic. Luckily, numbers—the subject of the next chapter—are precise, definitive, and not subject to shading. And if you believe that, let me tell you about my college days when I, too, did not inhale.

17

Note

1. "Nissan Agrees to Settle FTC False Advertising Allegations over 'Nissan Challenge' Campaign," Federal Trade Commission Press Release, March 9, 1994.

Chapter Two

Damn the Statistics

How to Lie with Numbers

The New College of the University of South Florida looks like a fine school, an excellent place to drop a few thousand in tuition. *Money* magazine ranked it #1 overall in 1994, based partly on the fact that the average SAT score was a whopping 1296. But that's not the only whopper from the New College of the University of South Florida. The other half of the story is that the University achieved its high SAT score average by simply *not counting the bottom 6 percent of students*, lifting the average by 40 points—a now discontinued practice its admissions director described as a "marketing strategy."[1]

Playing the numbers game is deceptively easy because we are respectful—practially worshipful—of numbers. Our attitude stems in part from the fact that numbers, and the people who manipulate them, have given us some apparent understanding of the world around us. Whoever invented the zero made complex calculations possible and gave birth to the modern economy. And when Newton perfected a calculus that allowed the use of small measurements to predict big ones—even predicting the existence of planets that no one had ever seen by measuring changes in orbits of planets we could see—we felt much more in control of the universe and our little part in it.

The extension of this concept is perhaps one of the most appealing, intoxicating, and hoped-for notions in all of human history: that somehow, *the same mathematics that predicted planets could be used to predict human behavior.* This notion had begun to develop real legs early in the Renaissance, when society developed a renewed interest in the potential of humans and how human behavior fit into the "scheme of things"—in the scientific patterns that govern the universe.

We can trace much of the application of scientific methods to social issues to a lawyer and philosopher named Francis Bacon (1561–1626). Bacon was among the first to argue convincingly that, in effect, experience was the best teacher and the best *predictor.* He perfected what came to be known as the scientific method, the idea that things are measurable and predictable.

The birth of the scientific method sent mathematicians and philosophers scribbling away like crazy in an effort to find a calculation that explained the strange ways in which people behaved. Thomas Hobbes (1588–1697) was inclined to use mathematical formulae to analyze behavior. Hobbes, who was an avid reader of Galileo and Copernicus, scientists who explained the physical properties of the universe, believed that similar mechanistic rigor could be applied to human behavior. Hobbes developed a formula for government involving imposition of pleasure and pain in precise ratios.

A contemporary of Hobbes, Rene Descartes (1596–1650), also believed that human affairs could be analyzed mathematically. Two centuries later, Auguste Comte (1798–1857) constructed a theory called "positivism," which held that society could be studied scientifically using universal scientific principles. Comte is usually credited with inventing the term "sociology."

This blending of philosophy and "hard science" opened up new avenues of exploration. Charles Darwin (1809–1882) applied mathematics to evolution, and one of Darwin's followers, Francis Galton (1822–1911), argued that intelligence was one of the characteristics inherited by the "fittest." Galton set about to develop new ways to measure and quantify intelligence and human behavior. Galton's innovations included fingerprinting and intelligence testing.

The fact that the mind itself could be studied and measured was fascinating to an Austrian psychiatrist named Sigmund Freud (1856–1839) and to a French sociologist named Emile Durkheim (1858–1917), both of whom fashioned theories to predict human behavior. Durkheim believed that societies were more than collections of individual minds; a collective society assumed a life of its own. Durkheim further believed that statistical sampling and mathematical measurement were essential to illustrating the workings of those societies. A German sociologist named Max Weber (1864–1920) used innovative research methods to study the ways in which economies developed, linking economic patterns to such underlying factors as religion.

Yes, believe it or not, there's a point to all this. The mixture of the factors described so far (the belief that there was some scientific and numerical consistency to human behavior and the notion that measurement of factors in society as a whole could cast light on the human condition) changed *everything*. We came to view society not as some random accident, but as an explainable and explorable phenomenon. The people who had measured minds and mankind were *heroic*, and we did our best to adopt their methods, or what we assumed their methods would be. By the 1920s, we were managing "scientifically," studying time and motion under the assumption that men were like machines and could be measured and adjusted accordingly. Through the 1920s and '30s we began using the opinion poll, which once again promised us that human behavior was quantifiable and therefore a little less scary. We also began to characterize the results of opinion polls as "public opinion," making the same rather arrogant assumption we had seized on when substituting the results of an intelligence test for "intelligence."

21

Is it any wonder that in the age of the information avalanche we cling to the spurious precision of numbers? An ad claiming that "four out of five dentists surveyed recommend sugarless gum for their patients" fits perfectly within our worldview. It appeals to scientific authority. No matter that no one tells us how many dentists were surveyed, or if the dentists surveyed were already predisposed to using the product.[2]

So that's why we're seduced by numbers. And here's how the game is played . . .

Technique #1: The Remade Measure

When you want to inflate or deflate a certain number, you don't have to tinker with the calculations. Simply *change what you choose to count*. To inflate SAT scores, for example, some colleges don't use the results from groups of students who usually score low, such as international students who don't do well on the verbal section of the test. Because the choice of what to count is made *without the knowledge of the ultimate consumer of the statistic*, the sleight-of-hand is virtually undetectable. Unless, of course, you ask what groups are included in the statistic. The *Wall Street Journal* caught dozens of colleges red-handed by comparing the statistics they reported to college guidebooks with the figures they reported to debt-rating agencies. Lying to debt-rating agencies, such as Moody's or Standard and Poor's, can be construed as a felony, and, after all, there are limits to marketing strategies. The full story is told in chapter 6.

You can now see the elegance of the Remade Measure from the tinkerer's point of view. Do you want, for example, to make your college appear more selective? Colleges are like Groucho Marx's country club: nobody really wants to attend one that would actually accept them. If you want to lower the acceptance rate you can simply encourage more applications from people who stand no chance of getting in, such as foreign students with no financial aid, and your college becomes instantly more selective. Another trick is to reclassify people who were initially put on a waiting list and then later admitted as "rejects." Your ratio of students who applied versus students who were admitted grows wider with each tweak of the statistics.

Remade Measures are ubiquitous and affect our outlook of the world around us in ways we might not initially consider. For example, many of us are increasingly content with city life because serious crime rates continue to drop in many major cities. But is this really reflective of a *reduction in serious crimes,* or is it a Remade Measure of *what we count as serious crimes*? Are incidents of theft, let's say, declining because actual thefts are declining, or because police officials under pressure to produce lower crime rates are reclassifying reports of "stolen" property as "lost" property, thereby taking them off the books?

Figure 2.1 shows an original crime report from the Philadelphia police department, one of those cities where "crime" has "dropped." Version one is the original report filed by the officer on the scene, and it says, "complainant stated that her wallet was taken." A later rewrite, the version that went into official department records, reclassifies the incident as "lost property" and eliminates any mention of theft.[3] Philadelphia was one of those suddenly safer cities caught with its hand in the statistical cookie jar. We'll follow up on that story in chapter 4.

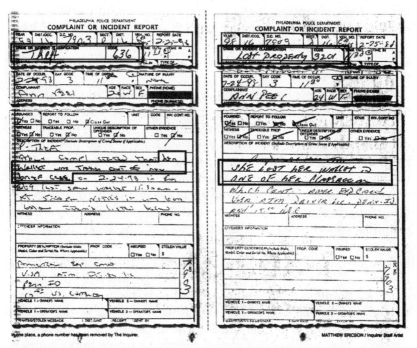

Figure 2.1: A crime report from the Philadelphia police department, as pictured in the *Philadelphia Inquirer*. The original says "complaintant stated that her wallet was taken." The rewritten report says the complaintant said that she "lost" her wallet.

* 23 *

Technique #2: Precision Garbage

Before I became totally honest, I dabbled in advertising and politics and learned a thing or two about numbers. First, nobody believes broad estimates, including Samuel Johnson, who wrote that "round numbers are always false." The solution to such skepticism is to provide a specific number, preferably with a few decimal points, that may be equally as bogus as the round number, but is much more believable. The number appears precise even though it was constructed from shreds of garbage.

As an example, a small-town radio station manager of my acquaintance was once under the gun to increase ad sales because merchants were skeptical that anyone would actually hear a commercial on his station. He asked exactly three people how long they listened to his station. The answers were, "about three hours a day," "maybe two hours a day," and "three hours, I guess." This exhaustive research mutated into the "fact" that a recent survey of the local listening area showed the average listener tuned in for 2.66 hours per day.

Measuring radio listening is a complex business and, when done correctly, provides important and meaningful data. But the point is that somebody intent on producing a precise-sounding number can do it easily. Unless the consumer of the statistic asks how the statistic was derived—and very few people think to do that—Precision Garbage can become an instrument of deception.

A determined manipulator can rig many factors in the derivation of a statistic that produces a precise but misleading result. For example, suppose you are managing a local municipal election and you want to produce a poll for public consumption a day or two before the election. What would you want the result to be? The ideal result, from my point of view, would be to show your candidate two points behind. Voters tend to root for the underdog and might be motivated to go to the polls. Also, two points is such a close margin that many potential voters for your candidate might be convinced to trek to the polls because their vote would make a difference. If the candidate is way behind, many voters don't want to waste their time and their vote; but if the candidate is far ahead, voters might assume that their efforts are not needed.

So, given the target result, how do you construct a poll that will give you what you want? One method is to assemble your pollsters, give them pages of a local phone book, a formula for whom to call (every twentieth number for example), and start the poll. If you keep a running tally through the early minutes and hours of such a poll, you'll find that the numbers in a small sample tend to swing in a pendulum-like manner. At 10 o'clock, your candidate may be ten points behind. At 10:30, your candidate might be six points ahead. At noon, your candidate is two points behind. And now it's time for lunch. And by the way, don't bother coming back.

The well-known professional polling organizations don't engage in these shenanigans, but remember that much of the data that assaults us daily does not come from these firms. Moreover, even a well-conducted poll is subject to all kinds of hidden distortion, including the construction of the questions. Remember, too, that a poll is just a snapshot in time, and you can't try to make a movie out of it. We'll look more closely at the use and misuse of polling data in chapter 9.

Technique #3: The Apple-and-Orange Average

An "average" is a slippery figure. First of all, there are three different ways to compute a measure of central tendency:

- the mode (the most frequently occurring number in a sample)
- the median (the number that would be in the middle if you lined up all the raw numbers from your sample from smallest to largest)
- the mean (the arithmetical average you get when adding all the raw numbers and dividing by the number of things in your sample).

The fact that there are different ways to compute an average gives you a lot of wiggle room to produce the number that paints the picture you want.

Figure 2.2 shows the price of all eleven houses that sold in one month in a "typical" town. You'll notice that, while there may be regional variations in pricing, this is probably a reasonable representation of the range of property that sells anywhere. Most houses are about "average"; one or two are beauties, and there's an occasional handyman special.

25

Computing the three averages produces some interesting results:

Median price of housing sold during the month: $119K
Mode price of housing sold during the month: $101K
Mean price of housing sold during the month: $202K

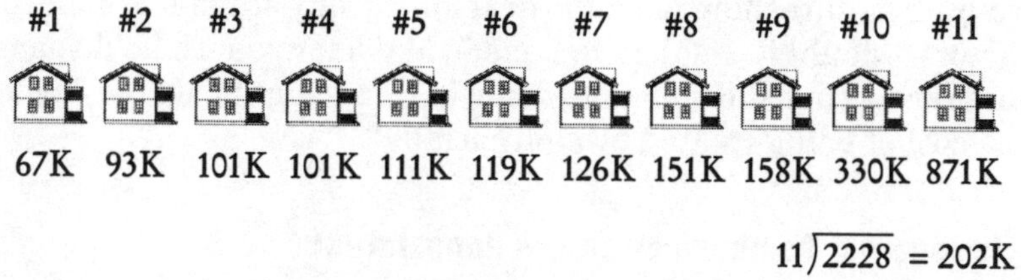

#1	#2	#3	#4	#5	#6	#7	#8	#9	#10	#11
67K	93K	101K	101K	111K	119K	126K	151K	158K	330K	871K

$$11\overline{)2228} = 202K$$

Figure 2.2: Prices of hypothetical homes. Note how the "average" can be skewed widely.

That's quite a range. All three figures can correctly be called the "average." Now, put yourself in the place of a real estate salesperson trying to sell House #7, offered at 126K. Is it a good bargain compared to other houses in the town, the customer asks? Is this an exclusive town? What is the average property value? Which number would you use?

In a similar vein, suppose you were the public relations officer for a company hit with a strike. How would you compute the "average" salary when responding to a reporter's inquiry about whether your workers were well-paid? Would you use the mean or the mode? Given typical ranges of salaries, including the fat-cat salaries of the top executives, the mean might push your average into the 40K range. But the median, the "halfway" point, can realistically fall in the range of the high twenties.

That is one of the problems with averages, especially means: they mix different things and then try to compare them. They attempt to compare apples with oranges: mansions with fixer-uppers, or executives with janitors. When you blend data that is even more disparate, the average can be used to "prove" just about anything.

For example, a chiropractor once informed me that "statistics show" the average person injured on the job recovers more quickly and more cheaply when he visits a chiropractor as opposed to a medical doctor.

26

I have no doubt that is true. But the "average" contains blended data:

- people who were injured on the job and were treated by a chiropractor, and
- people who were injured on the job and were treated by a medical doctor.

Those samples are not equivalent and produce an Apple-and-Orange Average. For instance, would a fellow who'd had his legs torn off by a threshing machine drag his bloody stumps to a chiropractor? I doubt it. He'd go to a medical doctor, where he'd spend years recovering and a fortune doing it, thus shooting up the "average" cost of being treated by a physician.

Technique #4: Comparison to the Nonexistent

One of the most effective ways to cosmetically improve a figure is to compare it to something that doesn't really exist. A common method of Comparison to the Nonexistent was illustrated in Technique #3 above, where we compared whatever we wanted to look good to an "average" that doesn't have any real grounding in reality. In place of the spurious average you can simply insert a "rack rate" or "manufacturers' suggested retail price" that nobody ever really pays. Then take 10, 20, or 30 percent off that imaginary rate.

The hotel industry has added some imaginative variations to Comparison to the Nonexistent with the introduction of weekend and summer "specials," deals that attract visitors who believe (by implied comparison) they are getting a deal because hotels are desperate to fill up rooms on weekends or in the summer. But when the *Washington Post* looked into these offers, they found the summer deals were simply minor reductions in the rack rate. In other cases, they were bargains on a very limited number of rooms in places where many people don't want to go.

The Wyndham Special Seasons package, for example, offers a $129 summer special. But that price is also good in the fall. But remember, the rate might not be available when you want it because only a limited number of rooms are available under most promotions. Doubletree's Dream Deals offers a terrific bargain: "Weekend rates from $40." But alas, the only hotel priced at that rate was in Mt. Laurel, New Jersey. New York is $229 and Baltimore is $144.[4] This representation blends Comparison to the Nonexistent with our next technique.

27

Technique #5: The Veiled Variable

At the heart of most numbers games is the variable that you're not told about up front, such as the fact that the rate "from" $40 is available only in Mt. Laurel (a lovely town about 30 miles from my home, but hardly a tourist mecca). Hotels do a clever job playing the Veiled Variable but credit card companies are the masters of the technique. Attractive rates often include landmines veiled in the fine print, such as stratospheric readjustments of the interest rates if you make one or two late payments. Cards that offer rebates, sometimes called "reward cards," give you points toward merchandise from the sponsor of the card. But the Veiled Variable is that interest rates are typically higher than those of standard cards, and any benefit you gain in accrued points is wiped out by the interest if you carry a balance. Other cards promise "up to" a certain percent cash back on charges but veil the fact that they pay only one-fourth of a cent per dollar on the first $1,000 in charges. Some offer you discounts on services but tack on membership and maintenance fees.

But no one can veil the variables quite like automotive firms (who richly deserve their own chapter in this book). Auto retailers often quote attractive lease rates but bury the down payment and other tacked-on fees in the fine print or a sonic blur of announcer copy. Car rental firms combine the numerical Veiled Variable with the verbal Tortured Definition to raise rates while claiming not to raise rates. While you might be quoted an attractive rate by a car rental agency, the final bill is often adorned with a mysterious variety of tacked-on additions, such as "occ.chg" (meaning other charges and credits) and "ex serv" (meaning extra services). Don't forget the LDW (loss damage waiver), airport concession fee, taxes, and other surcharges. Your final bill could easily add up to double the advertised rate.[5] Car rental companies claim these add-ons are costs of doing business. They include fees called "passthroughs" that technically cover costs such as auto licensing fees and rental of prime space in airports, and elected representatives in many states have passed legislation allowing them to do this.[6] Right. And imagine the reaction of a car rental executive who ordered a $4 martini and was billed $8 because the bartender included a $3 "bar rental fee" and a $1 "liquor license surcharge."

Notes

1. Steve Stecklow, "Cheat Sheets: Colleges Inflate SATs and Graduation Rates In Popular Guidebooks," *The Wall Street Journal*, April 5, 1995, p. A1.
2. This example is from a book I strongly recommend: *The Interplay of Influence*, by Kathleen Hall Jamieson and Karlyn Kohrs Campbell (Belmont, CA: Wadsworth, 1997). For other recommendations, see the list "Ten Books that Will Open Your Eyes about Communication, Words, Numbers, Persuasion, and Media," on page 139.
3. Michael Matza, Mark Fazlolloa, and Craig R. McCoy, "The Big Write-Off: When Stolen Goods are 'Lost,'" *The Philadelphia Inquirer*, November 2, 1998, pp. A1, A14.

4. Carolyn Spencer Brown, "Truth Squad: Summer in the Cities: Few Deals?" *Washington Post*, June 14, 1998, p. E03.
5. Alfred Brocover, "Car Confusion: Check Fine Print Before Jumping at a Rental Deal," *Chicago Tribune*, April 26, 1998, p. 11.
6. Thomas Goetz, "Travel: Cars Cost More to Rent as Surcharges Pile Up," *The Wall Street Journal*, May 5, 1998, p. Ba.

Chapter Three!

Seeing Is Believing? Don't You Believe It!

How to Lie with Images

Honesty is the best image. —Ziggy

✳Lying with images is the most diabolical method of pseudo-persuasion because we see the result with our own eyes and are, therefore, reluctant to believe that we could be hoodwinked. Moreover, putting up a chart or showing a photo has become synonymous with saying, "Look, here's proof."

We're all taught, at some point, the value of expressing our ideas with an image. Here's a perfect example from a college statistics textbook:

> A graph is a visual summary, and humans are visual thinkers. There is no culture of civilization that has not valued the visual image. . . . The reason that visual images are regarded as such a universally powerful form of communication is related to the way in which the eyes process data.... The brain's ability to process and to interpret images in the totality is a remarkable processing feat, whose functions even the most powerful computers cannot begin to duplicate. Although the eyes, in conjunction with our visual processing system, are a fabulous sensory system, they digest text or numbers rather slowly in comparison to the comprehension of a visual image.[1]

Images engage the audience and give the viewer the impression that everything has been impartially laid out before him or her. Moreover, the image—the nonverbal symbol—is compact, eloquent, and *needs no explanation*.

Here's an example provided by Kathleen Hall Jamieson and Karlyn Kohrs Campbell:

> Such events [eloquent images] rivet photographic attention because little or no commentary is required—the picture is the story. If such scenes were routine, they would not be newsworthy. It is both the freshness of the symbols and the ability to stand for more than themselves that make them attractive to news photographers. Non-verbal symbolic acts that require verbal commentary are less effective.
>
> [As an example] in spring 1990, the wife of former Philippines' president Ferdinand Marcos, Imelda Marcos, shaped national network coverage of her acquittal on charges of misuse of state funds and at the same time secured front-page newspaper access. Marcos accomplished this by inching her way up the aisle of a church on her knees in a black mourning dress to "thank God" for the trail's out-come. The black dress reminded viewers of her widowhood, kneeling suggested that she was religious, and movement up the aisle in the posture of a penitent suggested her humility and the injustice of seeking to convict her. How, after all, could one assume the guilt of a humble, religious widow, kneeling in a church?[2]

It's hard to overestimate the power of the symbol, the eloquent shorthand. Flags, crucifixes, uniforms, and military insignia all tell a story in short order. Corporate America did not overlook this lesson and set about to create its own family of icons: trademarks and logos.

Historian and author Daniel Boorstin summarized this perfectly in his book *The Image: A Guide to Pseudo-Events in America*:

> It was by elaborate design that the cumbersome name "International Business Machines Corporation" was made in the public mind into "IBM." This is probably the most expen-sive and most valuable abbreviation in history. Under the creative direction of Eliot Noyes and a design group consist-ing of Paul Rand, Charles Eames, and George Nelson, the firm developed its streamlined trademark, to project a

"clean, impressive image." Nowadays a trademark is seldom a simple by-product of other activities. It is not merely the name, initials or signature of the maker or owner, or a hallmark assigned by a guild. Usually, it is produced by specialists.

But the images which fill our experience are not only the few letters, the simplified picture, or the catchy slogan. They are not merely "IBM," "USS" staggered in a circle (for United States Steel Corporation), the graceful cursive "CocaCola." They are not merely "His Master's Voice (the RCA Victor Dog listening quizzically at the horn of a primitive phonograph), "Time to Re-tire," (a yawning infant wearing Dr. Denton pajamas and holding a candle). "Rock of Gibraltar" (Prudential Insurance Company), a Benjamin Franklin medallion (Saturday Evening Post), a sleek, speeding grey-hound (Greyhound Buses). Nor are they merely memorable slogans: "All the News That's Fit to Print," "I'd Walk a Mile for a Camel," "The Beer That Made Milwaukee Famous," "When it Rains It Pours," "Breakfast of Champions," . . . etc., etc.

While all these uses of the image have become more important with each decade of the twentieth century, a more abstract kind of image is the peculiar product of our age. Its tyranny is pervasive. An image in this sense is not simply a trademark, a design, a slogan, or an easily remembered picture. It is a studiously crafted personality profile of an individual, institution, corporation, product, or service. It is a value-caricature, shaped in three dimensions, of synthetic materials. . . ."[3]

33

Think about it: how much more does an image say than the obvious? On a basic level, a graph says more than "here is a visual representation of numbers." It says, or at least implies, that "here is something scientific, something beyond doubt." What does a colorful car ad *say*? "Here is a menu of opportunities for you to get what you want in any color you want for less money than you might think." (In fact, as we'll see, the abundance of prices, terms, and options can be used to obfuscate as well as to inform.) What does a picture of a fast-food hamburger communicate? Usually, an abundance of food, of meat in the middle, and, at a deeper level, a willingness to deceive ourselves because anyone who has bought a hamburger knows they don't look much like their inflated counterparts on the hanging menu. What does ten-point Times Roman type say? "Here is communication from an important, powerful organization, such as the federal government."

The image itself may be a distortion, or a caricature of the image may be a distortion—for example, a bogus sweepstakes notification in ten-point Times Roman type. Or a graph may visually distort accurate data. It's easy—distressingly easy. And here's how it's done.

Technique #1: Proportion Distortion

Let's say you want to "prove" that your over-the-counter headache medicine is more effective than aspirin. You can do it verbally, claiming it contains "more of the headache reliever doctors recommend most." (Which happens to be aspirin, and this happens to be a real advertising technique.) But the modern consumer knows that "seeing is believing" and has an appetite for scientific "proof." If I were you, I'd use a graph. The graph in figure 3.1, for example. Taken from a real ad, it clearly shows . . . well, I'm not exactly sure. The line on the Pain Relief graph shoots skyward for Anacin, while the plain old stuff limps along in the graph below. But what does the height of the graph represent? The vertical scale is *unlabeled*. It's supposed to represent "pain relief level," but level of what mea-

34

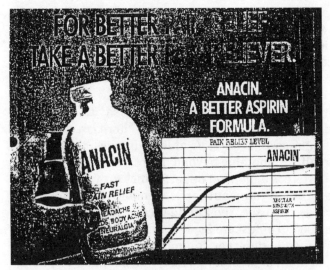

Figure 3.1: Ad showing an unlabeled graph. It looks impressive . . . but what does it mean?

sured in what? Painograms? Giga-painograms? Micro-paino-grams? We're in the dark. The horizontal scale is unlabeled, also. Does it represent pain relief level over hours or seconds?

Now you're beginning to see the real problem with graphs: their shape implies a proportion and a relationship between two mea-surements, but some creative tinkering with the X (horizontal) and Y (vertical) axes produces just about any value you want. In the case of the Anacin ad, the axes leave everything to the imagination. But you can use real numbers and still tinker with the overall impression.

Darrell Huff and Irving Geis wrote a wonderful book in the early 1950s titled *How to Lie with Statistics*, mandatory reading for any-one interested in decoding manipulation with numbers and images. Their undying contribution to the vocabulary of manipulative com-munication is the Gee-Whiz Graph. A Gee-Whiz Graph is designed to be eye popping, and it's usually created by chopping off (trun-cating) the bottom of the graph and/or changing the relationship between the axes.

For example, figure 3.2 shows a graph of earnings for a company over a one-year period. It's not very impressive and doesn't really convey the notion that a whole lot of progress is being made. To

* 35 *

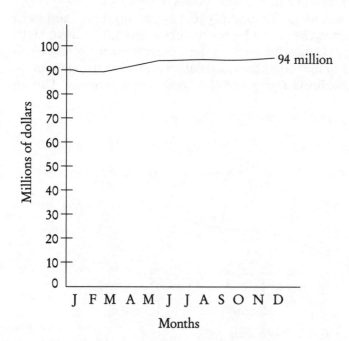

Figure 3.2: A graph of earnings.

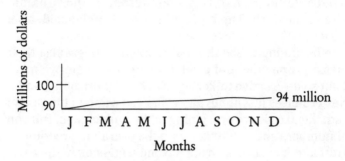

Figure 3.3: A graph after we've tinkered with it.
Much improved.

counteract that unfortunate visual neutrality, we can simply lop off the bottom of the graph, as in figure 3.3. The picture suddenly looks a lot better.

But the public relations people might want a graph that shows a *startling* improvement in earnings. We can do it with the same numbers. All we have to do in order to create a real Gee-Whiz Graph is to change the relationship between the X and Y axes by making Y represent smaller increments (figure 3.4).

A graph can be made to imply just about anything, and even sophisticated viewers can be hoodwinked using the above techniques. For example, figure 3.5 is an advertisement for *Investor's Business Daily* that compares circulation and advertising costs for *Investor's Business Daily* and the *Wall Street Journal*. The ad

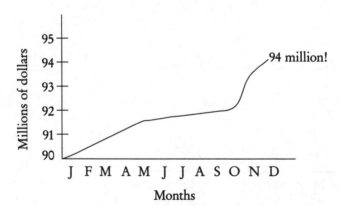

Figure 3.4: A gee-whiz graph.

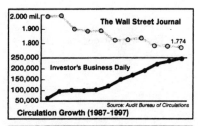

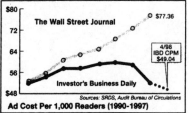

Figure 3.5: A graph that makes a
skewed comparison.

appeared in a magazine read by advertising executives, who ought
to know better than to be dosed with their own medicine.

The graph visually makes the point that *Investor's* is a better
advertising deal because its circulation is rising and the cost of
reaching advertisers is dropping. Two graphs are presented to
prove the case. Pretty impressive! But look at the numbers behind
the alternately skyrocketing and plummeting lines in the top graph.
The *Wall Street Journal's* circulation graph is severely truncated,
showing only the numbers from 1.8 to 2 million. A relatively small
change is made to look like a toboggan run. Moreover, the circula-
tions are made to appear *equivalent* because the graphs are the
same size. But the circulation of the *Journal* is 1.7 million compared
to *Investor's* circulation of 250,000.

The second graph is truncated too and would be nowhere near
as impressive if plotted from zero. I've taken the liberty of un-Gee-
Whizzing both graphs, and you can see the results in figures 3.6
and 3.7.

Technique #2: Graphic Garble

The eye is easily confused, and you can lead the viewer of a graphic
to a false inference by presenting an avalanche of juxtaposed
images that lead to a false inference. The ad for the Chrysler

37

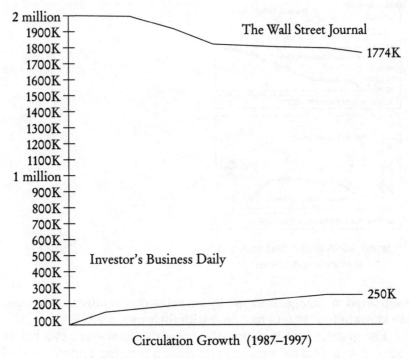

Circulation Growth (1987–1997)

Figure 3.6: An un-Gee-Whizzed graph.

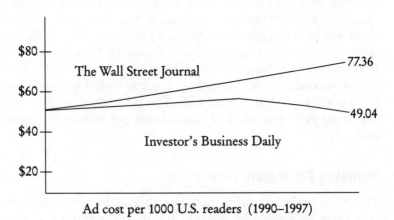

Ad cost per 1000 U.S. readers (1990–1997)

Figure 3.7: Another un-Gee-Whizzed graph.

Figure 3.8: Some important fine print on a car ad: the word "available."

Sebring convertible shown in figure 3.8 would *appear* to indicate that you can buy the car for $199 a month with $0 down. That's a terrific deal. Sorry. You didn't read the fine print. Underneath the big *"$0 down"* is the teeny-tiny word "available." This means that, as in any car purchase, you can get zero down if you want to make larger monthly payments. That, like any other opportunity to spend money, is "available." But for *this* car you need a down payment of $2,000 cash or trade. Also in mouse type is another surprise: when you finish paying your $199 per month, your last payment will be for *more than $11,000*. Yes, the disclaimers are there, and I caught them on the third reading after putting on reading glasses. But they're not easy to find, and anyone in the market for a Chrysler Sebring convertible might find himself drawn into the tent and switched into a far less attractive deal.

39

Graphic Garble techniques are also popular in political ads. A political action committee backing George Bush in his 1988 campaign against Michael Dukakis garbled information in the infamous Willie Horton ad, arguably the most infamous example of Graphic Garble in history. The ad made it appear that Dukakis had furloughed 268 first-degree murderers who had then gone on to commit other crimes. You probably remember the commercial: grim-faced convicts (most of them suspiciously dark-complected) marching through a turnstile symbolizing "revolving-door justice." What you might not remember is the Graphic Garble that led many viewers to form an incorrect inference about the figures presented in the commercial. The voice-over narration for the Willie Horton ad went this way:

> As governor, Michael Dukakis vetoed mandatory sentences for drug dealers. He vetoed the death penalty. His revolving-door prison policy gave weekend furloughs to first degree murderers not eligible for parole. While out, many
>
> —*Here the words "268 escaped" appear on the screen.*
>
> committed crimes like kidnapping and rape. And many are still at large. Now, Michael Dukakis wants to do for America what he's done for Massachusetts. America can't afford that risk.

The false inference was generated by placing the visual graphic "268 escaped" over the sound of the announcer reading ". . . first degree murderers not eligible for parole. While out, many committed crimes like kidnapping or rape." Yes, 268 did escape, but they weren't first-degree murderers. Four first-degree murderers did escape, and of them exactly one—Willie Horton—kidnapped and raped. But when the tape was played to focus groups many members interpreted the ad to mean the 268 first-degree murderers had been furloughed, escaped, and subsequently kidnapped and raped. I have a hunch that's exactly what the creators of the ad hoped people would think.

40

Technique #3: Image Engineering

This technique involves nothing more than using an attractive photo to distort reality in your favor or an ugly one to paint an unflattering picture of someone or something you don't like.

We're often seduced by glamour photos even when they make no intrinsic sense whatsoever. Note, for example, how Lane Bryant, a company that sells clothing for plus-size women, uses *thin models* in their catalog photos. We also tolerate photoflattery when it is obvious that the photo and the real thing are strikingly dissimilar. A case in point is the near-universal use of glamorized pictures of hamburgers in fast-food restaurants. The burger as it exists in the photo studio seems much bigger and better than the one taken out of the bag in the restaurant.

Manipulative photography is a staple of political advertising and journalism. Pictures of a candidate's political opponents in TV ads are almost always in unflattering black and white, sometimes projected in slow motion to give the opponent a menacing, dinosaur-like quality. Newspeople have a tendency to seize on photos that "illustrate" their point, but often distort reality. If the story is about a dejected president, or one who should be dejected, an appropriate photo is almost always available because it is a rare person indeed who never exhibits a momentary head-down posture.

This may seem trivial but pictures that say a thousand words have contributed to the downfall of many a politician. Witness Jimmy Carter's encounter with the killer rabbit. In case you don't remember, Carter was in a boat when he was accosted by a gigantic swimming rabbit who tried to get into the boat. Carter was shown trying to beat it off with a paddle. The picture came to "symbolize" the downward spiral of his presidency and his political impotence.

Technique #4: The Ambiguous Event

Picture this: Television news footage shows the runners in a major marathon staggering across the finish line. Exhausted competitors stumble past the line and reach into a barrel containing a well-known beverage. A *lot* of runners keep reaching into that barrel, and there are a lot of shots of them gulping the beverage down, usually with the label showing. In case you haven't caught on, the tape was produced by the manufacturers of the beverage and provided by satellite to local television stations. The TV news departments get free and well-produced footage of the race; the client gets a lot of publicity for the soft drink. Everybody wins. Except perhaps for the viewer, who's been force-fed a commercial in the guise of news. Several thousand video news releases, commonly called VNRs, are turned out each year, and virtually all television stations use them.[4] While some stations identify the footage as coming from video news releases, many do not, passing it off as a local station production.

The Ambiguous Event relies on the spurious linkage of an image to something "happening," and it has become a staple of political communication. The unchallenged masters of the craft were Ronald Reagan and his advisers, who not only manipulated the news media, but set the standard for future image crafters.

Reagan's advisers could turn the most humble "event" into a flattering video. On the day it was announced that housing starts were up, for example, advisers arranged to have the president don a hard-hat and tour a framed-out house in Texas. Gracing the network news that evening was a shot of the president touring the house, coupled with the news that housing starts were up. Good PR for the president, and a virtual must-carry story for the networks once the dry statistic was coupled with an attractive visual of the president doing something.

Think about it: What is the actual "event" that occurs when a ribbon is cut, or a presidential candidate tours a flag factory? Daniel Boorstin calls such happenings "pseudo-events," a fine name for what has become the coin of the realm in persuasive communication.

Technique #5: The Confusing Counterfeit

A couple of years ago, the treasurer of a nonprofit organization I founded received what looked exactly like the annual bill for our Yellow Page listing. We paid it without thinking. It turned out the bill was a phony—a bill for inclusion in a "directory" that, as far I know, doesn't exist.

The Confusing Counterfeit technique relies on the fact that people are busy, benighted, or boneheaded, or, as in my case when I paid that bill, all three. You've probably received many offers meant to look like mailings from a government agency. In fact, one book on mail-order techniques advises direct marketers to use a typeface that looks like something from the Internal Revenue Service.

Sweepstakes marketers use all sorts of visual counterfeiting to entice you to open the envelope. The outside of the envelope (figure 3.9) includes an imitation registered mail card, complete with little tear-off perforations. The address is computer-generated imitation handwriting. We are informed that the delivery has been approved according to USPS Section S916.1.1! There's even a little computer-generated check mark to show that this very important federal process has been complied with! (In case you're wondering, USPS Section S916.1.1 is the regulation that authorizes someone to send mail to individuals.) On the back of the envelope is a notice to open the "registered documents" (sounds a little like "registered mail," no?) on the front first, along with a notation "signed" in contrasting ink by none other than D. Doyle informing my wife that she has been approved for $31 million. Approval is very important to me,

42

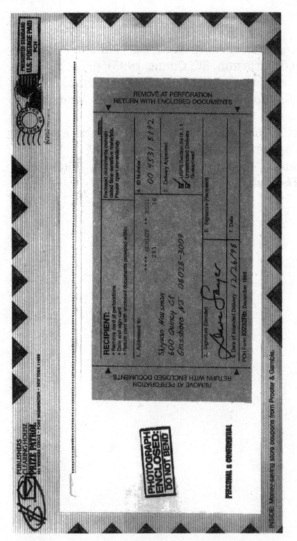

Figure 3.9: A sweepstakes "document" that
looks a lot like registered mail. But it ain't.

as I'm sure it is to you, but I have a feeling we'll still be waiting a
while for my $31 million.

There you have them: the basic techniques used to lie with
words, numbers, and pictures. The following chapters show how
various businesses and industries use these methods against you.

Notes

1. James S. Hawkes, *Discovering Statistics: An Adventure in Problem Solving* (Charleston, SC: Quant, 1995), p. 54.
2. Kathleen Hall Jamieson and Karlyn Kohrs Campbell, *The Interplay of Influence*, 4th ed., (Belmont, CA: Wadsworth, 1997), p. 129.
3. Daniel J. Boorstin, *The Image: A Guide to Pseudo-Events in America* (New York: Atheneum, 1987), pp. 185–87.
4. Joan Drummond, "Video News Releases Flood the Marketplace," *The Quill*, May 1993, p. 12.

Chapter Four

I'm from the Government and I'm Here to Confuse You

*On June 21, 1998, the U.S. Justice Department announced that background checks mandated by the Brady Act had prevented 69,000 people from buying guns in 1997. Later that same day, President Clinton proclaimed that since the implementation of the Brady Act (which he supported, by the way), "law enforcement officials have stopped hundreds of thousands of felons, fugitives and stalkers from buying handguns every year."[1] Aside from the vast discrepancy in the figures (which were explained by a Clinton spokesperson as an "editing error"), the statistic also produced a classic Apple-and-Orange Average, neglecting the fact that about half of rejections under the Brady Act were due to paperwork problems or traffic violations, not violent criminal offenses.[2] That's the way that government-generated misinformation often works. Whether the data are intentionally cooked or not, government officials (like most of us) tend to seize on "evidence" that seems to confirm the fact that we are doing a good job.

Statistics are persuasive creatures, and it is almost impossible to overstate the importance of statistics to the development of our government, culture, and worldview. For example, the mandate of a census—a head-count—was written into the Constitution. While the census was originally envisioned only as a method of gauging legislative apportionment, the statistical data gathered, sliced, and diced today are used to make far-reaching decisions about the allocation of government resources.

Interestingly, the census is probably responsible for the development of the computer. A scientist named Herman Hollerith designed punchcards for the 1890 census. He realized that the importance of the census went beyond the *collection* of data. Real gold nuggets could be uncovered by the correlation of those bits of information. For example, it's all well and good to know that a certain number of people live in cities, and a certain number live in poverty, but the correlation—how many live in cities and are poor—is the brush that paints the broad picture.

Hollerith borrowed from a centuries old idea: using paper with holes punched in it to automate a tedious process. (Punched paper had originally been used to actuate keys on a mechanical organ and later to change the pattern of a shuttle in automated looms.) But instead of rolls of paper, Hollerith used punch cards (the same size as dollar bills so that equipment of the U.S. Mint could be used to manipulate them) to allow mechanical tabulation and cross-tabulation of the data.

46   As so often happens with a technology, the fact that we could do something spurred us to actually do it, and the results exceeded anything the Founding Fathers could have imagined. We tracked the movement of population and, in 1920, noted the passing of a milestone as we discovered that, for the first time, more people lived in cities than in the countryside. Data on ethnic origin began to be employed for political purposes, with tabulations of immigrants living in the United States used to establish quotas for further immigration.

We developed what census scholar Margo Anderson calls a "census politics," with everybody from lobbyists to congressmen, from minority groups to majority groups, urging the Census Bureau to count certain traits so that they may be used in setting policy. Various constituencies have even sued the Census Bureau, claiming that members of certain groups, such as undocumented aliens and the homeless, are difficult to count and, therefore, underrepresented. Representatives of those groups, and the political constitutencies that would benefit from larger numbers of the individuals in those groups being counted, unsuccessfully attempted to introduce sampling into the year 2000 census. (A census literally means a count; sampling means counting a representative portion and extrapolating the results.)

Small wonder that the United States spends something like $3 billion per year gathering and analyzing statistics.[3] Statistics are the guideposts for public policy and can have an immediate effect on your pocketbook. Depending on what the government soothsayers predict based on their anayses of data, you may pay more for a mortgage or a student loan, or your company may decide that future economic trends do not include your continued employment.

But there are two problems with government statistics: they are often wrong, and even when they are right, the numbers can be manipulated to suit many purposes. An investigation by *USA Today* in 1996 showed that even government soothsayers themselves had little faith in their statistics. According to the official in charge of tabulating the gross domestic product, the government is wrong about 25 percent of the time when calculating whether the economy is growing or shrinking. And a former vice-chairman of the Federal Reserve Board, Alan Binder, added the heartening observation that it's not uncommon for economists—even the deified Alan Greenspan—to ignore government figures, essentially guessing at future trends because the government numbers can't be trusted.[4]

Part of the reason for the slipperiness of the figures relates to the notion that you can only read so much into data, and when we try to make numbers meaningful we can inject unintentional distortion. For example, the government counts the unemployed, in part, by monitoring company payrolls, but adds thousands of jobs per month to the total to account for new businesses that have not yet begun to file payroll reports. It's sophisticated guesswork, but guesswork nonetheless, and some analysts believe it masks real job losses.

At the same time, we often expend resources on measuring the wrong things. About 12 percent of the statistics budget goes toward measuring agricultural output, but farming makes up less than 4 percent of the total economy. The service industry accounts for about 75 percent of nation's economic output, but we spend less money analyzing it than we spend on assessing the mining industry.[5] Although, to my knowledge, no one has calculated the total, we probably spend more money spinning statistics than gathering them. And that is the real problem with what we might call "statistical politics." We prop up policy with shaky interpretations of data.

47

Richard Moran, a sociology and criminology professor at Mt. Holyoke College, offered a wonderful perspective on the problem when he noted that, in his thirty years of driving, he "had been killed or almost killed over 100 times." Obviously, he acknowledged, he'd been playing fast and loose with the definition of "almost killed." And by linking "almost killed" with "killed," he distorted and overdramatized how dangerous it is to drive a car.[6] His point was that when advocacy groups or government agencies make equally outrageous claims, no one gets upset. For instance, Former Rep. Pat Schroeder claimed that the "traditional" American family is a relic of the past, that only 6 to 10 percent of families now fit the traditional model. But the devil is in the definition. How do you define "traditional"? In this case, the definition was:

- a father who works
- a mother who does not work, even part time
- two dependent children at home (not one, not three, not four, but two).

By sifting the statistics differently, Moran points out, you can make exactly the opposite case: 73 percent of dependent children live in a home with two married parents.[7]

The applications of the Remade Measure offer enormous flexibility for justifying or attacking policy. All you need do is cite the statistic, but leave out the modifers or the potential modifiers. If you want to "prove" that the health care system in the United States is on the skids—and thus justify some sort of overhaul, such as national health insurance—you can trot out the factoid that that the United States has a relatively high infant mortality rate. While infant mortality may indeed be an indicator of the failings of the health care system, there are other factors that confound the statistic, such as the fact that U.S. doctors often undertake heroic and high-tech efforts to save high-risk babies who would otherwise be stillborn. Other factors unrelated to health care come into play as well, including drug abuse and the correlation between teen pregnancies and low-birthweight babies.[8]

Journalist Ramesh Ponnuru recently dissected several such statistics, including the persistent claim that guns in the home are 43 times more likely to kill a family member or friend than an intruder. Ponnuru notes that it's not exactly false, but it's plainly misleading. First, the statistic is based on a single study of Seattle reported in the *New England Journal of Medicine*. Second, it ignores a competing statistic that shows using a gun for defense kills the assailant only 1 or 2 percent of the time. The number of times an attacker is wounded or frightened away when the gun is brandished doesn't figure into the equation. And the majority of the deaths tallied in the "43 times more likely" factoid are suicides, which may have occurred even if guns were not present. Many countries with fewer handguns have higher suicide rates than the United States. People simply find other ways to kill themselves.[9]

Governments, the source of so many statistics, also twist them for self-serving reasons. The Commonwealth of Massachusetts recently claimed it had only a .5 percent escape rate for prisoners on furlough. But author Robert Bidinotto, in his book *Crime and Consequences*, examined that statistic, showing that it was derived by dividing 428 escapes by 121,713 furloughs. But (and you knew there was a "but" coming) the total number of furloughs was arrived at by adding *multiple furloughs* for *only 10,835 inmates*! The "real" escape rate, then, is more like one in 25.[10]

Such Remade Measures, coupled with Tortured Definitions, can dramatically alter the implied thrust of a "fact." I can maximize the perceived impact of disabilities, for example, by informing you that a 1996 report from the National Center for Health Statistics, widely reported in the press, noted that nearly 100 million Americans have "chronic diseases or disabilities" and that the cost of their care accounts for about three-quarters of U.S. health spending.[11] But I can mitigate the impact by telling you that the largest single category in this total was the 32 million Americans with sinusitis and hay fever.[12] Is unemployment up or down? That depends on how you measure it. In the long term, unemployment seems to be dropping steadily. But we've also been changing the way we count the unemployed in the past two decades, taking several categories of non-workers (such as recently discharged and currently unemployed military) out of the calculation. Is the number of AIDS cases rising or falling? Recent headlines noted, as in this example from the *Chicago Tribune*, that "Women Accounted for 19 Percent of All AIDS Cases, Their Highest Proportion Yet." True, but the proportion of women rose because of a drop in the number of men with AIDS.[13]

Perception can be altered by how data are reported, and in government, perception is often the reality. (Determination of reality is a broad and ancient question of epistemological inquiry, neatly

49

solved by Lily Tomlin, who correctly concluded that "Reality is a collective hunch.") For instance, it is likely that lately you feel safer on
the streets of major cities because crime rates have plummeted.
While there is good evidence to suggest that crime *is* dropping,
there is also an abundance of evidence to show that the Remade
Measure is hard at work cleaning up those mean streets.

To put it simply, police officials, under severe pressure to produce headline-grabbing reductions in the crime rate, have been
cooking the statistics using the verbal techniques of the Tortured
Defintion and the numerical chicanery involved in the Remade
Measure. Recent investigations in New York, Atlanta, and Boca
Raton, Florida, have led to the resignation or demotion of high-
ranking police commanders for manipulating crime data.[14] In
Philadelphia, the police department withdrew the local crime figures reported to the federal government when underreporting and
misclassification of incidents were discovered. But until the fudging was exposed, the "reduction" in crime was impressive.
Philadelphia Police Captain Daniel Castro, a rising star, reduced
serious crime in his precinct by 80 percent. But alas, Castro, the
youngest district commander in the city, was relieved of his command when internal affairs accused him of downgrading many robberies, burglaries, and thefts to "missing property."[15]

A *Philadelphia Inquirer* investigation concluded that the department as a whole was systematically using creative classification to
downgrade crimes and give the city a statistical makeover. When a
Fire Department jeep was taken by joy-riders, the incident was
classified as "investigate auto." A handbag containing $650 taken
from a salesclerk was classified as "lost property."[16] Many car thefts
were disguised with the classification "try and locate," a designa-
tion normally used on crime reports to indicate that the owners of
cars forgot where they parked them. Burglaries were commonly reclassified as property damage, leading one incisive watch leader to
observe that there were fewer burglaries on his beat but "more
vandalism to the door knob." Crimes against persons were also subject to creative bracket creep, a practice that not only is deceptive
but hurtful to the victims. In Pennsylvania, a state fund reimburses
hospital bills and lost income to victims of violent crime. But some
victims found themselves ineligible for reimbursement from the
fund because the crimes against them were downgraded to minor
offenses and no police reports of violent crimes were on file. The
techniques used to rewrite reports are nothing if not imaginative.

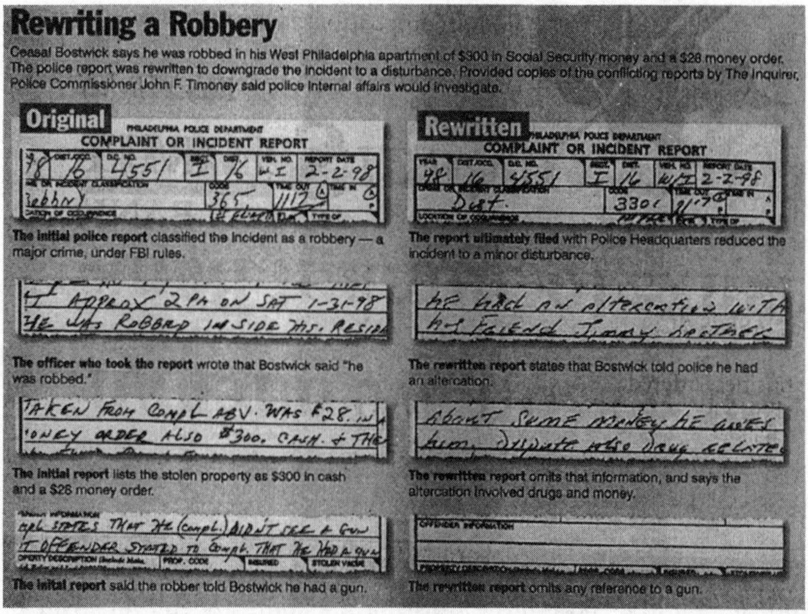

Figure 4.1: The original crime report said the victim was robbed, as seen in the *Philadelphia Inquirer*.

51

Caesal Bostwick told police he was robbed in his West Philadelphia apartment. The robber said he had a gun in his pocket and took $300 in cash and a $28 money order. The original police report classified the incident as a robbery, a major crime. The officer who took the original report noted that Bostwick said "he was robbed" (figure 4.1). But the revised version reclassified the incident to a "disturbance." Whoever rewrote the report deleted the reference to a gun. And the incident was characterized as a drug-related altercation, even though Bostwick says he never told police drugs were involved.

Crime in Atlanta seemed to be seeping away like the tide until some creative bookkeeping was uncovered. In 1998, the state of Georgia and the federal government audited the Atlanta Police Department's crime logs. This came after a public spat in which a deputy chief, since demoted, claimed that the police were tinkering with crime data, a charge the police chief denied. But the audit found a history of statistical chicanery, dating back to 1996 when fifty-six reports of rape were written off by the police department as "unfounded"—meaning that, in the eyes of the police, no crime occurred. More than one robbery occurred each day that the Atlanta police reports said didn't happen. The result was that the city put forth statistics claiming that rapes declined by 11 percent since 1995 and robberies dropped by 9 percent.[17] But the audit, released early in 1999, determined that, of about 5,700 cases reviewed by state and federal authorities from 1995 to 1997, 16.1 percent were improperly classified as unfounded. The *Atlanta Journal-Constitution* noted that a significant surge in unfounded crimes occured in 1996—a mayoral election year and the year the Olympics were held.

Crime statistics are notoriously slippery, and it's not necessary for someone to deliberately fudge them in order for the numbers to paint a distorted picture. Many crimes—some estimates peg the number at about a third—are not reported, according to door-to-door surveys conducted by the FBI in 1997. These may be largely minor and insignificant crimes, but no one knows for sure.

State statistics are also gathered and collated in fairly haphazard ways. Some police agencies report crime statistics to the state and some don't. Oakland, California, has not reported in several years. The unlikely possibility that there have been no crimes in Oakland casts some doubt on the state's figures as a whole.[18] California's state crime reporting system also mandates that fingerprint cards be sent along with arrest information forwarded to the state. When there's no fingerprint card, those crimes are not included in the report. Nobody knows for sure how many arrest reports come without fingerprint cards, but some estimates put the total at between 40 and 60 percent.[19]

So-called hate crimes—attacks based on racial or other prejudice—seem to ebb and flow depending on police cataloguing methods and the media's interest in such crimes. On the one hand, Orlando, Florida, exhibited a 100 percent drop in hate crimes between 1995 and 1996. Was there a sudden burst of brotherhood in the city of Disney? Perhaps, but the *St. Petersburg Times* said that the police simply had not reported about two dozen suspected hate crimes to the state. Such reporting failures occurred throughout the state, leading to an apparent 44 percent decline.[20]

But because alleged hate crimes are sometimes the focus of media attention, we may also be led to believe their prevalance is higher than it actually is. From 1997 through early 1999, there were at least five false reports of hate crimes on college campuses, cases which grabbed headlines but were later debunked as hoaxes.

The *Chronicle of Higher Education* reported that in some cases, the perpetrators appeared to be making a statement that "it could happen here" (even if it didn't) and were apparently emboldened by the fact that they expected others to rush to their defense, even if the crime reports were debunked. There may have been some truth in that belief, judging by the reaction of one college administrator who, in referring to a hate-crime hoax, told the *Chronicle* that "these are important conversations we are having, and we should carry them forward regardless of the reality of the initiating events."

Such is the problem with perception. We have to rely on amorphous "facts" to paint our picture of reality. As to the drop in crime, it is certainly not all illusory. I, and some people who actually know what they're talking about, believe that factors such as the aging of the population, the reduced popularity of crack cocaine, and aggressive police work have brought about a genuine reduction in crime. But the point is that it's a mistake to rely on government statistics alone to form a judgment about any social condition. Belief that things are getting better because the numbers say so won't provide any actual benefit if you're unemployed or being held at gunpoint. You'll be in roughly the same predicament as the statistician who drowned wading a river with an average depth of four feet.

53

Notes

1. James Bovard, "Truth Is the Casualty as Clinton Takes Aim at Guns," *The Wall Street Journal*, June 25, 1998, p. A22.
2. Ibid.
3. Beth Belton, "Bad Data," *USA Today*, December 3, 1996, p. 1B.
4. Ibid.
5. Ibid.
6. Richard Moran, "Statistics Are Misleading and Can 'Almost Kill'," "Morning Edition" commentary, National Public Radio, April 18, 1996.
7. Ibid.
8. Remesh Ponnuru, "The New Myths," *National Review*, Nov. 9, 1998, p. 42.
9. Ibid.
10. "True Numbers Escaped Them," *The Orlando Sentinel*, April 3, 1998, p. A8.

11. Scott Shane, "Making Sure the Figures Don't Lie," *The Baltimore Sun*, October 20, 1998, p. 2A.
12. Ibid.
13. Ibid.
14. Fox Butterfield, "As Crime Falls, Pressure Rises to Alter Crime Data," *The New York Times*, August 3, 1998, p. A1.
15. Ibid.
16. Michael Matza, Mark Fazlollah, and Craig R. McCoy, "The Big Write-Off: When Stolen Goods Are 'Lost'," *The Philadelphia Inquirer*, November 2, 1998, pp. 1, 14.
17. Ron Martz, "Crime Stats: Questions Linger after Atlanta Audit," *The Atlanta Constitution*, Jan. 28, 1999, p. C1.
18. Alan W. Bock, "There Are Reasons to Mistrust Crime Statistics," *The Orange County Register*, August 9, 1998, p. G5.
19. Ibid.
20. Leanora Minai, "Hate-Crime Statistics Misleading in Florida," *The St. Petersburg Times*, October 15, 1998, p. 1A.

Chapter Five!

I Lie, Therefore I Am

The Existentially Ambiguous Image in Politics

I tremble for my country when I reflect that God is just. —Thomas Jefferson

✱ Boston Harbor had been polluted ever since the colonists dumped tea in it, but that didn't stop candidate George Bush from blaming the mess on Michael Dukakis, then governor of Massachusetts. In what may be the granddaddy of all Ambiguous Events, Bush assembled a press conference on the docks of the harbor that Dukakis never got around to cleaning up. Pointing to the water in the harbor (which has approximately the same hygienic properties as a toilet bowl in the Port Authority Bus Terminal), Bush questioned Dukakis's claim that Dukakis would be "the environmental president." The soundbite appeared prominently on the network news programs that evening and was presented with an odd awareness of the pseudo-reality of the event. Reporters duly noted that the event was essentially a clever photo-op, but they still ferried along the video of George Bush wagging his finger at an open sewer in Michael Dukakis's home state.

You probably know the punch line: Boston Harbor is actually a *federal* harbor, and if anybody bore responsibility, it was probably Vice President Bush. While that fact eventually did surface, facts are rarely a match for a good television soundbite—the coin of the realm in modern TV-mediated politics.

While running for office, and then convincing voters they weren't hoodwinked, has never been an exercise in probity, the television age has ushered in unrivaled opportunities for telling half-truths with an Ambiguous Image. Television, you see, is a consummate liar. This isn't a personal attack against the people who run the medium, or the medium itself, but simply a reflection of the mechanics of the device. (As my late friend Edwin Diamond, the media critic, used to say, there's no point in getting mad at TV because it is what it is. Getting mad at TV is like getting angry at a duck because it has yellow feet. It is what it is.)

Here's how TV lies. First, it changes our point of view without our being aware of it. For example, the simple image of a man at a desk can have different effects dramatically: the technology of the medium changes the way we perceive the picture. If the camera angle is high and we're looking down on the man, he appears insignificant, submissive. If this were a scene from a TV show, and we were reading in a role, he might be a clerk we're going to berate for committing some bureaucratic error. If instead we're looking *up* at the man, he appears dominant and forbidding. Now, if we were scripting this scene, he might be a boss ready to fire an employee.

How do other technological manipulations influence the way you "decode" the television message? One example is when a TV producer chooses to use a close-up as opposed to a longer shot. Does the close-up have any deeper meaning, any visual grammar, so to speak? Sure it does. Under some circumstances, close-ups convey intimacy. Would an earnest conversation between husband and wife on a drama series seem convincing if it were all filmed with long-shots? But under other circumstances, close-ups convey the idea that the person pictured is under harsh scrutiny. If you were watching a news program in which a reporter grilled someone who was probably up to no good, do you think you would suspect the person to be more guilty or less if he was shown in a tight close-up with harsh lights bringing beads of sweat to his forehead? Here's a great example of how TV producers caught on to the visual grammar of TV right from the birth of the medium. Mike Wallace, who even back in the '50s had an aggressive demeanor and unnaturally black hair, described the set of his pioneering interview program "Night Beat" this way:

Not for us the traditional and cheerful living room set, with the standard soft lights, the comfortable sofa and fake flowers. Instead, our studio was stark, pitch black, except for the white klieg light glaring over my shoulder into the guest's eyes—and psyche. Nor was that all. Just as interviewers never cut too close to the bone in those days, neither did the cameras. They always had been kept at a decorous distance, a medium close-up, to assure the guest that he or she would be seen in the most flattering way. On Night Beat we used searching, tight close-ups to record the tentative glances, the nervous tics, the beads of perspiration—warts and all.

Not to put too fine a point on these remarks, but tics and sweat do not necessarily translate to guilt or wrongdoing on the part of the guest. We *associate* these traits with guilt. In our minds we construct a world in which the guilty tic and sweat, and through television technology in the form of hot lights and camera close-ups, we create conditions which cause the sweating, ticking wretch to *look* guilty.

This process illustrates what's wrong with the mixture of television and politics. The medium favors simple themes with compelling visuals, but political issues don't always come with such built-in shorthand. For example, conflict is the simplest element of any story, novel, or play. Most TV news stories feature conflict too, even if conflict is not an essential part of the story.

Here is the classic example, and as a former TV reporter I have been guilty of this. You are covering a city council meeting where some expensive and complex issues are being discussed. Boring. But then a shouting match breaks out between two windbags. The cameras turn—magnetized—and the windbags make the 11 o'clock news while the million-dollar sewer bill, or whatever, does not. The medium has obscured the message. The history of television and politics is indeed *the history of the medium trampling the message.* If you'll indulge me an extended side-trip here, let me illustrate how it happened.

The year is 1952. Richard Nixon is running as vice president on the Eisenhower ticket. Nixon is an ideal complement to Ike: where Eisenhower is profoundly uncomfortable with this new medium that has captured the imagination of the public, Nixon embraces it; Eisenhower is secure in his role as avuncular elder statesman, whereas Nixon is a tenacious political infighter. The campaign is running smoothly, but on September 18 a headline in the *New York Post* whips up the storm clouds: SECRET RICH MEN'S TRUST FUND

KEEPS NIXON IN STYLE FAR BEYOND HIS SALARY. Nixon, the *Times* claims, has possession of a secret fund set up by corporate fat-cats who hope to tuck the future vice president in their pocket. Eisenhower, running on an anti-graft "let's clean up the mess in Washington" theme, wanted no part of a scandal. Nixon was on his way off the ticket, but party elders told him he had one chance to save himself: Go on nationwide television and clear your name.

Nixon bought a block of network airtime and, in addition to giving the speech of his life, demonstrated what this new medium did best. With wife Pat sitting nearby, and occasionally pictured demurely on-camera, Nixon discussed his finances in excruciating detail, going so far as to disclose his mortgage balances and the loans he had taken from his parents. But some of the "secret fund" allegations were left hanging, and as the end of the broadcast approached, viewers were caught between the Scylla and Charybdis of two opposing sets of complex facts. But wait . . . in the closing moments of the broadcast, Nixon made a dramatic confession. He had accepted a gift from a political backer, after all. It was a little black-and-white cocker spaniel named Checkers. The kids, like all kids, loved the dog, so, no matter what anybody said, he was not going to give Checkers back. Nobody really wanted to confiscate Nixon's dog, of course, but by his appeal he used the heat of televised emotion to evade the light of reason. An emotional appeal that would appear ludicrous in print played beautifully on television, and Nixon saved his spot on the ticket.

The Checkers Speech made the emotional power of television undeniable and its use as a campaign tool essential. Even the media-phobic Eisenhower was dragged into the electronic era, although he expressed some prescient reservations about the intellectual honesty of the use of crafted images. For example, he filmed in one sitting several "answers" to questions. Later, his campaign handlers rounded up tourists from a line outside Radio City Music Hall—people who fit the visual roles of housewives, veterans, and plain folks who'd had it with the "goings-on in Washington"—and had them "ask" Eisenhower questions that were later inter-cut with his answers. (Question: "But aren't their intentions good?" Answer: "If a bus driver goes out of control, goes over a cliff . . . you don't say his intentions were good, you get a new driver.")

By 1960, after Eisenhower had completed two terms and Nixon was running for the top spot, a new TV gunslinger was pacing down Main Street. John F. Kennedy was as comfortable with the medium as Nixon, but had the distinct advantage of being photogenic. When the showdown came—the famous 1960 debate—Kennedy was a little faster on the draw. He'd slept most of the day in order to appear rested, and wore a TV-friendly dark suit. Nixon had put in a full day of campaign stops, was ill and feverish, wore a beige suit that made him blend into the background, and refused the makeup he badly needed.

A new bit of visual grammar also contributed to Nixon's downfall: the reaction shot. In 1960 television producers weren't entirely sure what TV was supposed to look like, just as there's no universal agreement today about how a web page is supposed to appear. Don Hewitt, today the executive producer of CBS's *60 Minutes*, directed the debate and decided to take a reaction shot of Nixon while Kennedy spoke. In 1960 reaction shots were a fairly new part of television's visual grammar, and while various accounts differ as to whether they were supposed to be used in the debate, they were. And the moral of the story is that, while the handsome young man from Boston was criticizing Mr. Nixon, an unexpected reaction shot showed Nixon doing what he did copiously and consistently—sweating. TV viewers put the images together and thought that Kennedy had made Nixon sweat. Viewers polled the next day thought Kennedy had won. But people who *listened on radio*, also polled the next day, thought *Nixon* had won. Don Hewitt said the experience demonstrated what's wrong with the mixture of TV and politics.

The power of the television image could not be denied or ignored any longer. Four years later, producer Tony Schwartz showed how emotional visual appeals could completely circumvent any recitation of fact with the "Daisy Commercial," arguably the most controversial and effective political ad in history. You probably know something about the Daisy Commercial. It featured a little girl picking flowers, counting the petals aloud, juxtaposed with a missile officer's voice as he counted down to nuclear Armageddon. The rest of what you think you know about the commercial is probably wrong, because in reality the infamous Daisy Commercial

- played only once and
- never mentioned Goldwater.

A couple of years ago Schwartz played a tape of the ad for me as we sat in the Manhattan brownstone he uses as an office. (It is an astonishing place, piled floor to ceiling with shelved tape boxes, and equipped with a TV camera and video link so that Schwartz, who detests travel, can teach college classes from his office.) He proved to my satisfaction that the tape never mentioned Goldwater, even though I could have sworn that it did. Schwartz explained that my confusion was the reason why the ad was so effective: it was like a Rorschach test. Like people who see dirty pictures in the psychiatrist's ink-blots, viewers blended their own conceptions into the drama, drawing on their deep-seated fears that Goldwater was a nuclear hothead. Incidentally, it was the controversy that followed the single airing of the commercial that seared it into the national memory. When newscasters discussed this Ambiguous Image, they really had no choice but *to repeat it and inadvertently reinforce it*.

Nixon exploited the power of the ambiguous and repeated image when he came out of exile to defeat Hubert Humphrey in 1968. Humphrey accepted the party's nomination after Lyndon Johnson, drained by the intractability of Vietnam, withdrew from the race late in his first term. The emerging antiwar faction viewed Humphrey's nomination as a product of insider politics. Outside the halls of the 1968 Democratic National Convention, demonstrators rioted, and Chicago police fought back. The carnage made chilling television. Nixon used riot footage in his commercials to associate Humphrey with the disorder in the streets. The logic of the connection was nonexistent, but the image was eloquent, and, in order to dispute it, Humphrey had to repeat it.

Eloquence in imagery was raised to an art form under Ronald Reagan, who, along with his handlers, understood the unassailable power of the image. When it comes to a test of the eye and the ear, the eye always wins, and even if your image is inaccurate, it is difficult to counter it without inadvertently reinforcing it. Reagan's images were beautifully choreographed, almost always making a specific point that may or may not have had any connection with reality. The framed-house mentioned in chapter 3 for example, showed the president touring a construction site on the day it was announced that housing starts were up. The image was elegant, the implication (that the president is responsible for this house being built) eloquent, and the logic nonexistent. Reagan used image-making to court southern blue-collar voters—vital to his reelection—by starting an auto race in Daytona and serving as commentator for the event, enlightening viewers with such observations as "somebody just passed somebody down there." And he was known to stop in for a choreographed "beer with the boys" in working-class neighborhoods—at least when a camera was present.

CBS's Leslie Stahl tried to expose the Reagan administration's use of creative imagery in a highly critical television report, in which she charged that images of supportive senior citizens and the handicapped used by Reagan were actually at odds with his policies. The evening after the piece aired, Stahl received a call from a White House adviser. Reluctantly, expecting to be lambasted for the critical piece, she took the call and was flabbergasted when the adviser *thanked her*. The Reagan adviser told her that viewers would only remember the visuals she showed in an effort to discredit them.

When George Bush reached for Reagan's mantle, he used the same visual strategy. He appeared at a flag factory, for example, almost literally wrapping himself in the flag, and declared that "flag sales are doing well, and America is doing well." (I am not making that up. He really said it.) Not to be outdone, Michael Dukakis then arranged to visit a flag factory himself to show that, he, too, had mastered the art of standing in front of television cameras while flags were cut and sewed.

This masterful illumination of policy, rivaling perhaps only the Lincoln-Douglas debates in its thoughtful depth, worked for Bush in 1988 because he tended to strike first, forcing Dukakis to return his serves. But the strategy failed him four years later. The economy had soured, and the post-Willie-Horton attacks—retargeted to sex rather than crime—failed to resonate with the public. Moreover, Bill Clinton turned out to be a master counter-puncher.

The Clinton White House refocused political image-making and counter-punching by launching what might be the most tightly organized spin machine in history. Spin Science under Clinton got off to a rocky start, but as his second term began, staffers such as Chief of Staff Leon Panetta, consultant Dick Morris, and Press Secretary Mike McCurry, developed a coherent approach to manipulating the media. Clinton, as media critic Howard Kurtz described it in *The Spin Cycle*, used "a carefully honed media strategy—alternately seducing, misleading and sometimes intimidating the press—that maintained this aura of success. No day went by without the president and his coterie laboring mightily to generate favorable headlines and deflect damaging ones, to project their preferred image on the vast screen of the media establishment."[1]

Clinton's spinners used the art of the image eloquently, but were eventually forced to engage in more-or-less continual damage control. Damage control usually involved some mixture of Ambiguous Images with Threading the Needle. But the president, perhaps the most steady-handed and sharp-eyed Needle Threader in history, was confounded by the events of January 21, 1998, when the *Washington Post* reported that Clinton had been accused of having an affair with a 22-year-old intern.

That morning, Clinton and his lawyers prepared a statement in which Clinton denied any "improper relationship" with Monica Lewinsky. And at a press conference that day, spokesman McCurry began threading needles and unraveling at the same time. The resulting exchanges would come to epitomize the Clinton spin machine.

The first question, of course, was what the president meant by an "improper relationship."

McCurry: "I'm not going to parse the statement."

But, the reporters continued, does that mean there was no sexual relationship?

McCurry: " . . . I'm just not going to parse the statement for you. It speaks for itself."

But what kind of relationship did the president have with Lewinsky?

McCurry: "I'm not characterizing it beyond what the statement that I've already issued says."

Later, a reporter from the *Washington Post* tried a different approach, asking McCurry if he would be at the podium, answering the way he did, if he were not absolutely confident the charges were untrue.

McCurry: "Look, my personal views don't count."

Sam Donaldson asked why the word "sexual" was never put in the statement.

McCurry: "I didn't write the statement."

The interview moved to a climax with a response that would be prophetic.

What, the press asked, was the administration's next move?

McCurry: "To get off this podium as quick as possible."[2]

Notes

1. Howard Kurtz, *The Spin Cycle* (New York: Free Press, 1998).
2. Ibid., pp. xiv–xvii.

Chapter Six

The Vying Game

Cooking the Books in College Rankings

Let's start a hypothetical college. I'll be president. (I have a Ph.D. that I paid quite a bit of money for and I want to put it to good use.) You'll be the admissions director. We'll call our institution Wassamatta University. Wassamatta U. is private, fairly small, on an attractive piece of real estate, and headed for trouble. The problem with our college (which, as admissions director, is now *your* problem) is that, despite my stellar leadership, the university has nothing special going for it. It doesn't have a big name, the test scores of the freshman class are pretty low, and we've gotten the unfortunate reputation of being practically an "open admission college"—meaning we take anybody with the cash to pay the tuition. We need good students, good students who also have money, and we need them right away. We're competing for the same pool of students with five or six nearby schools with marginally better reputations, bigger endowments, and better-looking cheerleaders.

There's another problem you need to fix. If we don't get our enrollments, "standards," and "reputation" up to snuff, we'll have more trouble recruiting faculty, and our current professors might go to other colleges, or even look for real jobs.

So what are you going to do? Before you answer I would like to remind you that being an admissions director is a pretty good job. You make about as much as the football coach, but you're equally as expendable if you don't put numbers on the board.

Now, how do we fix this problem? What's that, you say? We could aggressively recruit in high schools, hire well-known faculty, strengthen our current programs, and carefully monitor the progress of our students from their freshman to senior years. In the long run that would increase our average SAT score, help us be more selective when accepting students, and bolster our reputation. Well, in theory, that sounds good, but we can't afford to do all that and, in any case, it will take decades.

Since you're new at this, let me show you some tricks of the trade. The first thing you need to do is boost the average SAT score. Prospective students and their parents pay close attention to the averages reported in the college guidebooks, and if we look like we're a bunch of dummies, nobody's going to want to apply. Besides, those guidebooks use test scores to come up with their rankings, and if we slip below our competitors, the trustees will have my head on a platter.

How do we do that? Simple. We can boost the average SAT score by not including the lowest scores! Let's not count the verbal scores of the international students. Let's also admit the remedial students in the summer and not count them as "regular" students, so all those low SATs are off the books.

Wassamatta U. also needs to be more selective. "Selectivity" is one of those categories than can kill us in the rankings, so we need to accept a smaller percentage of those who apply if we want to look more "exclusive." Therefore, I want you to encourage more *applications*, even from people who don't stand a chance of getting in. Make the application form easier: split it into a couple of separate parts so prospective students can just fill in a form and not be bothered with all the essays. We'll count the form as an application. Encourage applications from students who don't have much chance of getting in. And as for the students we're going to admit, put some of them on a "waiting list." We'll let them in *eventually*, but we'll *count* them as rejects.

See? I've improved our numbers and it didn't take much work at all. All I did was remake the measure. Why didn't you think of that? Frankly, I'm not sure you're cut out for this line of work. . . .

In fairness to the president of Wassamatta U., he lives and dies by those numbers. If Wassamatta makes one of the popular guide-books' listings of "Top Colleges in the East," or "Best Buys in Liberal Arts Colleges," applications will spike, alumnae will be happy, and the trustees might renew his contract. But if Wassamatta drops from the list, or is surpassed by a competitor, angry alumnae and donors will be on the phone demanding to know what the hell happened.

All of this caught the higher eduction industry more or less by surprise. It's difficult to imagine, but competitive college admissions were not on the radar screen until after World War II. Prior to the war, the admissions office was usually a sleepy department, often run by one or two people. Not everyone expected to go to college or had the means to go, and, as a result, supply and demand stayed in balance. After the war, veterans on the GI bill flooded campuses. Then those college-educated vets set about producing a new gen-eration that expected a college education too. Admissions became serious business, and admissions officers became gatekeepers. But after the peak of the baby-boom generation went to college, demo-graphics changed. During the late 1970s, there were as many as three million graduating high school seniors a year. By the mid-1990s, the number was closer to two million, and there's no new baby boom in sight. This demographic downturn devastated some colleges. As one admissions official put it, "If you told a represen-tative of some other type of business that 'in the next ten to twelve years you'll lose 30 percent of your potential market,' you'd have people jumping out of windows."[1]   *65*

The gatekeepers suddenly found themselves with no one at the gates—except for the barbarians. But colleges didn't want to admit them, because it was important not to be perceived as an open admissions college. Ernest Boyer, president of the Carnegie Foundation for the Advancement of Teaching, pointed out that "there's still a feeling in higher eduction that there's some advan-tage in demonstrating that you're screening a lot of people out, even though many of the colleges that say they're selective might admit, frankly, 90 percent of the students who apply."[2]

So the hunt was on for high-quality students in the diminishing pool. The Harvards, MITs, and most of the other elite schools didn't have to worry: they were assured of a consistent stream of high-quality applicants. But the fair-to-middling colleges confronted disaster, and the gatekeepers turned to marketers.

College marketing is a tough business, and salespeople resort to some surprisingly intrusive tactics, including buying mailing lists of students who did well on the Preliminary Scholastic Aptitude Test (PSAT). The PSAT is taken in students' sophomore or junior year, and is more or less a warm-up for the SAT. Both tests are conducted by the same entity, the College Board, which sells names of students who scored within certain parameters on the test and who agree to receive marketing materials from colleges. Such students can expect to be inundated with glossy brochures and, perhaps, a few videos from prospective colleges.

The rapacious appetite for "quality" students can be hurtful, with some prospective students courted relentlessly but dropped at the last minute. Here's a typical scenario. A small liberal-arts college needs to fill 550 spots in its incoming freshman class. In order to meet this goal, the college will need about 3,200 to 3,500 applicants. Forty to 50 percent of these will be accepted. Let's assume the college accepts 1,600. The experience of prior years leads college officials to calculate that about 550 of the 1,600 accepted will actually enroll. Students who have expressed an interest in the college, or who have been identified through other means, and who fit the profile may be invited for campus tours, called by faculty, and generally given every indication that they will be welcome in the next freshman class. But as sometimes happens, the sports teams of this particular college have a good year, or a professor wins a major prize, or there's simply a glut in the particular demographic: as a result there are 4,200 applicants! The college then trims back its less-enticing candidates, and students who have been given every expectation they will be admitted are cut loose. And then this college will probably have the temerity to crow about it, pointing out how "selective" it was this year, because it only accepted a third of the applicants.

All this, of course, leads back to that statistical profile that will be reported to the guidebooks. We can feel some sympathy for college administrators, including the president of Wassamatta U., because this is not a game they invented (although, as we've seen, colleges do their own version of ranking and statistically collating). Americans are ravenously obsessed with ratings and rankings, and guidebooks satiate that appetite by taking numbers that may or may not hold any real informational value and ordering those in a chart that appears to be the result of a precise methodology. This appearance is the problem, because a lot of what comes out of the statistical grinder is Precision Garbage.

Here's an example. The California Institute of Technology took a statistical hit in the rankings in 1996 when *U.S. News and World Report*, which publishes the best-known annual college guide, added a new category called "value added." As part of the computation for this category, *U.S. News and World Report* calculated a "predicted" graduation rate for each college based on test scores and "educational expenditures per student." The magazine then compared their predictions with actual graduation rates. Cal Tech dropped in the "value added" category because it has a graduation rate of only 85 percent, while the magazine's predicted rate was 99 percent.

Putting aside the odd notion that a predicted graduation rate can be concocted from a ratio of expenditures and test scores, the conclusion that a rigorous college that does not make it easy to pass courses somehow lacks "value" is absurd. Of course Cal Tech could fix this lack of "value added" by giving a lot of automatic As and passing everybody.

While we can sympathize with a college's position in all this—that it is being held to absurd standards—fudging data compounds the problem. While my hypothetical example may seem extreme, there's a lot of sleight-of-hand used in SAT and admission numbers. An admissions director for a top liberal-arts school, who insisted on anonymity, told Deirdre Carmody of the *New York Times* that about a quarter of the students in the most competitive colleges are going to be N.I.P.s, meaning "not in profile," and hence their SAT scores are not going to be reported to the guidebooks.[3] N.I.P.s often include children of alumnae, athletes on scholarships, foreign students, students admitted under special programs, or any other group with a score low enough to pull down the average SAT score of those who applied to a particular college and were accepted.

67

By excluding a group from the profile, the average SAT score can be altered significantly. Reporter Steve Stecklow of the *Wall Street Journal* found that New College of South Florida lifted its average SAT score by about 40 points by simply lopping off the bottom 6 percent of students, a device termed a "marketing strategy" by the admission director (who also said the practice had been discontinued).[4] The strategy did, however, help secure the college a Number One ranking in a category in *Money* magazine—based partly on the impressive freshman SAT average of 1286. Northeastern University excluded foreign students and remedial students—who represent about 20 percent of the freshman class—and raised its average SAT by about 50 points.[5]

Colleges also manipulate acceptance rates. One administrator, who spoke on condition of anonymity, told me that some colleges have recently started encouraging applications from foreign students—most of whom stand little chance of admission because they are ineligible for student loans and must foot the entire yearly tuition and housing bill—in order to be able to reject a greater number of those who apply.[6] The tactic of putting students on waiting lists and not counting them as admitted is also widespread, as is the practice of counting a student who was rejected by one program within the university. The most nettling part of this is that, in the absence of any uniform standards, it's very difficult to compare data harvested under differing measures. And colleges have every incentive to fudge the figures because college guides cannot or do not audit every piece of the data. Besides, there's no law against lying to a college guidebook.

But there are some pretty severe legal consequences involved in lying to a debt rating agency, such as Moody's or Standard and Poor's. *Wall Street Journal* reporter, Steve Stecklow, scored one of journalism's great gotchas by comparing data reported to college guidebooks and data reported to the rating agencies. Stecklow and the *WSJ* staff conducted an audit of credit reports and bond prospectuses for one hundred colleges, and uncovered more than two dozen discrepancies in SAT scores, acceptance data, and other enrollment information. In almost every case where there was a discrepancy—prepare yourself now, because this will be quite a shock—the information reported to the guidebooks was more favorable than what was reported to Moody's or Standard and Poor's.[7] Contacted by the *Journal*, the college officials who proffered the data offered a variety of explanations, including "transcription error," or mistakes made in "pure innocence." One administrator claimed that because college guides "abuse" such numbers, "then what you've got to do as an admissions person is jiggle them in such a way so the abuse is minimized."

Fingers continue to point in both directions regarding who's to blame. In 1998 Stanford University, which has attacked the reliability of college guide data for several years, began offering audited data on its web site. College guides routinely say they are verifying more of the data reported to them and tightening methodologies. But changes in methodologies often are denounced by the colleges, who claim that such mechanical alterations produce mechanical changes in rankings. Such changes, they contend, in turn spur continued sales of magazines, as readers devour the annual college horse race, following which college is closing in and which fell back in the pack. Many variables contribute to who finishes in what order and sometimes the result isn't fair. In that respect, the college ranking business really is analogous to a horse race. But unfortunately, the variables used to determine the winner are much more analogous to what's left on the track after the race.

Notes

1. "Colleges Compete for Fewer and Fewer Freshmen," National Public Radio *NPR's Morning Edition*, April 29, 1994.
2. Ibid.
3. Deirdre Carmody, "Colleges' S.A.T. Lists Can Be Creative Works," *The New York Times*, August 30, 1995, p. A18.
4. Steve Stecklow, "Colleges Inflate SATs and Graduation Rates in Popular Guidebook," *The Wall Street Journal*, April 5, 1995, p. A1.
5. Ibid.
6. You really didn't think I was going to tell you, did you? I told you he insisted on anonymity.
7. Stecklow.

Chapter Seven

The Veiled Variable Rides Again

Tricks of the Trade in Financial Institutions

When 18-year-old Erian McKinley received a mail offer for a platinum card with a low interest rate and a credit limit of "up to $100,000," he was delighted. And when a representative of the credit card company called him a few weeks later to repeat the offer, he signed up. But when the card arrived, it wasn't platinum, and the credit limit was $500.[1] Mr. McKinley did, however, get something valuable out of the deal: an early introduction to the ways that credit card companies and other financial institutions play what amounts to a financial shell game.

The Veiled Variable and the Incognito If are the most common numerical and verbal techniques used by financial institutions. In the case of the credit card offer, the tacit modifier was the verbally vacuous phrase "up to," meaning that the $100,000 credit limit would be offered to very few people.

More useful from the credit card issuer's point of view are the interest rate calculations, variables, and fees buried in the fine print or contingent on a host of other factors. For example, among the estimated two to three billion credit card promotions mailed each year are little gems like: "Offered by invitation only," "4.9 Percent APR," and "Credit line up to $100,000." Only in the mouse type are the ifs and variables explained. In a few months the finance charge will skyrocket to 14.99 percent. In a variation of the Incognito If in credit card come-ons, the attractive low rate may take effect only after a balance transfer. Jacked-up rates may take effect sooner if a payment is late by so much as a day.[2] And don't count on your friendly customer service representative disclosing the Veiled Variable. *Boston Herald* reporter, Robin Washington, received an offer for a Chase Manhattan Shell Mastercard that promised a 9.9 percent interest rate on the life of a loan after a balance transfer. The offer claimed that "unlike teaser rates that go up after a few months, this rate will not change." The *Herald* called Chase's customer service line twice and was told that there was no way that the rate could be changed. But in the fine print of the offer was the nitty-gritty: mail two payments late in a six-month period, and the rate skyrockets to 22.49 percent. Some card companies are not only quick to penalize delinquents, but also slap you on the wrist for paying on time. If you don't pay enough in annual finance charges, some cards hit you with an annual fee.

Buried or disguised fees are, in the words of one industry analyst, "juicy" for the industry. In addition to imposing usurious late fees, credit card companies have been quietly hiking cash advance fees. By raising them to as much as 4 percent of the advance, credit card companies manage to bring in an extra billion dollars a year.[3]

While we're tossing around big numbers, consider that consumer debt in the United States has reached $1.2 *trillion*. About half the families in the United States regularly use credit cards for borrowing, a figure that rose more than 8 percent from the mid-1980s. Median balances carried on credit cards have been climbing steadily too, as have credit limits. And so have personal bankruptcies, which are about three times higher today than they were in 1980.[4] While the fault for this most directly lies with consumers, and liberalized bankruptcy laws, remember that credit companies make a lot of money from people who can barely afford the credit, and debt, they assume. Think about it. Someone who stretches to the maximum and can only make minimum payments is a gold mine! Suppose you take out a $1,000 credit card loan and pay it off with minimum monthly payments. At a 14 percent interest rate, you'll need *14 years* to pay off the loan. The interest will total $935, practically as much as the original loan.[5]

Incidentally, 14 percent is a pretty good rate as credit cards go, but the less credit-worthy you are, the more credit will cost you. On the face of it, that's reasonable because a firm extending credit to bad risks will need to cover higher losses. But the less credit-worthy are often the least sophisticated and the most desperate. Low-income borrowers sometimes pay double the average rate of 15 percent for an unsecured loan. Finance companies serving low-income clients sometimes charge as much as 40 percent interest.

The Atlanta Journal and Constitution—serving a metropolitan area that carries one of the highest per-capita levels of consumer debt in the country—looked into the lives of low-income borrowers and found that many were not only locked into high-interest loans, but suffered the further indignity of being "flipped" from loan to new loan, with generous fees and insurance premiums tacked on each time. Many such borrowers fit a common profile: people with low incomes but high equity in their homes.[6]

Low-income borrowers are also not very good at decoding fine print. The *St. Petersburg Times* did its own investigation of a segment of the credit industry: firms offering secured credit cards to clients with low incomes and poor repayment records. In one case, a company allegedly implied in its telemarketing pitch that the people they called had qualified for a credit card with a $500 credit limit. Many cardholders, who paid a $79 nonrefundable initiation fee, said they were surprised and chagrined to learn that it wasn't a real credit line at all. They built up their $500 "credit" by payments made to the bank that held the card, and they could take out only what they put in. After two years, if they made timely payments, they would graduate to a regular credit card with a $500 or more credit limit. The bank claimed it was clear in its explanation of the $500 credit limit, but refused to release its telemarketing script to the newspaper.[7]

Standard advice to the consumer, of course, is to read the fine print in any credit card deal. But you need to *keep reading* the fine print because *credit card companies can change the rules anytime they want simply by providing you with a notice buried in more fine print*! If you don't believe me, check the mouse type in the original document you signed and you will see that it says something to the effect that the lender can change the agreement as long as they notify you fifteen days in advance.[8] If your credit card bill is anything like mine, that notification comes in an avalanche of Graphic Garble, including statement-stuffer ads for anything from insurance to luggage. If you don't respond, you tacitly "accept" the new terms.[9]

That's how credit card companies can pull such lures, offering, for example, an attractive rebate and then, when the company has lured a huge customer base, cap the rebate or make it more difficult to acquire points.[10] Some companies, such as Blockbuster Video, just drop the rebate cards if they prove to be too good a value for their users.[11] Others subtly change the rules, such as offering frequent-flyer miles based on balances carried over from month to month, when the original deal was computed on all dollars charged to the card.

Rebates themselves are of dubious value because whatever benefit you gain from these so-called rewards cards—issued under the name of a company or organization and offering points toward purchases of related products—can quickly be wiped out if you carry a balance or get socked with additional fees.

Fees are easy to hide or disguise, and anyone intent on manipulating a financial transaction can always claim indignantly that it is unreasonable for a consumer to expect to get something for free. But in the low world of high finance, you might actually be charged for something that is free. That's increasingly the case with so-called reverse mortgages, loans offered to older Americans through a federal program. "Reverse mortgages" are a loan against the value of the property which the homeowner does not have to repay until he or she moves out of the home or dies. A variety of firms have put themselves in the business of "arranging" these mortgages. In other words, they put the borrower in touch with the program—for a fee. One woman found herself on the spot when the salesman who arranged the loan delivered a check for $42,000 and asked for a fee of $5,571 for putting the elderly woman in touch with a lender. That, quite literally, is paying something for nothing.

Home refinancing in the private sector is a high-profit business and the sales pitches are often aimed at the elderly. NBC News recently reported on a come-on that often impresses the uncircumspect: Confusing Counterfeits featuring government-style, brown manilla envelopes adorned with an American Eagle and, inside the address panel, a hint of a check for big money. As an 81-year-old man, now deeply in debt, put it, "That looked official to me." [12] In fact, many come-ons for home refinancing come in disguise. My personal collection of come-ons includes envelopes bearing the return address "Mortgage Service Department," an effective ruse because it convinced me that the correspondence might be from a real lender concerning my current mortgage.

Financial maneuvers often rely on the customer not knowing exactly what's involved in the transaction and that, of course, opens the door to an uninvited collection of fees. The insurance industry is notorious for such practices as "churning," where customers are led to believe they are adding additional coverage to a current policy, when in fact, they are buying a new policy. For example, two years after buying two $50,000 life insurance policies, a Pittsburgh couple heard from their agent who explained that a special benefit of one of the policies would allow them to increase coverage by $28,000 at no extra cost.[13] They bit—but weren't told that they were actually buying a new policy, that part of the premiums of the old policy were being diverted to pay for it, and that the old policy's cash value was used to pay for the new one.[14] The motivation behind churning, of course, is that a fresh commission fee is generated for the agent. The reason the agents can get away with it is that the complexity of insurance allows for an Evil-Twin Substitution of a new policy for an old one.

Now, if you happen to thrive on complexity, I would invite you to check out the newest product in the insurance industry, variable universal life insurance (VUL). Such policies offer the opportunity to invest in mutual funds and enjoy tax-free growth. But according to *Business Week,* the plans are so mind-bogglingly complex that sometimes the agents can't understand them, and comparison shopping is virtually impossible because the fees and terms differ from company to company and are buried in the fine print of the prospectus or herded together under asterisks in the sales material.[15]

And the fees are *enormous*. For one popular VUL policy, insurers deduct about a 4 percent sales charge (called a "load") from each premium. Other fees include a first year administrative fee, a "mortality expense fee," whatever that might be, a state premium tax, and a fund management fee. If you cash in before holding the policy fifteen years, you'll be charged a surrender fee. The bottom line is that you'll stand a chance of profiting only if you can hold onto the policy more than fifteen years. According to industry estimates, however, more than half the customers who buy VUL policies cash them in before the surrender fee expires. *Business Week* concludes that this statistic suggests agents are marketing the policies to the wrong people. They have a strong incentive to do so: commissions of at least 55 percent of the first year's premium.[16]

There's a movement underway, propelled in part by consumer

75

demand, to simplify VUL policies, and the insurance industry is now reforming sales practices after coming under the scrutiny of state attorneys general and insurance commissioners. Credit card companies have, in recent years, been forced to disclose their terms more clearly, and the Securities and Exchange Commission has mandated less arcane language in prospectuses for financial documents. But the overall problem probably won't go away soon, because for every new regulation there is a new financial product to confuse and conquer the buying public. As author Robert Byrne put it, getting caught is the mother of invention.

Notes

1. Stephen E. Frank, "Credit Cards: Credit-Card Pitches Promise More, But Not All Deliver," *The Wall Street Journal*, Sept. 18, 1997, p. B1.
2. Fred Hiatt, "The Credit Card Lure and Bankruptcy," *The Cleveland Plain Dealer*, June 18, 1999, p. 11B.
3. Linda Stern, "Read the Fine Print," *Newsweek*, June 15, 1998, p. 74.
4. Frances Smith, "Are Consumers Sinking in Debt?" *Consumers' Research Magazine*, February 2, 1998, p. 10.
5. Carrie Teegardin, "Forgive Us Our Debts," *The Atlanta Journal and Constitution*, December 7, 1998, p. E1.
6. Ibid.
7. Jeff Harrington, "Customers Claim Bank Preys on Credit Woes," *The St. Petersburg Times*, Feb. 7, 1999, p. 1H.
8. Dan Oldenburg, "More Dope on Credit Cards," *The Washington Post*, August 26, 1998, p. D4.
9. Kathy Kristof, "Watch out for the Fine Print: Credit-Card Companies Legally Add Charges and Fees after the Expiration of Introductory Terms," *The Chicago Tribune*, July 28, 1998, p. 7.
10. Ibid.
11. "Credit Card Rebates Are Littered with Fine Print," *The Dallas Morning News*, October 12, 1998, p. 2S.
12. Jim Avila, "Families Losing Their Homes to Misleading Financing Loans," NBC, *The NBC Nightly News*, October 12, 1998.
13. Kristin Davis, "When Your Insurer Plays Churning Games," *Kiplinger Online*, July 1994, p. 29.

14. Ibid.
15. Adele Malpass, "Life Insurance Drowning in Fees," *Business Week*, April 13, 1998, p. 111.
16. Ibid.

Chapter Eight!

There's a Special on Fine Print in Aisle 9

The Tricky Business of Retailing

My local Shop-Rite recently offered what seemed to be a pretty good deal on Diet Pepsi, so I bought two cases. At the register, one case rang up at the sale price featured on the big sign near the stacks of cans. But I was charged full price for the other. I complained to the service desk, where an assistant told me that the display was clearly marked "limit one." But I hadn't seen the "limit one" sign, and when I went back to the display I still couldn't see it. I then asked the service clerk to show me the sign. Sure enough, there it was. Well, I *think* it was there, because it wasn't actually visible. "Limit one" was printed in small type inside a graphic about the size of a standard business envelope posted about twelve feet off the ground (figure 8.1).

I have 20/20 vision and I couldn't see it, and I don't think the average consumer under twelve feet tall could see it. But the clerk (who couldn't see it either) assured me that, if I *could* see it, I would see that I was only entitled to one case at the sale price.

The business of retailing depends on persuading a consumer with appealing signs and ads, and it is one of the toughest businesses in the world. Supermarkets face fierce competition for hitting the lowest price level, and many department stores are beat-

Figure 8.1: A "limit one" sign that Daniel Boone couldn't read
with the Hubble Telescope.

ing the wolf away from the door. So many stores were opened in
the 1980s, that it's virtually impossible for the customer base to
support them all. Couple this with the dominance of a few eight-
hundred-pound gorilla discount chains, and it's no surprise that
second-tier retailers constantly flirt with bankruptcy or a slide into
liquidation.

Advertising—inside and outside the store—is the life raft for
retailers trying to attract the choice-glutted consumer. While low
price is often the theme of retail advertising, stores also seek to dif-
ferentiate themselves by image advertising. Sears, for example,
undertook some research showing that most shopping decisions
were made by women, and boosted its sales with its "Softer Side of
Sears" campaign.

Such campaigns are boons for media, especially newspapers,
which are particularly amenable to store ads, because their pages

can contain dense detail and large listings of sale items. A chain like Sears can drop $100 million a year on newspaper ads. Newspapers, for their part, are usually as desperate for the ad revenue as stores are for shoppers. The newspaper industry is facing a triple whammy: declining readership, the aging of the newspaper demographic to a level unappealing to many advertisers, and the high price of transportation and paper. Consequently, they welcome the ad revenue from retailers. Retailers, in fact, comprise one of the few newspaper advertiser segments that is increasing.

Actually, retailers have been the lifeblood of advertising ever since the first merchant tacked up a sign. If you'll allow me a brief digression, let me trace the role of the retailer in the history of the ad industry—an industry that has been called everything from "the life of trade" (President Calvin Coolidge) and "the greatest art form of the twentieth century" (communications scholar Marshall McLuhan), to "a black art" (Judge Learned Hand) and "the rattling of a stick inside a swill bucket" (author George Orwell).

I personally like the definition proffered by ad executive Fairfax Cone. "Advertising is what you do when you can't go see somebody. That's all it is." There's some truth in that. When the industrial revolution powered a geometric increase in the number of goods for sale, it became impossible for salespeople to see all their potential customers. Person-to-person sales had been the norm since trading and commerce developed. While there is no definitive history or definition of the first ads, they probably consisted of signs or symbols over shops. In some cases those signs used symbols instead of words. For example, the well-known barber pole with its red stripes is a symbol dating back to the Middle Ages. Barbers used to cut all parts of the body, and a pole with bloody rags wrapped around it indicated the inviting parlor of a barber-surgeon.

Newspapers in the seventeenth and eighteenth centuries carried advertising, but the process of developing and selling the ads was usually half-hearted and done without any particular science or strategy. In the mid-1800s, the first advertising specialists mainly brokered space and did not offer advice or guidance on the advertising content. But around the turn of the century many ad agents began writing copy and in the age of patent medicines, it was not surprising that many of these claims were outlandish. (A "patent" medicine was a nonprescription drug allegedly containing a secret ingredient protected by a patent or a trademark. Sometimes these drugs, often marketed through traveling medicine shows, were pejoratively called "snake oil." During the second half of the nineteenth century there was a brisk trade in these drugs, which were hardly ever patented nor particularly medicinal. However, they often did make people *feel* better, at least temporarily, since some were mostly alcohol and a few were laced with morphine.)

Ad agencies would later attempt to reclaim their image, putting a sheen of businesslike respectability on their craft. An interesting example of the problems of the dual burden of hype and respectability at the time was provided by N. W. Ayer, a young man who added "and Son" to his shingle to overcome the reluctance of patrons to deal with him because of his youth.

Market research became part of the advertising strategy in the 1920s. George Gallup, of Gallup Poll fame, made considerable contributions to advertising strategy by conducting surveys of consumer reading habits. During the 1920s and '30s, two "schools" of advertising competed: the type that relied heavily on market research, and the variety that tended to employ intuition.

Radio added a new dimension to advertising in the 1920s, even though advertisers were at first reluctant to place their message on a medium so ephemeral and "personal." The radio waves reached right into people's living rooms, and there was vigorous debate about whether items like toothpaste should be advertised, lest listeners be offended.

Incidentally, the toothpaste and toothbrush industries were in a way invented by advertisers. Americans did not always pay much attention to their teeth in the early part of the century. Many people had never actually used (or seen) a toothbrush until they were issued one after World War I. Soldiers brought the habit home with them, and advertisers were more than happy to help sell them the necessary tools, powders, and pastes.

The invention of television opened the floodgates to a new style of visual advertising, the, at the time, bafflingly indirect "image" approach. An ad executive named David Ogilvy, for example, decided to sell Hathaway shirts without the traditional detailed copy extolling the benefits of the item. Instead, he hired a middle-aged male model, a distinguished man with a mustache, and gave him an eye-patch. Hathaway shirts flew off the racks, and it became obvious that customers identified with the distinguished, but nonetheless rakish, image of the one-eyed man. Image advertising became a staple of the new medium, television. And although they were skeptical at first, advertisers soon flocked to television, and the money spigot was cranked open.

Advertising agencies became a powerful influence in the TV of the 1950s, choosing which programs to back with their accounts. Some advertisers took it on themselves to actually produce the programming. This worked particularly well with quiz shows. The ad agencies' producers had a good handle on what would captivate an audience. On one program, for example, the producers would put the contestant in a glass "isolation booth" (apparently so confederates could not whisper answers to them). The final question—always extraordinarily difficult—would be posed, and the contestant would visibly and literally *agonize* inside the booth. He would mop his brow, bite his lip, look heavenward for the answer, and at the very last second, that answer would usually appear. It was compelling television, so intoxicatingly suspenseful that it seemed too good to be true. Which of course it was. The agencies sponsoring some quiz shows had supplied the most appealing contestant with both the answers and dramatic coaching on how to look properly agonized. When the scandal broke, it became the subject of congressional hearings and strict regulations were adopted to keep advertisers out of the production business. This was not the first time that advertisers had taken a lead in creating content; after all, many early magazines were created as advertising vehicles with the content as an afterthought. But the quiz show scandals provided a startling example of the power and influence of the advertising industry.

The point is that advertising and the media grew up hand-in-hand, and were it not for advertising there would be many fewer media outlets, and were it not for media outlets there would be fewer businesses. But despite the mammoth impact of advertising on media revenues, we're still not exactly sure how or why it works. What we do know is that advertising *itself* secures very few sales. There are many steps in the journey between attracting a customer and closing a sale. And that brings us full-circle back to the modern version of the barber-surgeon pole, the sign.

After the sales clerks, who are almost always on break or enrolled in the witness protection program and, therefore, unable to help close the sale, the sign is the store's last chance to lure you into action. But often the signs are simply not accurate, and the consumer must decode a pattern of Graphic Garble that makes shopping more difficult and expensive than it has to be.

Signs usually get the blame when there's a disparity between posted prices and what the scanner rings. That was the standard excuse when NBC's Dateline accompanied staffers from the Michigan Attorney General's office, as they visited twenty major retail stores, spending about $150 at each location on at least a dozen items, all of which were advertised in flyers or on store signs. During their shopping spree, about one out of every seven items rang up incorrectly![1]

Dateline repeated the investigation at various locations around the country. At a Sears store, Dateline staffers bought thirteen items, and seven scanned wrong: six overcharges and one undercharge. At a Hecht's, an overcharge was pointed out to the sales staff, but repeated three times when staffers returned. All in all, Dateline found one in four sale prices scanned incorrectly during its Christmas sale rush test.

While far from a scientific test (I don't have the same research budget as NBC), I visited two K-Marts in Southern New Jersey on the same day and bought an item in each store that was prominently marked as being on sale at a substantial discount: a winter hat and a toddler's shirt. Both rang up at full price. What's going on here? Stores consistently maintain they are not trying to cheat customers. Spokespeople for the retail industry point out that checkout error works both ways. However, a Federal Trade Commission study confirmed what my experience leads me to believe: about two-thirds of checkout errors are overcharges. And overall, the claimed disparity rate between marked prices and checkout prices is smaller than Dateline's experience: retailers peg it at about 5 percent on sale items. An industry spokesman told Dateline that being wrong 5 percent of the time wasn't so bad: "In any other aspect of business if you are right 95 percent of the time, that's darn good." Well, now. Aside from the fact that putting up a correct sign does not seem that darn difficult, I can't help but wonder how many nanoseconds it would take for corporate management to fix the problem if scanner error resulted in consistent *undercharges*.

Graphic Garble is not limited to pricing matters. The visual jumble in a retail store can be used for all sorts of purposes. For example, bottled water sometimes features pictures on the label that distinctly imply a virgin land of bubbling streams, but about 25 percent of all bottled water comes from *municipal water supplies*. (Yes, that means "out of the tap.") Once the water is purified, the distributor does not have to tell you its source.[2] The bottles are often covered with official-looking stamps and seals, but they are often meaningless, such as "EPA Certified" or "FDA Approved." The federal government doesn't endorse or certify products. Sometimes there are association seals on the bottle, but often that means that the particular association awarding the seal found that the bottled water meets at least the same health standards as tap water.[3] And speaking of visual marketing, check out the subtle downsizing of product packages that occurs while the price stays the same. Tuna cans, for example, used to contain seven ounces. Now they've mostly shrunk to six.[4]

Comparison to the Nonexistent is another favorite technique in retailing. It's intoxicatingly simple: make up a high price, mark down from there, and advertise big sale reductions. While there are rules and guidelines for what a retailer may advertise as a sale or markdown, they are difficult to enforce because retailers sometimes actually *do* put the items on sale for a few days at an inflated price. While the Federal Trade Commission requires that the price be offered on a regular basis for a "reasonably substantial" period of time, that standard obviously leaves a lot of wiggle room.

The Evil-Twin Word Substitution is occasionally employed in retail. My favorite example is a national jewelry chain that used the term "Kultured Pearl." Its "Kultured Pearl" was really an imitation pearl, which is not the same thing as a cultured pearl. According to the Federal Trade Commission's complaint against the stores, a cultured pearl is a pearl formed by a mollusk as a result of an irritant placed in the mollusks's shell by humans. An imitation pearl is a manufactured product that is designed to simulate in appearance a pearl or cultured pearl.[5] (While this spelling trick could appear to be deliberately deceptive, I am sure it was a mistake and this company is completely "Honist.")

Stores—especially grocery stores, that have little differentiation in their inventory and, therefore, not much room for image advertising—like to claim they have the "lowest" prices, and creative use of a Remade Measure can help make their case. The Stop & Shop chain recently opened a new store near Boston and proclaimed in its advertising that the store had "the lowest grocery prices." A competitor, Star Market, took Stop & Shop to task and printed several pages of comparisons showing that many of Star's prices were lower. A report from the *Boston Globe* compared prices and found the same to be true.[6] Stop & Shop responded by claiming that the overall price of a "market basket" of 2,000 to 2,500 items would be

85

Figure 8.2: Some exclusions in Macy's ad—a lot of them.

lower at Stop & Shop than at any other store in the area. The "lowest price" ads made no mention of a comparison of only select items.[7]

But few stores can compare to Macy's when it comes to making comparison shopping difficult. As we noted in chapter 1, Macy's ads sometimes make it look like they're in the business of selling asterisks. The fine print produces several Tortured Definitions. My favorite: "TAKE AN EXTRA 20% OFF ANY SINGLE SALE OR CLEARANCE ITEM STOREWIDE.*" But look at the exclusions in the fine print (figure 8.2)! The ad excludes no fewer that twelve departments, twenty-two designers, and twenty collections!

Retailing is a tough business, to be sure, and advertising, whether in-store or on the printed page, has to compete with an avalanche of other messages. But a consumer should not have to decode microscopic mouse type or keep track of the accuracy of every sign in the store. Store advertising is unconscionably tricky and I leave you with this warning paraphrased from Aaron Levenstein's famous quote about statistics: Ads are like bikinis. What they reveal is suggestive, but what they conceal is vital.

Notes

1. "The Price Is Wrong: How Accurate Are Checkout Scanners?" Dateline Archives, www.msnbc.com/news/224089.asp.
2. "Bottled Water's Worth Is Debatable," *The Sacramento Bee*, November 8, 1998, p. B13.
3. Ibid.
4. Bruce Mohl, "Edgar Dworsky's Consuming Passion," *The Boston Globe*, September 27, 1998, p. 12.
5. United States of America, Federal Trade Commission, *In the Matter of Zale Corporation*, Docket no. C-3738, Complaint.
6. Patricia Wen and Bruce Mohl, "'Lowest-Price' Isn't Right in Grocer Circular, Survey Shows," *The Boston Globe*, August 16, 1998, p. B2.
7. Ibid.

Chapter Nine

Driven to Distraction

How Car Retailers Confuse the Consumer

Q: How do you bring a sturdy Federal Trade Commission Chairman to his knees?
A: Have him try to read the fine print in a car ad disclaimer.

That's exactly what FTC Chairman Robert Pitofsky was reduced to when his agency began cracking down on the auto industry a couple of years ago. "I actually got down on my hands and knees in front of my TV set," he recalled, "and tried to see if I could read what these disclosures were and find out what the balloon payment was, how much money you had to put down. And I simply couldn't read those disclosures even though I was waiting for them and looking for them."[1]

Five automakers settled the suit that followed the investigation without admitting wrongdoing. While auto advertising has improved marginally with each resulting federal and state action, fine print abuses are essentially dealt with on an after-the-fact, case-by-case basis. As a result, there is plenty of fine print left over to serve as fodder for this chapter.

Why is it that auto ads and sales seem so often to tread the fine line between ethical behavior and deception? Part of the reason is the sheer amount of money on the table. A staggering $500 billion dollars per year is spent in the United States on light cars and trucks. With so much hanging in the balance auto retailers take chances, as do the agencies that produce the ads and the media outlets that carry them.

The media in the United States reap about $5 billion per year in auto advertising revenue.[2] Auto advertising is a particular boon to newspapers, which count the auto industry as their top advertising revenue producer, and which garner about 52 cents of every auto advertising dollar, compared to 17 cents for TV and 16 cents for radio. The conventional wisdom in the auto and advertising industries is that newspapers really pull the freight. Television builds demands, but it's hard print that brings buyers into showrooms.[3] Newspapers tout their appeal to car buyers, compiling statistics to show that 71 percent of newspaper readers actively seek out ads for used cars, and 64 percent seek ads for new cars.[4] Newspaper publishers also point to statistics showing that the public believes newspapers are the most believable of all media.[5]

As you can imagine, advertisers are under pressure to produce campaigns that will bring those buyers in. The ad business, itself, is brutally competitive and risky. One ad agency that "pitched" a car company—and didn't get the account—expended $400,000 and ninety-five working days of seventy-five staffers.[6]

In such a competitive marketplace, getting the buyer in the showroom can boil down to who can produce the most alluring ad. And fine print is a fine tool. While auto sellers are required to disclose certain particulars of the sale or lease conditions, burying the fine print in a clutter of Graphic Garble can distract the customer from the unpleasant truth. For example, in a reprise of a technique we examined in chapter 3, look at the ad for a Nissan Sentra XE shown in figure 9.1. This ad takes advantage of the eye's tendency to focus on the highlights as it travels through a complex path of information. Reading from left to right, it appears that you can lease the car for $89 per month. With ZERO CASH! In fact the banner headline for the page also trumpets LOW PAYMENTS & ZERO CASH! Uh-oh. You missed the fine print. That's ZERO CASH "AVAILABLE," which of course means that you'd have a much higher monthly payment. But to get this car for $89 per month you'll need to cough up $3,127 at the start of the lease.

A Veiled Variable in the fine print in figure 9.2 also allows the confection of an attractive bottom line. From each price listed the advertiser has subtracted $2,500 for "cash or trade." Meaning, essentially, that if you give them $2,500, that's $2,500 you don't have to pay.

There's a *really* nasty variable buried in figure 9.3. While the big print implies that you can buy a Chrysler Sebring convertible for

Figure 9.1: Zero cash *Available*. Better not miss that.

Figure 9.2: Where'd that $2,500 go?

Figure 9.3: Don't miss that part about the balloon payment at the end.

ZERO DOWN and $199 per month, the fine print shows that the ZERO DOWN is "available." For this car, however, you'll need $3,000 down. And when your low monthly payments come to an end, you'll owe a lump-sum balloon payment of $11,803!

Why is it so difficult to sort out car ads? Part of the reason is the complexity of the financial arrangements. Leasing has become popular in the past few years. About one-third of new cars are leased today, and in a few years that figure is expected to reach about half. When you combine the intricacies of a lease with the wheeling and dealing endemic to car sales, you've whipped up a recipe for abuse. You can hide an enormous amount of money in the fine print. For example, New York Attorney General Dennis C. Vacco went after BMW in 1997, claiming that BMW attracted customers with ads that disguised fees in fine print, and in some cases consumers would be required to pay "as much as $5,000 or more up-front before they could drive the advertized car off the showroom floor."[7] BMW agreed to modify its advertising without admitting any violation of law.

Variations of the Tortured Definition come into play when the consumer negotiates leasing or purchase options. Many customers want to buy rather than lease because they invest some equity in the car and, of course, own it at the end of the payments. But spiraling car costs have put the monthly purchase payment out of the reach of many buyers. A practice called "residual-based financing" is sometimes offered to customers who want to buy. Basically, it's a plan in which the customer makes small payments for sixty months, and then either pays off the remaining value of the car, or turns it in. It's still a lease, even though it sounds like a purchase plan.[8]

One variable frequently buried in the blur of the transaction is the interest rate on the loan. The way the variable is veiled is by the salesperson talking about the monthly payments and not the purchase price. Remember, even if the payments are attractive, the interest rate on the loan adds up to hard money! A word of advice: find out what the interest rate is and what the loan will cost you. The rate on your loan will depend on your credit history, and loan rates vary in different areas of the nation. In general, though, they hover at 8.5 to 11.5 percent for new car loans, and 8.8 to 12.2 percent for used car loans.[9] Be aware too, that car dealerships generally go through another lender to secure your loan. If you get a call back the day after the deal has been made in the showroom and are asked to sign some "additional paperwork," be sure you're not signing up for a new loan at a higher rate, because the lender did not approve the rate you and the dealer agreed on.[10]

Speaking of Veiled Variables, keep an eye out for administrative fees buried in the terms of the lease. So-called acquisition fees are routinely bundled into some leases, often with the stated intent of making the lease simpler or more "consumer-friendly." But this gentle favor leaves consumers without the option of negotiating the fee or walking away from the deal if they object to it.[11]

As annoying as these tacked-on fees are, the consumer generally operates from a position of relative strength when negotiating the purchase or lease of a car because he or she retains that all-important option—the ability to walk away from the deal. But short-term auto rental is a different story. Few of us can walk away from the airport in a strange city, and a consumer hit with unexpected hidden fees at the car checkout counter really has little choice but to cough them up. The add-ons can be substantial: A ten-day charge of $600 can include $200 in fees and taxes.

Car rental agencies hide fees so thoroughly that Ken Starr probably couldn't uncover them, even if they somehow involved sex. Sometimes the fees are written in code (occ.chg for "other charges and credits"). In some cases, compliant state legislatures have written new laws allowing rental firms to tack on extra costs. Minnesota, for example, allows rental firms to add 3 percent to customers' bills to cover the costs of auto registration. Why would Minnesota state lawmakers allow this? One reason might be that any money left over from the registration fund goes back to the state.[12] Car-rental agencies claim they are just passing along fees that somebody else sticks them with, such as extra airport charges for premium counter space, or local taxes; they also argue that all travel-related industries have increased prices. Maybe so, but when you purchase an airline ticket, you know the total price. Also, in some circumstances there's no practical way to know what your car rental price will be because taxes don't show up on all travel agents' computer screens, and the ads detail the prices ambiguously: "At many airports, an 8.5–11.5 percent airport concession fee recovery applies on car rentals."

The point is, anything to do with purchase, lease, or rental of a car is bound to be complex, and likely to be confusing. And more than in most transactions, the devil is in the details. Some observers less charitable than I would say that in the business of car-selling, the devil wrote the details, but that's beyond the scope of this chapter.

Notes

1. "Automakers Settle Lawsuit Regarding Auto Leases," Transcript, CNBC News, November 21, 1996.
2. Emily Hebert, "Ford Dealer Consolidation Worries Media," *Indianapolis Business Journal*, September 8, 1997, p. 13.
3. "Auto Advertising Statistics Strong, but Slipping," *Editor and Publisher*, April 26, 1997, www.mediainfo.com.
4. Joe Consoli, "Good News for Publishers," *Editor and Publisher*, June 22, 1996, p. 14.
5. Ibid.
6. David Lieberman, "Behind the Scenes of an Ad Agency," *USA Today*, March 28, 1995.
7. "Vacco Announces Lease Advertising Settlement," June 1, 1997, www.oag.state.ny.us.
8. Craig Anderson, "Car-Buying Secrets," *The Arizona Republic*, July 21, 1998, p. E1.
9. Ibid.

10. Ibid.
11. Nedra Pickler, "Attorney Files Lawsuit Against Ford Alleging Deceptive Leasing Practices," *Associated Press*, November 24, 1998, BC cycle.
12. Thomas Goetz, "Travel: Cars Cost More as Surcharges Pile Up," *The Wall Street Journal*, May 5, 1998, p. B1.

Chapter Ten

Reach out and Confuse Someone

Baffle-Gab on the Phone Line

What a deal! One of the most heavily advertised "10-10" numbers offers 99 cents for calls up to twenty minutes. And that's actually a good buy under certain circumstances. But there's a Veiled Variable lurking in the circuits. The 99-cent charge is a blanket price, you pay 99 cents regardless of whether you talk for one minute or for nineteen. So a one-minute call—a connection, perhaps, to somebody's answering machine—is going to cost you roughly a dollar a minute. Another "10-10" service requires you to talk at least ten minutes to get the advertised savings. Anything below that, and you pay at a higher rate. Another buries a 10 cent per call "connection fee" in the fine print at the bottom of its TV ad.[1] These services, called "dial-around" services because you literally dial around your long-distance carrier by entering the 10-10 code, have become popular. About 11 percent of American households use them. In 1998, consumers spent about $2 billion on dial-around services, and the total is expected to reach about $3 billion by the end of 1999.[2]

But the 10-10s don't always provide the savings the customers anticipate. J. D. Power and Associates found that about 36 percent of dial-around customers classified themselves as "extremely or very satisfied" with the service—less than half the satisfaction rate with regular long-distance carriers. "They're horrible," Power spokesman Kirk Parsons told the *Dallas Morning News*. "They promise a lot of things, but the cost savings aren't there." Welcome to the mysterious and expensive world of the telephone, a land where charges are buried in a topsoil of fine print, and comparisons slide by in an avalanche of conflicting and confusing claims.

In today's deregulated marketplace, hundreds of firms, some reputable, some not, compete for a share of that line that connects you with the person you call. Deregulation allows almost anyone to gain entree into the telecommunications business and puts few restrictions on the types of services they can offer. Deregulation has, in fact, changed the entire telecommunications landscape. As you may remember, prior to 1984, telecommunications was a cozy little monopoly for AT&T. AT&T effectively owned almost every link in the chain, right down to the phone and the wiring in your house. In return for the government allowing near-total dominance in the market, AT&T was subject to strict government controls on price and service.

But many people suspected there were better deals to be found if competition were injected into telecommunications. Among those people was Federal Judge Harold E. Greene, who approved the breakup of AT&T after prodding the Justice Department to aggressively pursue it. AT&T was allowed to keep its long distance service, manufacturing arm, and some other service and product components, but had to divest itself of local phone service companies.

The theory was that, by cracking the phone monopoly, intense competition would produce limitless choice and result in lower prices. It didn't exactly work that way in 1984, or when the other shoe dropped in 1996, when Congress and the Clinton administration pushed through the Telecommunications Act. The Telecommunications Act of 1996 significantly relaxed ownership regulations and—most importantly—removed most restrictions on the type of content that a communications company could provide. For example, prior to 1996, cable companies were prohibited from offering telephone service and telephone companies couldn't provide cable TV programming. When the ban was lifted, the expectation was that the competitive scramble would produce a creative and financial, supercompetitive free-for-all, with small companies taking the innovative lead. As for telephone companies, they would move into other branches of the business: long distance companies would provide local service, and local companies would provide long distance, with competition driving those prices even lower.

Wrong again. What happened is that telecommunications companies took advantage of loosened regulations and merged like crazy, on the expectation that whoever can provide the biggest package deal will emerge victorious in the $80-billion telecommunications market. A merger between a telephone company and a cable company, for example, opens the door to bringing entertainment over phone wires. That's something cable firms drool over because, while cable penetration is about 60 percent nationwide, telephone penetration is pretty close to 100 percent. The lure of "package deals" is irresistible too. Imagine being able to offer a deal on long-distance service to someone who orders cable service.

Deregulation also allowed phone companies of all stripes to make some subtle changes you may not have noticed. One is a hike in the rate for in-state calls. Check out your bill. You might be surprised to find your regional calls cost more than cross-country calls. Many phone companies have also quietly changed their peak and off-peak hour schemes. Peak (full-price) hours used to start at 8 A.M. Check your bill and you may find that the start of the peak period has crept back to 7 A.M.[3]

Another subtle change is that deregulation and computerized technology allow almost anyone with a little knowhow to nibble around the edges of the phone business, providing 900 pay-per-call numbers, voice-mail services, and even long-distance service. In theory, this is free enterprise at its best. In practice, it's often a feeding-frenzy at the shark tank. As we'll see a little later in this chapter, "crammers" take advantage of the telephone free-for-all by providing (and charging for) services no one really asked for, and "slammers" switch your long-distance services without your informed consent. It's a big problem. In 1998, the FCC received about 4,500 complaints against crammers, and 18,000 complaints against slammers.[4]

All in all, the telephone makes deception easy for several reasons. First, it provides anonymity. At the instant the conversation or transaction occurs, you don't necessarily know who is on the other end of the line. Second, you often don't know exactly who you are dealing with or where to lodge complaints. For example, did you know that there are several sources for "directory assistance"? When you're away from home and you call for information, you usually dial an area code and the numbers 555-1212, which con-

99

nects you to a long distance carrier's directory assistance operators who provide directory assistance at a per-call rate. But the long distance carriers give wrong information as much as 15 percent of the time,[5] errors due in part to the fact that the long-distance companies sometimes do not buy the updated listings from the local telephone companies. (This recently happened to me when I was in New York and needed to call my son's pediatrician in Southern New Jersey. The long-distance information operators informed me three times in three separate calls that there was no listing for a doctor by that name when, in fact, it is printed in the local phone book.)

Given the explosion in area codes, you might even be scammed internationally. A popular ruse begins with you receiving an urgent message to call back a number with an area code beginning with 809. You're kept on hold for as long as you'll tolerate, not knowing that you've called a Caribbean version of a 900 number. In other words, you're billed directly and exorbitantly for each minute you're on the line.[6]

Finally, telephone bills come at the end of the month, and by that time you have forgotten many of the details of your calling activity. The bill itself may be less than clear in laying out the charges. And even if you have a good memory and want to dispute a charge, you may still face a run-around because almost anyone, anywhere, who has the energy and ambition can engage in an enterprise that tacks charges onto your phone bill. Ethics do not necessarily accompany energy and ambition.

* 100 *

A case in point is the cramming business. Cramming is when a company uses an Incognito If to induce the consumer to sign up for unwanted services. The modus operandi usually involves a scenario such as entering a contest, where the hidden "if" buried in the fine print of the entry from is that you have a chance to win a prize *if* you change long-distance carriers, or sign up for some other phone-related service. One consumer entered a contest to win a Jeep, and found she'd missed the fine print on the entry blank and inadvertently signed up for voice-mail services.[7] Cramming typically follows this pattern: give the consumer something they don't want, perform the unrequested service badly, and charge an exorbitant rate—the same strategy perfected both by men with squeegees who wash your windshield at tunnel entrances, and by the federal government.

Television ads for dial-around services use Remade Measures to demonstrate that they offer the lowest prices. Here's how it works:

One dial-around says it saves over AT&T on every call, but the fine print on the ad says the comparison is to AT&T's *basic* rates, which are quite high and are the rates you'll pay if you don't have sense enough to enroll in a calling plan. New York State Assemblyman Scott Stringer researched this particular comparison and found that a ten-minute state-to-state call on Sunday using the dial-around cost $1.30, while the same call cost 50 cents using an AT&T calling plan called "Simply Minutes."[8]

Comparison shopping becomes even more difficult when marketers employ Comparison to the Nonexistent in their ads. The New York State Attorney General's office undertook a massive study of prepaid calling cards and found that advertisements for the cards dangled many a comparative. Something called "Pronto Card" offered "more minutes," without saying more minutes than *what*. A firm called PTI claimed that the consumer can "[s]ave up to 70% percent on all . . . long distance" calls, but that does not answer the question of 70 percent compared to *what*.[9]

Comparison shopping, in fact, seems next to impossible with many of the dial-arounds because there's no way, at least as far as I can deduce, to call a representative of the services and find prices in advance. I tried. I listened to a dial-around radio ad for 10-10-566 and called the number announced in the disclaimer. (It was read so quickly that I couldn't understand it and called the radio station to get it.) But that number connected me with a recorded message that only gave me details of a contest associated with the calling service, and no other number for information.

The anonymous nature of telephone commerce opens the door to more serious problems, including plain-vanilla telemarketing fraud. While blatant bunko goes beyond the techniques of half-truth and distortion we're discussing in this book, it's worthwhile to take a quick look at the use of the Evil-Twin Word Substitution as it's practiced on the telephone.

Some varieties of the technique are reasonably benign, such as the currently popular practice by telemarketers of implying that they are policemen, war veterans, or parole officers seeking donations. What sometimes happens in these cases is that telemarketing firms raise money on behalf of legitimate organizations, but keep a sizable cut of the proceeds. They also seem to take considerable liberties with the truth along the way.[10] In a six-month period, I received at least half-a-dozen calls from telemarketers who clearly implied they were calling "from" a police department or a parole officers' association. In each case I asked for written information, on letterhead, about the organization. To my astonishment, nothing came in the mail, although I'm still holding out hope. And when I once asked the friendly voice on the phone—who was telling me in excruciating detail about what it's like fighting crime on the streets—if he actually was a cop, as he implied, he simply hung up the phone.

But there's a wrinkle to this technique that is simply deplorable, practiced by men and women with the apparent moral development of shower-curtain bacteria. As was briefly mentioned in chapter 1, some unscrupulous entrepreneurs have opened charities with names similar to the real things. I won't compound the confusion by listing them here, but as you might guess, they often involve the words "cancer," "heart," and "children," and sound enough like the real charities with those words in the title that consumers become confused.[11] People unsure of the precise wording of the name can, therefore, be misdirected by directory assistance. As a result, callers—some of whom are seeking information about crises facing them or their family—can be milked for donations to fake charities. When a woman named Linda Blue, desperate for advice about her husband's brain cancer, called a sound-alike "charity," the "charity" wanted to charge her for advice. In fact, they went so far as to ask for her checking account number so they could call the bank and get her money immediately.[12] That's so awful I can't even come up with something sarcastic with which to end this chapter.

102

Notes

1. "Dialing around with 10-10 Long Distance Numbers Aren't Necessarily Cheaper," Ann Thompson, NBC Nightly News, *NBC News Transcripts*, December 29, 1998.
2. Jennifer Files, "10-10 Numbers Don't Always Equal Savings," *Dallas Morning News*, December 27, 1998, p. 19.
3. "Protect Your Dream," CNBC, *Protect Your Dream Transcript*, November 29, 1998.
4. Ibid.
5. "Long-Distance Information Calls Are Fleecing Americans Because up to 15 Percent of the Information Given Is Incorrect but You Still Pay," Fred Francis, The NBC Nightly News, *NBC News Transcripts*, November 11, 1998.

6. Fay Faron, "Another Five Ways Scammers Can Get You," *Dallas Morning News*, January 1, 1999, p. 6c.

7. Kalpana Srinivasan, "FTC Slams Crammers," *The Associated Press*, archive.abcnews.com/sections/business/dailyNews/cramming980717/.

8. "10-10 LD Savings Questions," CNN-FN, Fred Katayama, Kelli Arena, *Digital Jam*, Dec. 7, 1998, transcript #98120702FN-L11.

9. New York State Attorney General, *Pre-Paid Phone Cards: The Facts*. Dennis C. Vacco, Attorney General of the State of New York, www.oag.state.ny.us.

10. Rehema Ellis, "Tele-Marketers Hired to Raise Money for Charities Are Sometimes Going beyond the Limits and Harassing Potential Donators," *NBC Nightly News*, December 18, 1997.

11. Gary Cohen, "Charities Abound but Laws Are Few," *U.S. News and World Report*, Dec. 8, 1997.

12. Arnold Diaz, "What's in a Name: Cashing in on Charity Name Confusion," ABC News, *20/20*, September 27, 1998.

Chapter Eleven

You May Already Be a Sucker!

Misrepresentation by Mail

*I am indeed a lucky man. In today's mail I received a document that "serves as official notification" that "the holder of this document" (that's me, as you can see by the fact that my name is officially typed on the line) is "confirmed," and, "as a result of this offer," my "ticketing and confirmation number" have been "identified and issued" (figure 11.1). On the inside flap of my official (looking) document there's a ticket! (figure 11.2). Or maybe it's a check! I can't exactly tell, but it does say, "To the order of" Carl Hausman, and that's me![1] And my ticket number and confirmation number are on the right. On the attached leaflet, inside the official-looking scroll-work edging, Robin Leach tells me to PACK MY BAGS! But before we open my underwear drawer, let's take a look at figure 11.3.

And now look at figure 11.4.

What word did you miss in figure 11.3? Probably the second "the" in "PARIS IN THE THE SPRING." Yes, there are two *the's*. What I've shown you is an old graphic-arts trick used to demonstrate how easy it is to miss a typo on the beginning of a line, especially when the text is contained within decorative boundaries and you're filling in words in your mind, jumping ahead to what you

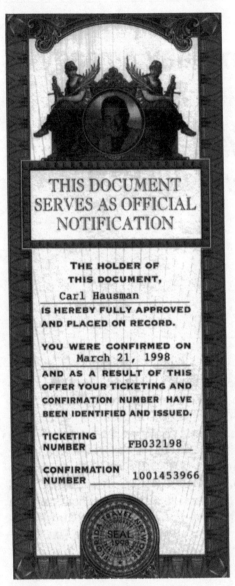

Figure 11.1: My "official notification"
that I've won.

Figure 11.2: And there's a check, or a ticket, or something. It certainly looks official.

Figure 11.3.

Figure 11.4: A close-up of my prize notification document.

think is coming. And if you're like me, with a tendency to read things quickly and rush impatiently to the middle of a line of type, you might have missed the first word on the second line of Mr. Leach's congratulatory message: "*offer*."

Yes, I've won not a . . . "World Class Florida/Tropical Caribbean Vacation Package," but only a "World Class Florida/Tropical Caribbean Vacation Package offer." In other words, I've won the chance to buy something.

The modus operandi here is a combination of two techniques, the Veiled Variable and the Confusing Counterfeit. While I can't prove that the word "offer" was intentionally veiled by putting it at the beginning of the line, note that it appears in the identical location farther down in the text (figure 11.5).

As you can see, the rest of the document brazenly imitates a travel ticket and an award certificate. Yes, you know and I know that it's not a real ticket, and after some detective work we know it's only a sales pitch. After all, you and I are a sophisticated group, people who, respectively, read and write books by Carl Hausman.

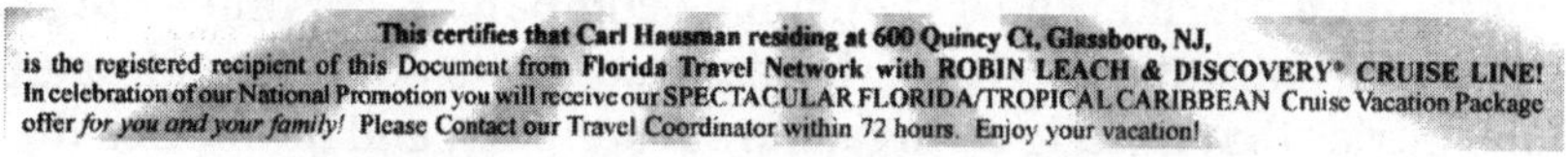

This certifies that Carl Hausman residing at 600 Quincy Ct, Glassboro, NJ,
is the registered recipient of this Document from **Florida Travel Network** with **ROBIN LEACH & DISCOVERY® CRUISE LINE!**
In celebration of our National Promotion you will receive our SPECTACULAR FLORIDA/TROPICAL CARIBBEAN Cruise Vacation Package
offer *for you and your family!* Please Contact our Travel Coordinator within 72 hours. Enjoy your vacation!

Figure 11.5: Another close-up: hidden "offer"?

Others might not be so lucky as to share our education, intellectual vigor, or health. Some people simply don't read very well. Others do not read well any more because their eyesight is failing, as are their memories and, perhaps, sadly, their faculties.

That's what makes the Confusing Counterfeit so pernicious and predatory. It can be used to deceive the vulnerable into believing they've won a sweepstakes. According to testimony presented before the U.S. Senate Governmental Affairs Committee by Florida Attorney General Bob Butterworth,[2] an 80-year-old Seattle woman postponed surgery so she could be home when Ed McMahon and Dick Clark arrived to deliver her $10 million dollar check. One sweepstakes by American Family Publishers led twelve people to fly to a Tampa subscription office to collect their expected multi-million-dollar prize.[3] Cab drivers had to be notified to take passengers who thought they were winners to the attorney general's office instead.

Sweepstakes are a big business and the competition is intense. In 1999, the issue was spotlighted when the Senate held hearings on the industry. Representatives of Time Inc., Publishers Clearing House, Reader's Digest, and American Family Enterprises were asked to defend practices such as telling millions of potential sweepstakes entrants that "it's down to a two-person race for $11 million," and they were one of the lucky two.[4] During the hearings, senators displayed a letter from Publishers Clearing House with the salutation "Dear Eustace Hall," in which a contest manager wrote that her boss had come into her office to say, "It's not right when someone as nice as Eustace Hall doesn't win." The "personal" letter urged Ms. Hall to "return the Guaranteed Winner Document." The elderly Eustace Hall had broken down in tears while testifying that she thought the letter was personal.[5] Later in the testimony, an official from Publishers Clearing House testified that the same letter had been sent to nine million people, each identified as the subject of the same office "conversation."

Many entrants mistakenly assume that their chances of winning are better if they buy the magazines touted in the sweepstakes promotional material. The sweepstakes companies say that's not so, but some entrants noted that there are separate addresses for mailing entries that include a magazine subscription and for entries that don't, and conclude that not subscribing will somehow penalize them.

Sweepstakes promoters argue that their wordings are very clear. You be the judge. Here is a look at the techniques used by Publishers Clearing House. Publishers Clearing House seems to have informed my wife that she's a big winner, which gives me even more incentive to stay on her good side. Let's open that envelope I told you about in chapter 3, the one with the ersatz registered mail card on the front and the red stamp on the back noting that my wife, or perhaps the envelope, or something anyway, is APPROVED FOR $31 MILLION.

Inside is—heavens!—a PRIZE ACCEPTANCE AFFIDAVIT (figure 11.6). And the folks at Publishers Clearing House have even provided a box for my wife to check to indicate if she prefers her money in certified checks or deposited directly to the bank.

Also included in the package is a PRIZE AWARD TIME CARD (figure 11.7) that lists twenty-four unfortunates who won only a few thousand dollars each. My wife, on the other hand, is scheduled— yes, scheduled at 9 P.M., that's what it says on the "time card"—to receive $31 million.

There is her name! And in big red letters the card says APPROVED TO WIN. But in small black letters it says, PROVIDED THE RECIPIENT NAMED ABOVE HAS AND RETURNS THE WINNING NUMBER. We are heartbroken, but we did somehow suspect there was a catch. We'll have to wait until next year.

And there probably will be a next year, and many years after that. While there are sporadic legal actions against sweepstakes promoters and occasional calls for legislation to rein in their more flagrant abuses, sweepstakes work. Sweepstakes promoters send out a billion pieces of mail a year, and each year 29 percent of the American public enters a sweepstakes. The magazine industry gets a third of its new subscriptions through sweepstakes.[6] Sweepstakes are backed by some heavy corporate hitters, and according to sponsors, previous legislation at the state level has fallen victim to intense lobbying.[7]

According to Florida Attorney General Bob Butterworth, some players in the sweepstakes business are expanding their business in troubling ways. His office recently filed suit against one firm for

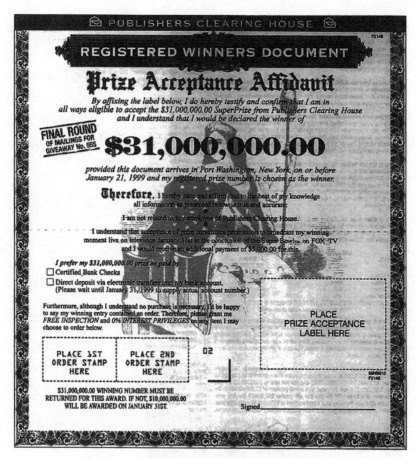

Figure 11.6: My prize acceptance *affidavit*.

allegedly targeting the elderly through deceptive solicitations, and for trying to sell the names of nearly half a million seniors and retirees to other contests. Some companies, he claims, intentionally send elderly customers a second bill for magazine subscriptions they've bought through sweepstakes, even though they've already paid. "They don't refund the money," Butterworth told the Associated Press. "What they do is give you another year's subscription. What we are finding is that many seniors have subscriptions to the year 2020."[8]

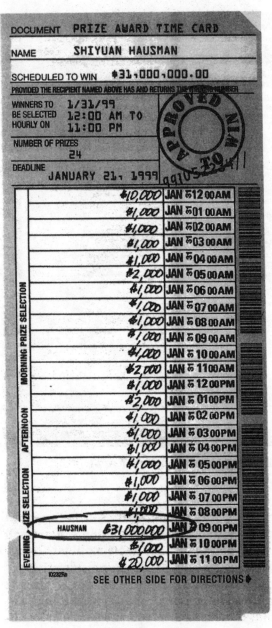

Figure 11.7: The time card showing me when I
can expect my prize.

Notes

1. Even William Safire has given up on saying, "That is I," even though it's technically correct.
2. Tamara Lytle, "Senators Focus on Big Sweepstakes; Promotions Described as Deceptive," *The Chicago Tribune*, Sept. 2, 1998, p. 12.
3. Dan Abrams, "Florida Attorney General Investigates American Family Publishers for Misleading Claims in Sweepstakes Mailings that Have People Believing They Won When They Haven't," NBC, *NBC Nightly News*, February 4, 1998.
4. Bob Dart, "Senators Threaten Sweepstakes Crackdown," *The Atlanta Constitution*, March 10, 1999, p. 4A.
5. Ibid.
6. Lytle.
7. Jeffrey McMurray, "Legislators Propose Cracking Down on Deceptive Contests," The Associated Press State and Regional Wire, November 18, 1998, BC cycle.
8. Ibid.

Chapter Twelve

Brave New Bamboozle

Tricky Business over the Internet

Signing up for an Internet service is easy. Canceling is another matter. If you can decode America Online's cancellation policy, ("You will not be charged your first monthly fee unless you don't cancel within the first 30 days."), you still face formidable obstacles in the form of various Incognito Ifs.[1]

The problem dates back about two years, when, fresh from its debacle of late 1997 in which new subscribers essentially purchased the right to listen to a busy signal, AOL set out to recruit even more subscribers by mailing out discs that offered fifty hours of free service. But you only got the free hours *if* you used all fifty hours in one month. And, the trial period would only end *if* the consumers canceled. Otherwise, the service automatically continued and consumers were billed monthly. At the time, AOL prohibited canceling by e-mail. Later, AOL did allow cancellation by e-mail, but then retracted that option. The reason was that too many people were quitting.[2]

On-line services are nothing if not inventive when it comes to putting obstacles in the way of customers who want to quit. The *Wall Street Journal* looked at AOL's sign-up materials and noted that the printing on the diskette did not disclose the need to cancel the introductory service, and once on-line, subscribers had to wade through several screens of information before learning that they were responsible for cancellation. Further, it would be difficult to cancel by mail, because there was no address on the diskette.[3]

A different on-line service used a more passive/aggressive strategy for retaining members. When one customer from Southern California, who was trying to cancel his service, called the New Jersey–based internet provider's toll-free number, he was told he could not cancel on that number and would have to call long-distance to New Jersey during business hours. He told the *Journal* he called five times, waiting as long as 40 minutes on hold at a time.[4]

State attorney generals, noting the avalanche of Incognito Ifs and obstacles to cancellation buried in Internet service provider sales material, took action. In the spring of 1998, America Online entered into a settlement with forty-four attorney generals and agreed to explain its charges more clearly.[5]

What makes this so ironic is that these companies are allegedly in the communications business! Moreover, they're in the trust business because there's still a big job ahead in trying to convince consumers that transactions on the Internet are safe and honest. But Internet service providers routinely bury information in fine print, making the communication process as Byzantine as possible when it suits them to do so.

116

As a side note, I believe that most computer-related industries take a much different view of customer service than do other enterprises. *Wall Street Journal* columnist Walter Mossberg nailed it when writing about AOL's various boondoggles.

> In general, the computer industry seems to suffer from two cultural attitudes that make these stunts likelier than they ought to be. First, many people in high tech maintain a self-congratulatory belief that they are dong the hardest, most cutting-edge work in the world, so it's OK to sell products or services with known defects. Secondly, many people in the industry still labor under what I call the 'science-project mentality' of computing. This is the attitude that all this stuff is so new and experimental that the customers can be thought of as trial-and-error testers, instead of people expecting to buy products that work.[6]

I might add that there's also a perceptible "Wild West" feel to the Internet. The novelty of the technology gives license to an anything-goes, frontier-style business ethic.

Outright deception is relatively easy. Someone running a stock market investment scam can construct a web site that rivals those of major, legitimate firms. But a shoestring scamster can't construct a suite of offices in a Wall Street building. The problem is compounded by the fact that legitimate financial businesses have established outposts on the web, habituating traders to visiting cyberspace. According to some estimates, one in four trades is conducted on the Internet.[7] Since the Federal Trade Commission launched an Internet antifraud campaign, the number of complaints it receives daily totaled two hundred per day in spring 1999. The moral: The Confusing Counterfeit has become coin of the realm in an uncharted land where most visitors are just learning the landmarks.

For example, children on the net can be lured into revealing personal data about themselves and their friends, data which are invaluable to marketers eager to harvest the next generation of consumers. At the Mars Inc. web site, kids who played a game called "Imposter Search" were asked to fill out a form entitled "Alert Your Friends" in order to help find the "imposter" M&M. The form requested the names and e-mail addresses of playmates, who were then sent an automatic "wanted" poster by e-mail.[8]

117

There's nothing new, and maybe nothing wrong, with gathering names of children; the practice dates back at least to contests entered with tear-offs from cereal boxes and the exchange of proofs of purchase for model rockets and decoder rings. But there's something fundamentally different about a medium that appears to be a game venue, but in reality is a marketing device. Add to that the capability of web marketers to track the movements of users in cyberspace by copying so-called cookies (identifier codes) on to their hard drives, as well as correlating e-mail addresses with physical addresses, and we appear to have a troubling issue.

There is also a problem with "spam"—electronic junk mail that clogs computers—and "spamouflage," junk e-mail that appears in your mailbox under the guise of legitimate messages. (For example, in my mailbox this morning was an ad for a porno site sent with the message header, "Error on your invoice.") Spamouflagers also create false return addresses to outwit e-mail blocking software.[9]

Navigating around web sites can be a tricky business too. Click

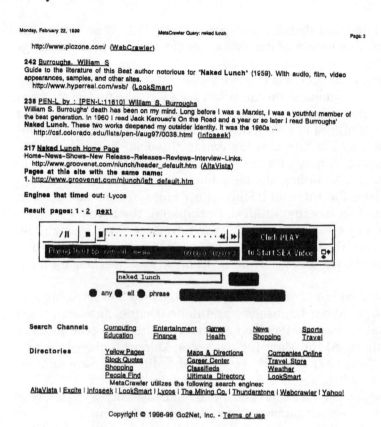

Figure 12.1: The play control doesn't deliver.

on a graphic that looks as though it's an adjustment panel to speed up your access rate, and you land in an ad page for a firm selling high-speed Internet access. Entering words on a search engine revs up custom-targeted advertising that suddenly appears on your screen, whether you wanted to see it or not. The robotic sales force sometimes takes a laughably mechanical view of where your interests lie. For example, when I used the search engine Metacrawler to hunt for information on William Burroughs' *The Naked Lunch*, the search engine seized on one word (guess which one) and assaulted me with a banner ad that is meant to resemble the play control panel on a computer video program (figure 12.1). The counterfeit command console even told me that it was playing a 16.0 KBS buffered stream. But when I hit the "play" command I found that the console was simply a link to a pay porno site full of stuff that would make Bill Clinton blush. (And the site, *Tease.com*, was reluctant to let me leave. *Tease.com* automatically opened another window to a site elegantly titled *Slutfest* when I closed the *Tease.com* window.)

Any webmaster determined to lure his or her audience into clicking to somewhere they didn't intend to go, can visit a site (which I won't publicize) specializing in deceptive graphics designed to hijack the unwary. Here's the text on the first page of the site.

> Below is an assortment of graphics (gifs) you can include in your web ads to deceive individuals into clicking your ad. I will add more as I see a demand for. Please e-mail me, if you want a custom made button, bar, etc.
>
> Provided the idea, sentance [sic], phrase, etc. is provisional to future web advertising I will be happy to create it, and place it here for all to use.

Included for free are phony windows applications boxes and "more text" buttons that lure surfers to a link.

But even the most mainstream of all web marketers don't seem averse to stretching the truth a little via a robotic counterfeit. These "skewed searches," as the *New York Times* christened them, are one of the ways the line between editorial and advertising content is being blurred. The *Times* reports that:

119

- Clicking on a solution for diaper rash at an internet site about babies produces a recommendation for a brand of baby powder. Unknown to the searcher is the fact that the product is placed there as an ad.
- Searching for a Mexican restaurant at newspaper's web site produces the recommendation of a sponsor who has paid for favorable placement.
- A page on hair loss in AOL's health section features three links, two leading to articles in on-line publications, but the third leading to a site selling baldness treatments.
- The site for the television series "Dawson's Creek" has stories about its characters getting their hair done at the Dep Capeside Salon, and features paid promotions for Dep products.

Reporters Saul Hansell and Amy Harmon conclude that "trusting an internet site to navigate the web, in short, is akin to following a helpful stranger in Morocco who offers to take you to the best rug store. You may well find what you're looking for, but your guide will get a piece of whatever you spend."[10]

The relationships between advertisers and search results can be exploited in intriguing ways. For example, if I click over to Lycos.com, a major search engine, and search for the term "low fat cooking," the return screen notifies me that I can find "books about low fat cooking at barnesandnoble.com." Clicking on that notification sends me to Barnes and Noble's search utility on its site, which churns for a minute and, indeed, produces hundreds of entries on low fat cooking. The implication is that Lycos has searched the universe of low fat cooking sources and found and returned results from Barnes and Noble. But I'm not the trusting type. Back at Lycos, I try another search, this time for "marinating brontosaurus rectums." And wonder of wonders, what looks to be a research result from Barnes and Noble pops up again, and I am one click way from "books about marinating brontosaurus rectums."

Alas, I've been hijacked in my journey along the information highway. After churning for a few seconds, Barnes and Noble's web site informs me it has no books about "marinating brontosaurus rectums," after all. The result on the search engine was a hollow promise. But Barnes and Noble does have one title that "may be close" to what I'm looking for—a collection of sheet music by Scott Joplin.[11]

Notes

1. "AOL Pricing under Scrutiny," National Public Radio, *Morning Edition*, Jan. 23, 1998, transcript #98012315-210.
2. Jared Sandberg, "On-Line Services Make It Hard for Users to Quit," *The Wall Street Journal*, Jan. 20, 1997, p. B1.
3. Ibid.
4. Ibid.
5. Robert D. Hershey, Jr., "Information Age? Maybe Not, When It Comes to Prices," *The New York Times*, August 23, 1998, Section 3, p. 10.
6. Walter S. Mossberg, "Personal Technology: Users Are Starting to Resent Taking Part in Science Projects," *The Wall Street Journal*, May 15, 1997.
7. James L. Tyson, "Cyberspace Scams Lure Online Investors," *The Christian Science Monitor*, February 8, 1999.

8. Jared Sandberg, "On-Line Ply and Pry: How Business Pumps Kids on Web," *The Wall Street Journal*, June 9, 1997, p .B1.

9. Jared Sandberg, "Advertising: Recipe for Halting Spread of 'Spam' Is Proving Elusive," *The Wall Street Journal*, June 13, 1997, p. B1.

10. Saul Hansell and Amy Harmon, "Caveat Emptor on the Web," *The New York Times*, February 26, 1999, p. A1.

11. I don't know why. There's a piano piece called "Baby Brontosaurus Rag," but that's not by Joplin, and there were no references to it in the Joplin listing. And you thought that just because there was a footnote you'd find out the answer. Well, I can be tricky, too.

Chapter Thirteen

Reality (Sound)bites

How Made-for-Media Pseudo-Events Distort Our View of the World

 In the 1920s, a journalist named Walter Lippmann wrote a seminal book entitled *Public Opinion*. It would probably make Ben Stein's eyes glaze over, and, therefore, is not much read anymore, but it contains some terrific ideas with which I'd like to close this section of the book.

Lippmann was a reporter, and for a brief time a propagandist, during World War I. He wrote surrender pamphlets that were dropped behind enemy lines. He came up with the brilliant idea of writing different versions of the pamphlets and asking surrendering soldiers which ones they had read, thereby learning what worked and what didn't.

After the war, Lippmann retained his interest in how people are affected by communication, and, in particular, how the media shapes their view of reality. In his book, Lippmann analyzed press reports of the war, showing how they were filtered through government sources who arranged the facts in the order most favorable to the government's needs at the moment. The newspaper reader got a different view of reality than the "actual" reality. Although Lippmann didn't use the word, he was writing about spin.

In *Public Opinion*, Lippmann argued that there is a world outside and "pictures in our heads," and that the two don't necessarily jibe. In other words, the world and our conception of the world are two different things. Because we can't directly know much of what goes on in the world, we rely on media to shape those pictures in our heads. But the problem is that "reality" and "mediated reality" are two different things.

Part of the reason is that we cannot conceive of facts as facts. I can't hand you the "facts" about an issue; even when I bend over backward to give you what I think is a neutral accounting of an event, my views are diffracted through the prism of my language, my preconceptions, and my biases. I may not *think* I have biases, but biases are unavoidable. Someone growing up in suburban Rochester will have an entirely different mindset than someone who grew up in Beirut. When I recount my views of the Middle East, they are bound to be biased, and so are the views of the person from Beirut. Thus, our indirect view of the world is often distorted, shaped by our preconceptions and those of the all-too-fallible humans in the media, who give us second-hand accounts of a world we cannot entirely know and of people we usually cannot meet.

About forty years later, historian Daniel Boorstin picked up on this theme in his book *The Image*. In his book (which is very readable and still in print), Boorstin continued the discussion of mediated reality and extended it to show how media create a *separate* reality using events that never *quite* happen. The development of powerful media capable of reproducing images had an unfortunate side effect: folks with something to gain from publicity learned that they could confect media "events" that would produce as much or more benefit as a real event. For example, in the days before widespread media, a hotel owner looking to increase business might have repainted the lobby, or hired a new chef, rational actions directly related to the quality of hotel service. But after the media placed a premium on images once-removed from reality, the owner might have been more likely to hire a PR specialist and stage a "thirtieth anniversary dinner," inviting the press and local dignitaries. The *celebration* of the hotel is a *verification* of its quality. Image becomes substance. Boorstin called these types of events pseudo-events: events that are not spontaneous, that are created solely for the purpose of being reported, that hold a great deal of ambiguity as to their underlying meaning, and are meant to be self-fulfilling prophecies.

The culture of pseudo-events we've served up for ourselves goes beyond the Ambiguous Event technique described in chapter 3. The pseudo-event culture is a simmering stew of all the methods we've examined in this book: verbal chicanery using the Tortured Definition, Reduction to the Ridiculous, the Evil-Twin Word Substitution, the Incognito If, and the Logical Leapfrog; numerical skullduggery with the Remade Measure, Precision Garbage, the Apple-and-Orange Average, Comparison to the Nonexistent, and the Veiled Variable; or tricks with imagery, such as Proportion Distortion, Image Engineering, and the Confusing Counterfeit.

Each technique further erodes our contact with "reality," and, in fact, we've handed over some civic functions—such as elections— almost entirely to those who tell half-truths and manipulate pseudo-events. In chapter 5 I related how politicians have adopted the pseudo-event as their own—how, for example, Richard Nixon deflected threats on his honesty by declaring that nobody was going to take his dog away. I think that little black-and-white cocker spaniel and his clever, if furtive and unshaven, owner forever changed the culture and complexion of society. The Checkers Speech was the little lever that television used to shift our entire society's universe of knowledge.

The outgrowth of our reliance on second-hand reality has pro- *125*
duced almost unbelievable results. Let me illustrate by telling you my favorite story about mediated reality and pseudo-events. It's an old story, but an illustrative one, and, as far as I know, it hasn't been told publicly before.

When Congress was debating the removal of the possibly car- cinogenic sweetener saccharine from store shelves in the early 1980s, the public relations firm Hill and Knowlton was called in to sweeten up the image of the substance. A group of saccharine manufacturers calling themselves the Calorie Control Council funded the campaign. It was a giant account for the environmental and consumer affairs division of Hill and Knowlton, who embarked on a dual campaign, attempting to reach both the public and the congressional representatives who would vote on the issue. Executives from the Calorie Control Council were "media-trained," meaning that they learned effective techniques to use while being interviewed. Op-ed pieces were written for the Council and circu- lated to major newspapers. Lobbyists became active in the effort. They buttonholed congressional representatives and staffers, both in Washington and in their home states. To cap off the campaign,

Hill and Knowlton gathered a group of diabetic children—children who could not eat sugar—and lined them up outside the Capitol. As a former Hill and Knowlton staffer, Jim Lichtenberg, recalls the incident, the children shrieked at the congressmen: "Please don't take away our artificial sweetener."

What congressional representative wants to be pictured on the evening news *as the person who ignored the shrieking diabetic children?* Saccharin's handlers bought the substance some time, although it was eventually replaced by other sweeteners. But the incident might sour you on the idea that the media provide a picture of reality on which the citizen can act.

That's a good thought to keep in mind as we stealthily move this book to a close: *Who the hell wants to be the guy who ignored the chorus of shrieking diabetic children?* Who can fight the perfectly orchestrated pseudo-event? Moreover, how did we maneuver ourselves into becoming a society in which fragmented, out-of-context information is the coin of the realm, a place in which "events" one step removed from reality paint the pictures in our heads?

It really began well before Nixon's dog—probably, in fact, with Christopher Columbus, the world's first PR man. As he traveled through Europe trying to raise money to finance his voyages, Columbus used the brand-new Gutenberg press to create pamphlets extolling the virtues of his trips to the New World (and stretching the truth about the wealth to be found in the New World). The humble pamphlet is a powerful device. We Americans might still be paying taxes to the Monarchy were it not for Thomas Paine's pamphlet "Common Sense."

But the role of the media changed drastically when high-quality presses began to crank out newspapers in earnest around the time of the Civil War. Those papers were purchased by readers, who demanded interesting stories. And because the papers were produced regularly, the editors needed an endless stream of material.

Something known as the "press agent" literally invented itself and fulfilled the mutual demands of the newspapers, the readers, and *the people who benefitted from publicity.* P. T. Barnum, arguably one of America's first "press agents," built an empire devising stories that the press and the public found irresistible. They were rarely true, but they were still irresistible. For instance, Barnum engineered nationwide publicity with his promotion of Joice Heth, a former slave whom Barnum hired in 1835. Barnum maintained that Heth was 161 years old and was once a nurse to

George Washington. After she died, an autopsy revealed that she was about 80.

The modern image industry emerged in the second half of the nineteenth century. American business had been wounded by press exposés and antitrust crusades and wanted to reclaim a good image. Also, business found that persuading the public could be profitable. It therefore moved away from brazen "press agentry" to the new field of "public relations." Westinghouse, which is usually credited with establishing the first corporate public relations department, hired former journalists to convince the public that the electrical standard for the U.S. should be alternating current rather than direct current. This was an amazing battle, much of it waged in the media and fueled by an insane pseudo-event. The chief purveyor of direct current, Thomas Edison, noted that alternating current was used in the new electric chair and began a publicity campaign calling A.C. the "death current." Proponents of alternating current countered, charging that direct current was too weak to power entire cities. Edison retaliated by staging a media event in 1903 on Coney Island. He "proved" the power of direct current by electrocuting an elephant!

Before World War I, advertising and public relations became firmly established as professions. During the war, the government followed Westinghouse's lead and hired a former newspaper reporter to head its public information office. The trend of hiring journalists, who understood what form information should take and how to package it so journalists could use it, as *persuaders* continued through World War II.

After World War II, a revitalized corporate economy and an increasingly influential mass media contributed to the explosion of the image empire. Today, millions are employed in businesses involved in the creation of image. There are an estimated half a million people involved in the many forms of public relations alone, more than the number of people employed in the business of writing and producing actual news. As a result, we're never quite sure where a particular image came from or what an event means. Does the dead elephant mean direct current can really power households? Do the shrieking diabetic children mean that the humane thing to do is to approve the continued sale of a risky substance? Often our confusion with images is benign, with one world of images intersecting with another, such as when local television stations use electronic publicity kits featuring interviews with top movie stars. The kits are put together by the studios and designed so that local reporters can re-ask questions and edit themselves into the shot and make it appear that they are actually talking with the star. The media kits are expensive—as much as $125,000 per kit— but produce publicity that would cost the studios more than $700,000 if they had to buy the airtime.[1] Odds are you've been fooled by one of these media kits, and maybe you're a little irritated by it. But it's only fantasy.

But maybe you've also been hoodwinked by American presidential candidates who visit flag factories to provide themselves with photogenic backdrops for speeches in which they say little of substance. Or who lead parades, or recite the Star-Spangled Banner, or strip to their shirtsleeves to wire a school for the Internet. Maybe you're a little irritated by it. But it's only fantasy. It makes us feel good about ourselves, this skein of colorful, vigorous, compelling, and seductive images. We like our images. Maybe more than we like our reality.

Boorstin summed it up pretty well when he wrote that we've come to the point where the American citizen

> lives in a world where fantasy is more real than reality, where the image has more dignity than its original. We hardly dare face our bewilderment, because our ambiguous experience is so pleasantly iridescent, and the solace of belief in contrived reality is so thoroughly real. We have become eager accessories to the great hoaxes of the age. These are the hoaxes we play on ourselves.[2]

128

Notes

1. Kathleen Hall Jamieson and Karlyn Kohrs Campbell, *The Interplay of Influence*, 4th ed., (Belmont, CA: Wadsworth, 1997), pp. 133–34.
2. Daniel Boorstin, *The Image: A Guide to Pseudo-Events in America*, (New York: Atheneum, 1987), p. 37.

Ten Lists of Ten Guidelines for Becoming a Better Consumer of Information

The following pages contain ten action plans—each a ten-point program—for dealing with information, media, and sales pitches. I also recommend a reading list of ten books.

HOW TO DETECT REPORTER-INJECTED DISTORTION

Intentionally or not, reporters can handle information in such a way that its impact and meaning are altered.

Here are some ways this happens:

1. *Speaking through sources*. Any experienced reporter knows which sources will agree with the reporter's views. By accident or design, those sources wind up on the speed-dial.

2. *Inventing a trend*. A powerful and well-known editor once confessed to me that information for her "trend" stories about fads sweeping the nation often came from her teenager. She had no idea whether these fads were real, but they became real after she carried stories about them.

3. *Favoring the dramatic*. Debate about how to spend millions of dollars of taxpayer money at a city council meeting is important, but the resulting story might be tedious and complex. Two council members shouting at each other, however, looks more like a "story," and it's likely the confrontation will wind up on the 11 o'clock news.

4. *The reaction shot*. Reaction shots are used in TV news to cover edits. The on-the-scene interview is usually done with one camera, and the shots of the reporter nodding or re-asking the questions are taken later, sometimes even after the subject of the interview has left. Sometimes reporters spruce up their original questions to make them appear more aggressive, to indicate that they forcibly extracted information from a villain, when that information was, in reality, offered up quite willingly.

5. *The empty ending*. In television news, the reporters usually shoot the wrap-up from the scene of the story first, but they may do several hours of research after that back at the station. That's why so many TV reports end with vacuous conclusions: "We'll know more when we know more, at which point we'll know more. This is Bob Hairspray, Eyewitness News."

6. *The extremist roundup.* Reporters in all media tend to gravitate toward the sources that hold more radical viewpoints. Such sources produce the best quotes. But that leaves out a lot of people from the middle.

7. *The seductive source.* A source who is available, well-spoken, and who can painlessly give a reporter a good story tends to be used over and over, tilting the news toward the source's point of view.

8. *The seductive visual.* This is the same as #7, except that it involves a great picture the media can't pass up.

9. *Lights, camera, distortion.* Do you want to make somebody look guilty? Throw a lot of light on him and take a close-up.

10. *The one-person cross-section.* Generalizing from the circumstances of one individual is usually misleading. Unfortunately, it is the extreme case—the fellow leaving town because he can't find a job, for example—who makes the best copy.

HOW TO READ A NEWSPAPER

Newspapers set the agenda for the nation's information system. Even though most Americans get their news from TV, if you hang around a TV network you'll notice the news executives come in with papers tucked under their arms.

Here are some points to remember when reading a paper:

1. Newspaper reporters usually know more about the subjects they cover than broadcast reporters. It's not that they're necessarily smarter or better reporters; it's because newspapers usually have more reporters, and those reporters cover regular beats.

2. More and more newspapers have been gobbled up by chains. That's not necessarily bad, but you will note a certain similarity of content among chain-owned papers. Some receive canned editorials from the chain, and they often endorse the same presidential candidates.

3. Newspapers are desperate about their future. The average age of the reader is skyrocketing, and older readers are not appealing to most advertisers.

4. As a result of #3, a lot of newspapers are skewing their content in an attempt to reclaim younger readers.

5. Also as a result of #3, newspapers are starting to look more like television. If you doubt this, look at the *USA Today* vending machines. Their glass has rounded edges and they're tilted upward for easy reading. In short, they look like TVs—not a coincidence,

because that's exactly what Al Neuharth, the founder of *USA Today*, dictated.

6. There's an increasing emphasis on softer feature stories because that's what sells. Again, that is not unlike TV.

7. Largely because of #6, international news is fading from most newspaper pages.

8. Newspaper pictures can severely distort reality. By their nature, they capture an instant in time. If an editor wants to show a political candidate as dejected, it's not hard to find at least one second in the day when the candidate's head was lowered.

9. Remember that the amount of news you get in a newspaper is pegged to the amount of advertising the paper sells. Newspapers don't like to vary their ratio of news to advertising. Too much news and too little advertising is not cost-effective. The reverse drives away readers.

10. Having said all this, I should note that newspapers do a pretty good job, and their content is generally reliable. But blunders do happen, especially in web editions. Most newspapers don't let their web editions scoop the printed version, but some do, and in the rush to make it to the electronic page, big blunders can occur.

HOW TO WATCH TV NEWS
131

TV news is not exactly the same thing as "news," if you define news as a recounting of the the events of the day. This is not to say that television news is inferior to news on other media; it's just different. TV favors certain events at the expense of others.

You can be a better consumer of TV news if you keep these points in mind:

1. Television news competes for the same viewers who watch heavily produced entertainment programs. Therefore, it must mimic, to a certain extent, entertainment TV.

2. As a result, the people who choose what goes on TV favor stories that involve conflict, that have good visuals, and that revolve around easily grasped ideas.

3. The average television newscast has many minutes of pure promotion and show-biz. Much of the apparatus of TV news is designed to induce you to stay tuned through the commercials. Note how many "teasers" there are before commercials, some of them pretty shameless. We've not yet reached the point where the anchorman says, "Shots fired at the President! Did they hit?

You'll find out after these messages . . . ," but I think we're close.

4. Remember that there is nothing random in the selection of elements designed to get you tuned in and keep you there. TV anchors are chosen as much for their warm fuzziness as their journalistic abilities. The company that measures "Q-factors," for example, mails out questionnaires asking about anchors' likability and appeal, not their news backgrounds.

5. Also, be aware that all those homey touches that appear so natural are there for a reason and are carefully worked out. Sometimes we're not sure exactly why they work—why there is appeal and chemistry with the combination of a gray-haired male anchor paired with a young blonde female anchor and a goofy sports guy who acts like Biff in *Death of a Salesman*—but these formulae seem to work consistently from market to market. And if you have any doubt about the type of planning that goes into a TV news program wait until you read #10.

6. Consultants often have a strong say in the news process. Consultants frequently implore local news stations to load their newscasts with "people" and medical stories.

7. TV news is all kinds of news, not just the front page. There's a lot of feature news, and that's OK. But note how often the feature news is somehow related to the big entertainment show at 10:00. ("Tonight, in a *real* E.R. . . .")

8. TV programmers think we're lazy, and they're probably right. We tend not to change channels, and that's why local stations put high audience draws on right before the 6 o'clock local news. This is not in itself sinister, but it does bring home the fact that the news business is part of the entertainment business.

9. Pictures drive TV news. News directors often spend tens of thousands of dollars per year subscribing to several video services so they can get the most memorable, colorful picture. While there may not be anything wrong with that, remember that some of that money could be used to pay for additional reporters.

10. Remember that TV news is part show business. There are superb journalists working on TV, but you cannot take the show business aspect out of the equation, and no matter how you slice it, show-biz changes the complexion of what we watch. My favorite quote about TV news illustrates this. Here's how former CBS Legal Correspondent Fred Graham describes what happened when he decided to return to his hometown of Nashville and become principal anchor of WKRN-TV. According to Graham, his tenure was not

a happy one because of his profound inability to engage in Happy Talk.

> The plan had been to weave some of my knowledge and experience into the conversation at the anchor desk. The results suggested that either I was not adroit at doing it or that "meaningful happy talk" was a contradiction in terms.
> During my anchor training in Iowa, the Frank Magid Company [the nation's top TV-news consulting firm] handlers had come up with a technique for injecting my own thoughts and personality into the format. The voice coach suggested that when a scripted news item caught my attention, I could add a "dollop" of my own insights as I tossed the conversation to [his coanchor] for her next story.

Graham concluded rather acidly that the only real result of this strategy was his discovery that his coanchor knew six different ways of saying "that's interesting."

HOW TO READ A MAGAZINE

Some magazines, particularly major news magazines, are pretty reliable and objective. But many magazines present a very slanted view. You might say this is part and parcel of being a magazine, because many magazines simply echo the point of view of their readers. But note that magazines are also beholden to advertisers, and that may further distort their editorial slant.

133

Here are some thoughts to keep in mind when taking home your quota of titles from the magazine rack:

1. Remember that most magazines appeal to a very narrow demographic. You won't find views far outside the mainstream of opinion for that particular readership.

2. As a result, a magazine is often like a mirror, reflecting and reinforcing predetermined views.

3. Magazines usually get most of their money from ads, not subscriptions or individual copy sales.

4. Magazines have a limited universe of advertisers. An auto magazine, for example, won't get many ads from soap companies.

5. As a result of #4 and #5, magazines are susceptible to advertiser pressure. Advertisers can and do influence news coverage in the pages of some magazines.

6. Magazines often sell "adjacencies," meaning ad placement near articles dealing with the particular product.

7. While there is (usually) no explicit promise that the mention of the product in the news copy adjacent to the ad will be favorable, it often works out that way. Surprise.

8. Some (but not all) trade journals—magazines that serve members of a particular profession—actually make it a policy to show prepublication news copy to people who are mentioned, seeking their approval.

9. Sometimes trade journal writers and editors even show article copy to advertisers for approval.

10. Bottom line: In many magazines, advertising and news have an unhygienically close relationship, one that distorts the "news" that you read.

HOW TO MAKE SENSE OUT OF A POLL

Polls often mislead because of flaws in the way they are conducted or because we simply try to read too much into them. When somebody tries to convince you of something using poll data, remember these points:

1. A poll is a snapshot it time. You can't make a movie out of it. In other words, what's true now may not be true tomorrow or next week.

2. You need to know the question before you can figure out what the results mean. We have a tendency to generalize poll results— "75 percent of Americans think . . . "—when we don't know what question was asked.

3. The question is important. You can literally reverse the percentage of "yes" replies by taking a question like "Do you favor increasing veternans' benefits even though it means raising taxes?" and rephrasing it as, "Do you favor raising taxes to pay for increased veteran's benefits?" It'll probably come up 75 percent yes asked the first way, 25 percent yes posed the second way.

4. Remember that polls ask questions of anybody who is contacted by the poll taker. While pollsters attempt to obtain statistically representative samples, that doesn't mean the people questioned really care about the issue, or that they know anything about it. So a lot of polls are really surveys of people who don't know and don't care.

5. People sometimes bluff or lie to pollsters. Try this experiment. Ask somebody if they favor the president's policy on aid to the

nation of Fredonia. Most of the president's supporters will tell you yes, and most of his detractors will tell you no. Hardly anybody will tell you they don't know where Fredonia is, which is the honest answer because Fredonia existed only in the minds of the Marx Brothers as the setting for one of their movies. Interestingly, *Spy Magazine* asked the Fredonia question of congressmen, and many of our representatives gave extended disserations about the importance of Fredonia to our national security.

6. Find out the source of the poll. Political pressure groups sometimes "poll" their members and produce results that—surprise—echo the pressure group's manifesto. They publicize this "poll" without reference to its source.

7. Any self-selected poll is not particulary useful. People calling in to a 900 number are not a statistical representation of society at large.

8. Polls cannot measure all things with the same precision. Pollsters have been pretty successful at predicting the outcome of elections. But that's a specific question asked of likely voters a short time before the event. Anyone who says, "this is what the public thinks" about an issue, and who also says "this result must be accurate because look how pollsters predict elections within a few percentage points" is comparing two different sets of data.

135

9. Pollsters have gotten pretty good about keeping bias out of their sample. But remember that somebody taking a poll on a streetcorner is unlikely to approach a surly-looking thug, even though with some topics the thug's opinion might be important to the poll.

10. Polls are narrow sets of numbers that don't apply in all circumstances. Just because a poll says most people feel safer on the streets doesn't necessarily mean the streets are safer, and even if that were true it doesn't necessarily apply to your street.

TEN THINGS TO REMEMBER WHEN YOU READ ABOUT A SCIENTIFIC "BREAKTHROUGH"

We're often frustrated because we read an article or see a TV news report about a new miracle cure, or new form of energy, or whatever, only to hear nothing about the "breakthrough" ever again. Why does this happen?

1. Mice are not people. You can't always extrapolate what happens in a lab to real life.

2. Scientists and their institutions have an agenda that often includes publicity. Press exposure begets grant money and higher student enrollments.

3. Sometimes the importance of a scientific study is overblown because public relations people, who live and die by press coverage, trumpet a dubious breakthrough for reasons explained in #2.

4. Many reporters don't know much about science and they can't critically evaluate the information.

5. But reporters do know that a story about a cure for cancer on the cover sells a lot of magazines.

6. Reporters are human. They'd like to believe in a wonderful breakthrough as much as you do.

7. Journalists and PR people sometimes put words in the mouths of scientists because they are convinced that the scientists need to be "drawn out."

8. The press is convinced that science stories have to be simplified for the public to understand them. To an extent that's true, but a lot of science and medicine coverage becomes simplistic, not simplified.

9. #8 means that a lot of the detail, especially the qualifying and counter-balancing detail, is left out.

10. A lot of junk science winds up on TV because medical and science stories have good pictures: labs, flashing lights, operating rooms, and so forth.

HOW TO DETECT PROPAGANDA

Propaganda has various definitions, but we usually think of it as a one-sided, deliberately misleading message, often designed to be hurtful to a person or group.

Here are ten warning signs that the message you are reading, seeing, or hearing is propagandistic in nature:

1. The person presenting the message figuratively turns over card after card after card and everything squares with the message. All the cards are in the dealer's favor, and turn over exactly at the right time. If you get the gut feeling the deck is stacked, it probably is.

2. The message contains vague, but appealing, terms, such as "red-blooded Americans" or "progressive freethinkers."

3. The message contains vague, but somehow repellant, terms, like "card-carrying member of the ACLU."

4. There are many references to vague authority. "Professors at

leading universities say. . . ." Who are they? What universities? Or there are many testimonials when the connection between the person (usually famous) and the message are tenuous.

5. The message tries to convince you to do something because everybody else is doing it. You don't want to be left off the bandwagon.

6. The message or the messenger appeals to "plain folks." Be on guard when someone, particularly someone with a lot of power and money, tries to convince you that he or she is just one of the "ordinary people."

7. Name-calling is used as a device to reinforce the message. Note, for example, whether the messenger uses words like "terrorist" or "freedom fighter."

8. The whole message seems deliberately confusing.

9. The message centers on transferring the attributes of one thing, like the Bible or the flag, to another person or thing.

10. The attribution is biased. Be on guard when sources are not quoted as "Smith said," but rather "Smith gloated" or "Smith tried to defend his actions by saying. . . ."*

*Several of these points were originally proposed by the Institute for Propaganda Analysis, an educational group that tried to inform Americans about propaganda methods in the years leading up to World War II.

TEN RED FLAGS THAT MAY SIGNIFY YOU'RE BEING SWINDLED

There's no magic formula that will tell you that the person you're talking to is up to no good, but here are some pretty good indications:

1. You are told you have to act immediately. There are few legitimate deals that will evaporate if you need a little time to think things over.

2. You are given testimonials from the likes of "Mark S. from New York City." Real people have last names, not initials.

3. You are told that this is an "exclusive" offer. It's probably exclusive to anyone who has money.

4. You're not supposed to tell anybody about the deal, usually because it's so good everybody will want in. (Yeah, like the bunco squad.)

5. You'll get something for nothing, with virtually no effort.

6. You will have to put up "good-faith money." There are cer-

tainly legitimate cases where a deposit of some sort is a reasonable requirement, but if there doesn't seem to be any rational reason for you to put up your money, don't.

7. You can't contact other clients or customers for references. Not even "Mark S. from New York City."

8. The person trying to persuade you to do something acts annoyed if you ask detailed questions, or tries to give you the impression he's offended by your questions.

9. You're asked to sign something that's not completely filled out.

10. There's nothing in writing about this particular deal, and nobody wants to put anything in writing.

HOW TO SHORT-CIRCUIT SOMEBODY WHO'S TRYING TO BAMBOOZLE YOU ON THE PHONE

The telephone is a great convenience when you have to call home, order a pizza, or fool someone. The problem with trying to ascertain truth on the telephone is that you're missing a lot of the cues that fill in your gaps of knowledge about the communication situation, such as the location of the caller, the demeanor of the person you're talking to, and whether the "clergyman" on the other end of the line is wearing a nose ring and a Grateful Dead tee shirt.

Here are ten methods you can use to keep callers honest:

1. If your suspicions are aroused, ask for a number and call back. Crooks don't usually welcome return calls.

2. If you're really suspicious, and need an instant clue as to whether the person on the other end is for real—for example, if he claims he's a police officer and there's an emergency, but you're suspicious—ask for a switchboard number. Or tell him you'll call back through the police department main switchboard and look it up yourself.

3. Get the person's name. This is helpful if you need to sort things out later. Ask for both names. Some places assign a phony name, such as "Mr. Robert," to everybody. If the person on the other end refuses to give you his or her name, that person is either very stuffy or is hiding something. If the person can't seem to remember his name, hang up.

4. When the sales pitch gets too intense, ask for the details in writing. Tell the caller you don't do business with anybody who can't afford paper.

5. If you're suspicious, plainly state that you are concerned about

doing business over the phone because of the prevalence of telephone fraud. I say this to all telephone salespeople, and about one-quarter hang up as soon as they hear me say this. I don't think I'm missing anything.

6. Press for details on what, exactly, the person's affiliation is. Some pseudo-charities would like you to believe the caller is a priest, rabbi, or whatever and will come close to saying that, but not actually say it, to avoid legal trouble. Make them put up or shut up. Are you a priest? (A police officer? A firefighter?)

7. If the person on the phone says he's conducting a survey, and you are inclined to participate, let him know that you'll hang up immediately if he tries to sell you something. Legitimate survey-takers won't mind this threat. The people trying to sell you something might give up.

8. But there's no guarantee. So if they do try to sneak in a sales pitch, deliver a stern lecture about how they are making it difficult for real researchers to conduct legitimate research. They probably won't care, but you'll have some fun.

9. If a caller says he's conducting a political poll, ask if it's a "push poll." A push poll is a series of questions that are designed to "push" you toward a certain conclusion or candidate.

10. If he tries to sneak in a push poll, repeat the lecture described in #8.

TEN BOOKS THAT WILL OPEN YOUR EYES ABOUT COMMUNICATION, WORDS, NUMBERS, PERSUASION, AND MEDIA

1. *Technopoly: The Surrender of Culture to Technology*, by Neil Postman (New York: Vintage, 1993). A terrific look at how technology overwhelms our culture and decision-making—and about ways in which media technologies make you less aware of what you don't know.

2. *How to Lie with Statistics*, by Darrell Huff (New York: W. W. Norton & Company, 1954). A classic: a short, intriguing book that shows how numbers can be manipulated.

3. *Dirty Politics: Deception, Distraction, and Democracy*, by Kathleen Hall Jamieson (New York: Oxford University Press, 1993). Eye-opening, sometimes enraging study of how the electorate is manipulated by media.

4. *Ogilvy on Advertising*, by David Ogilvy (New York: Random House, 1997). An insider's view of the advertising world. Gives you

an understanding not only of how advertising works but its place in our culture.

5. *The Media Monopoly*, by Ben Haig Bagdikian (New York: Beacon, 1997). Bagdikian's theme is the centralization of control of the media, but perhaps his most telling observation is how corporate ownership of news media has escalated the expectation of profit—and changed the news business.

6. *The Image: A Guide to Pseudo-Events in America*, by Daniel J. Boorstin (New York: MacMillan, 1987). The definitive guide to the ongoing struggle between reality and image.

7. *Breaking the News*, by James Fallows (New York: Vintage, 1997). A clear-headed look at how the news trivializes complex issues. Also focuses on the impact of big money on the news business.

8. *Language in Action*, by S. I. Hayakawa (New York: Harcourt, 1941). How words are distorted, and how they sometimes become a barrier to communication.

9. *The Interplay of Influence: News, Advertising, Politics, and the Mass Media*, 4th edition, by Kathleen Hall Jamieson and Karlyn Kohrs Cambell (International Thomson Publishing, 1996). A very readable textbook that investigates the melding of persuasive processes—the interplay between politics, political advertising, and product advertising are a few areas covered in this fine book.

10. *Crisis of Conscience: Perspectives on Journalism Ethics*, by Carl Hausman (New York: Harper Collins, 1992). As reluctant as I am to plug my own book, I urge you to buy this one (perhaps several, as gifts). It explores the way media distorts "reality," and the difficulty in finding where that "reality" lies.

How and Where to Complain: A Resource Guide for Consumers

There are good ways and bad ways to complain, the bad ways being unproductive methods that simply cause aggravation for all involved. I've studied what works and what doesn't and would like to pass along some brief suggestions, followed by addresses, names, and web sites particularly relevant for consumers. Although consumer issues are only one area of focus in this book, it is the topic that lends itself most directly to making a phone call, writing a letter, or otherwise seeking some action. The people and places listed here should help.

First, advice on how to complain:

1. Be sure you do complain. Many of us think to ourselves that we'll make a call or write a letter but never get around to it. Complain regularly. Make a schedule; write one complaint letter a week, if that's your style. I doubt you'll have trouble finding material.

2. Think of your complaint as a positive expression. Seriously. I've had several restaurant owners thank me after I informed them that the pastrami was tough or the soup tasted metallic. They don't want to serve unappetizing food to the rest of their customers, most of whom will simply suffer in silence, but never come back. The same applies to many businesses. You're helping them out, whether they realize it or not.

3. Keep track of your letters and phone calls. I have a secret to keeping track of calls: I put spiral notebooks by every phone and tape them to the table. I also keep a pad of Post-It notes by the phone to help me resist the temptation to rip pages out of the notebook, which would defeat the purpose of the system. Force yourself to make a note of whom you called and what you said. It only takes a second.

When the person you're complaining to tells you that this is the first time he's heard of this problem, you can remind him that you brought it to his attention on October 15, 18, 22, 27, and 28, and he never returned any of your calls. That sort of documentation is effective, and its existence is a powerful threat if your case ever goes to court.

4. While complaining by phone is effective, it's always a good idea

to put something in writing. Make sure your letter is addressed to a specific person, is dated, and lays out your case completely. Be sure to list relevant dates when something happened (or didn't happen) in the letter. Also be sure to ask for something specific—a refund, a timely repair, or so forth. If appropriate, give the person a deadline by which to respond or take other action.

The model below is suggested by the Federal Trade Commission:

Sample Complaint Letter

(Your address)
(Your City, State, Zip Code)
(Date)

(Name of Contact Person)
(Title)
(Company Name)
(Street Address)
(City, State, Zip Code)

Dear (Contact Person):

On (date), I purchased (or had repaired) a (name of the product with the serial or model number or service performed). I made this purchase at (location, date, and other important details of the transaction).

Unfortunately, your product (or service) has not performed well (or the service was inadequate) because (state the problem).

Therefore, to resolve the problem, I would appreciate it if you (state the specific action you want). Enclosed are copies (copies, NOT originals) of my records (receipts, guarantees, warranties, canceled checks, contracts, model and serial numbers, and any other documents).

I look forward to your reply and to the resolution of my problem, and will wait (set a time limit) before seeking third-party assistance. Please contact me at the above address or by phone (home or office numbers with area codes).

Sincerely,
(Your name)
(Your account number)

5. Resist the temptation to carbon-copy several people when you write a complaint letter. What sometimes happens is that all the recipients will assume it's somebody else's problem.

6. If you seek third-party remediation, start your complaints with someone who is close to the situation at a local level. A list of local and regional consumer protection agencies is provided in this section. People in these offices know their way around and can often resolve disputes expeditiously.

7. You can file complaints with federal agencies, but those agencies often don't become directly involved in resolution. But you can put yourself on record. The Federal Trade Commission (FTC.gov) and the Federal Communications Commission (FCC.gov) have an explanation of how to complain on-line.

8. Experienced scamsters may thumb their noses at the law, but few will have the same cavalier attitude about adverse publicity. For obvious reasons, people with something to hide hate publicity. You can call consumer reporters at local media outlets, or check out the Call for Action list provided in this section.

9. If you're dealing with a bureaucracy, learn your way around the agency through the switchboard or through a chatty secretary or clerk. You want to find out not only who to complain to, but also *the name of that person's boss*. Why? Because you can use the following technique, which is the radioactive rat poison of complaining, and should be used with discretion. If Mr. Big won't give you what you want, or you are stalled at Mr. Big's secretary, ask to be transferred to Mr. Bigger. This won't work if you don't know the real name of Mr. Bigger. You'll be amazed at how often Mr. Big will capitulate or suddenly "walk into the office."

★143★

10. In some cases, writing to the president of the company produces a quick resolution. It's not that the president will read your letter and pound the desk in outrage; rather, executive offices typically have clear complaint resolution strategies and your letter will probably get passed along to the right people. Your local librarian will be able to lead you to directories of company CEOs.

Consumer Issues Websites

I have not listed a large number of sites because the major ones included here will link you to literally thousands of relevant sites. You might try starting with "Consumer World" and the "U.S. Consumer Gateway."

Consumer World
http://www.consumerworld.org/

A huge, well-organized resource. Over 1,800 destinations catalogued in a very logical scheme. One of the most useful and interesting categories is the resource section on finding a better loan or credit card. Give it a try. Consumer World is a carnival of consumer news.

The U.S. Consumer Gateway
http://www.consumer.gov/

Your tax dollars invested wisely! Here's a one-stop link to federal information services available online. The categories (such as food, health, product safety, and transportation) are logically laid out and divided into sensible subcategories. Of particular interest is ScamAlert!, a feature that provides current information on fraudulent and deceptive practices in the marketplace.

The Bills Project
http://www.consumerwatchdog. org/public_hts/bills/

Ralph Nader's latest project was created to monitor billing errors, deception, and fraud. The web site offers insights into the problem (which is much more serious than you might suspect) and offers some solutions.

The Foundation for Taxpayer and Consumer Rights
http://www.consumerwatchdog. org/public_hts/home/

This California-based organization works with public interest groups headquartered in Washington and elsewhere. The site contains useful links and articles.

Consumer ACTION & ADVICE Ring
http://www.webring.org/cgi-bin/webring?ring=consume;list

A collection of consumer links.

Consumer Reports OnLine
http://www.consumerreports.org/

You can access the magazine's archives for $2.95 a month, and there are also plenty of free articles on this excellent site. Clear buying advice and well-written features.

Telephone Preference Service
http://www.the-dma.org/con sass5/consasst-tps5a2.shtml

Direct Marketing Association
P. O. Box 9014
Farmingdale, NY 11735-9014

At this web site, you can fill out a form (which you have to snail mail) to have your name removed from some telemarketing lists. It won't stop all calls, and crooks are not likely to voluntarily adhere to the service's guidelines, but you may be able to finish dinner in

peace a little more often.
There is a mail version of the
same service:

Mail Preference Service
http://www.the-dma.org/con
sass5/consasst-mps5a3.shtml

Direct Marketing Association
P. O. Box 9008
Farmingdale, NY 11735-9008

State, County, and City Government Consumer Protection Offices

City, county, and state consumer protection offices, a list of which I
have provided below, provide consumers with important services.
They mediate complaints, conduct investigations, prosecute offend-
ers of consumer laws, license and regulate a variety of professionals, promote strong consumer protection legislation, provide   *145*
educational materials, and advocate in the consumer interest.
    City and county consumer offices are familiar with local busi-
nesses and local ordinances. The cities where these offices are
located are in bold type to help you find the office closest to you. If
there is no local consumer office in your area, contact your state
consumer protection office. State offices, whether in the attorney
general's office, the governor's office, or in a separate department
of consumer affairs, are familiar with state laws and look for
statewide patterns of abuse. Consumer protection offices in the U.S.
territories also are included in the list. To save time, call the office
before sending in a written complaint. Ask if the office handles the
type of complaint you have, and if complaint forms are provided.
Many offices prepare consumer alerts on local problems and issues,
with specific information on the applicable state and local laws.
Call, send an e-mail, or visit the web sites listed below for more
information.
    A personal note: It's been my observation that local problem-
solving organizations are the best. The local folks really know their
way around.

Alabama

State Office

Chief Director
Consumer Affairs Section
Office of the Attorney General
11 South Union Street
Montgomery, AL 36130
334-242-7334
Toll free in AL: 1-800-392-5658
Fax: 334-242-2433
Web site: e-pages.com/aag/cus
    pro.html

Alaska

The Consumer Protection Section
in the Office of the Attorney
General has been closed.
Consumers with complaints are
being referred to the Better
Business Bureau, small claims
court, and private attorneys.

American Samoa

Assistant Attorney General
Consumer Protection Bureau
P. O. Box 7
Pago Pago, AS 96799
011-684-633-4163
Fax: 011-684-633-1838

Arizona

State Offices

Chief Counsel
Consumer Protection
Office of the Attorney General
1275 West Washington Street
Room 259
Phoenix, AZ 85007
602-542-3702
602-542-5763 (consumer infor-
    mation and complaints)

Toll free in AZ: 1-800-352-8431
TDD: 602-542-5002
Fax: 602-542-4377

Assistant Attorney General
Consumer Protection
Office of the Attorney General
400 West Congress South Bldg.
Suite 315
Tucson, AZ 85701
520-628-6504
Toll free in AZ: 1-800-352-8431
Fax: 520-628-6532
E-mail: NMATTS@AG.state.az.us

County Offices

County Attorney
Apache County Attorney's Office
P. O. Box 637
St. Johns, AZ 85936
520-337-4364, ext. 240
Fax: 520-337-2427

County Attorney
Coconino County Attorney's Office
Coconino County Courthouse
100 East Birch
Flagstaff, AZ 86001
520-779-6518
Fax: 520-779-5618

County Attorney
Gila County Attorney's Office
1400 East Ash Street
Globe, AZ 85501
520-425-3231
Fax: 520-425-3720

County Attorney
Graham County Attorney's Office
Graham County Courthouse
800 West Main
Safford, AZ 85546
520-428-3620
Fax: 520-428-7200

County Attorney
Greenlee County Attorney's Office
P. O. Box 1717
Clifton, AZ 85533
520-865-4108
Fax: 520-865-4665

County Attorney
La Paz County Attorney's Office
1320 Kofa Avenue
P. O. Box 709
Parker, AZ 85344
520-669-6118
Fax: 520-669-2019

County Attorney
Mohave County Attorney's Office
315 North 4th Street
P. O. Box 7000
Kingman, AZ 86402-7000
520-753-0719
Fax: 520-753-2669

County Attorney
Navajo County Attorney's Office
P. O. Box 668
Holbrook, AZ 86025
520-524-4026
Fax: 520-524-4244

County Attorney
Pima County Attorney's Office
1400 Legal Services Building
32 North Stone
Tucson, AZ 85701
520-740-5600
Fax: 520-791-3946

Pinal County Attorney
Pinal County Attorney's Office
P. O. Box 887
Florence, AZ 85232
520-868-6271
Fax: 520-868-6521

County Attorney
Santa Cruz County Attorney's
   Office
2100 N. Congress Drive, Suite 201
Nogales, AZ 85621
520-761-7800, ext. 3121
Fax: 520-761-7859

Yavapai County Attorney's Office
Yavapai County Courthouse
255 East Gurley
Prescott, AZ 86301
520-771-3344
Fax: 520-771-3110

County Attorney
Yuma County Attorney's Office
168 South Second Avenue
Yuma, AZ 85364
520-329-2270
Fax: 520-329-2284

City Office

Deputy City Attorney
Consumer Affairs Division
Tucson City Attorney's Office
110 East Pennington Street
P. O. Box 27210
Tucson, AZ 85726-7210
520-791-4886
Fax: 520-791-4991

Arkansas

State Office

Consumer Protection Division
Office of Attorney General
200 Catlett Prien
323 Center Street
Little Rock, AR 72201
501-682-2341
TDD toll free in AR: 1-800-482-
   8982
TDD: 501-682-2014
Web site: www.ag-state.ar.us

147

California

State Offices

Director
California Department of
  Consumer Affairs
400 R Street, Suite 3000
Sacramento, CA 95814
916-445-4465
Toll free in CA: 1-800-952-5210
TDD: 916-322-1700
510-785-7554

Attorney General
Office of Attorney General
Public Inquiry Unit
P. O. Box 944255
Sacramento, CA 94244-2550
916-322-3360
Toll free in CA: 1-800-952-5225
TDD: 916-324-5564
Web site: caag.state.ca.us/piu

Chief
Bureau of Automotive Repair
California Dept. of Consumer
  Affairs
10240 Systems Parkway
Sacramento, CA 95827
916-445-1254
Toll free in CA: 1-800-952-5210
  (auto repair only)
TDD: 916-322-1700

County Offices

Commissioner
Alameda County Consumer Affairs
  Commission
1328 Via El Monte
San Lorenzo, CA 94580
510-535-6444

District Attorney
Contra Costa County
District Attorney's Office
725 Court Street, 4th Floor
P. O. Box 670
Martinez, CA 94553
510-646-4500
Fax: 510-646-2116

Senior Deputy District Attorney
Business Affairs Unit
Fresno County District Attorney's
  Office
1250 Van Ness Avenue, 2nd Floor
Fresno, CA 93721
209-488-3156
Fax: 209-495-1315

District Attorney
Criminal Division
Kern County District Attorney's
  Office
1215 Truxtun Avenue, 4th Floor
Bakersfield, CA 93301
805-868-2340
Fax: 805-868-2700

Director
Kern County Department of
  Weights & Measures
1116 East California Avenue
Bakersfield, CA 93307
805-861-2418
Fax: 805-324-0668

Director
Los Angeles County Department of
  Consumer Affairs
500 West Temple Street, B-96
Los Angeles, CA 90012
213-974-1452 (public)
213-974-9750 (private)
Fax: 213-687-0233
Web site: www.co.la.ca.us/con
  sumer-affairs

Marin County Mediation Services
4 Mount Lassen Drive
San Rafael, CA 94903
415-499-7454
Fax: 415-499-6978

Deputy District Attorney
Consumer Protection Division
Marin County District Attorney's
    Office
Hall of Justice, Room 130
3501 Civic Center Drive
San Rafael, CA 94903
415-499-6450
Fax: 415-499-3719
E-mail: consumer@marin.org
Web site: www.marin.org/mc/da

District Attorney
Mendocino County District
    Attorney's Office
P. O. Box 1000
Ukiah, CA 95482
707-463-4211
Fax: 707-463-4687

Monterey County District Attorney
Consumer Protection Division
P. O. Box 1369
Salinas, CA 93902
408-755-5073
Fax: 408-755-5608

Deputy District Attorney
Consumer Affairs Division
Napa County District Attorney's
    Office
931 Parkway Mall
P. O. Box 720
Napa, CA 94559
707-253-4211
Fax: 707-253-4041

Supervising Deputy District
    Attorney
Consumer/Environmental
    Protection Unit
Orange County District Attorney's
    Office
405 West 5th Street, Suite 606
Santa Ana, CA 92701
714-568-1200
Fax: 714-568-1250

Supervising Deputy District
    Attorney
Economic Crime Division
Riverside County District
    Attorney's Office
4075 Main Street
Riverside, CA 92501
909-275-5400
Fax: 909-275-5470

Supervising Deputy District
    Attorney
Consumer and Environmental
    Protection Division
Sacramento County District
    Attorney's Office
P. O. Box 749
Sacramento, CA 95812-0749
916-440-6174
Fax: 916-440-7660

Director
Consumer Fraud Division
San Diego County District
    Attorney's Office
P. O. Box X-1011
San Diego, CA 92112-4192
619-531-3507 (complaint mes-
    sage line)
619-531-4040

Consumer Protection Unit
San Francisco County District
   Attorney's Office
425 Brannan Street
San Francisco, CA 94103
415-552-6400 (public inquiries)
Fax: 415-552-7038

Supervising Deputy District
   Attorney
San Joaquin County District
   Attorney's Office
222 East Weber, Room 412
P. O. Box 990
Stockton, CA 95202
209-468-2315
Fax: 209-468-0314

Director
Economic Crime Unit
Consumer Fraud Department
County Government Center
1050 Monterey Street, Room 235
San Luis Obispo, CA 93408
805-781-5856
Fax: 805-781-1173

Deputy in Charge
Consumer Fraud & Environmental
   Protection Unit
San Mateo County District
   Attorney's Office
401 Marshall Street
Hall of Justice and Records
Redwood City, CA 94063
650-363-4656
Fax: 650-363-1681

Senior Deputy
District Attorney
Consumer Protection Unit
Santa Barbara County District
   Attorney's Office
1105 Santa Barbara Street
Santa Barbara, CA 93101

150

805-568-2300
Fax: 805-568-2398

Deputy District Attorney
Consumer Protection Unit
Santa Clara County District
   Attorney's Office
70 West Hedding Street
West Wing, 4th Floor
San Jose, CA 95110
408-792-2568
Fax: 408-279-8742

Director of Mediation Services
Santa Clara County Consumer
   Protection Unit
70 West Hedding Street
West Wing, 4th Floor
San Jose, CA 95110
408-792-2880
408-792-2881 (small claims)
Fax: 408-279-8742
Web site: claraweb.co.santa-clara.
   ca.us/da/compform.htm

Coordinator, Division of Consumer
   Affairs
Santa Cruz County District
   Attorney's Office
701 Ocean Street, Room 200
Santa Cruz, CA 95060
408-454-2050
TDD/TTY: 408-454-2123
Fax: 408-454-2227
Web site: www.CO.Santa-
   Cruz.CA/US

Deputy District Attorney
Consumer Affairs Unit
Solano County District Attorney's
   Office
600 Union Avenue
Fairfield, CA 94533
707-421-6859
Fax: 707-421-7986

Deputy District Attorney
Consumer Fraud Unit
Stanislaus County District
    Attorney's Office
P. O. Box 442
Modesto, CA 95353-0442
209-525-5550
Fax: 209-525-5545

Supervisor
Consumer Mediation Section
Ventura County District Attorney's
    Office
800 South Victoria Avenue
Ventura, CA 93009
805-654-3110
Fax: 805-648-9255
E-mail: on web site
Web site: www.Ventura.Org/VCDA

Chief Deputy District Attorney
Special Services Unit-
    Consumer/Environmental
Yolo County District Attorney's
    Office
P. O. Box 245
Woodland, CA 95776
916-666-8424
Fax: 916-666-8423
E-mail: YOLADA@aol.com

City Offices

Supervising Deputy City Attorney
Consumer Protection Division
Los Angeles City Attorney's Office
200 North Main Street
1600 City Hall East
Los Angeles, CA 90012
213-485-4515
Fax: 213-237-0402
E-mail: dkass@atty.ca.la.ca.us

Head Deputy City Attorney
San Diego City Attorney's Office
Consumer and Environmental
    Protection Unit
1200 Third Avenue, Suite 700
San Diego, CA 92101-4106
619-533-5600 (consumer com-
    plaints)
Fax: 619-533-5504

Deputy City Attorney
Consumer Protection, Fair
    Housing & Public Rights
    Division
1685 Main Street, Room 310
Santa Monica, CA 90401
310-458-8336
310-458-8370 (Spanish hotline)
Fax: 310-395-6727
TDD/TTY: 310-458-8696
E-mail: teresa@pen.ci.santa-
    monica.ca.us

Colorado

State Office

Consumer Protection Division
Office of Attorney General
1525 Sherman Street, 5th Floor
Denver, CO 80203-1760
303-866-5189
Toll free: 1-800-332-2071
Fax: 303-866-5691

County Offices

District Attorney
Archuleta, LaPlata and San Juan
    Counties District Attorney's
    Office
P. O. Drawer 3455
Durango, CO 81302
970-247-8850
Fax: 970-259-0200

151

Chief Deputy District Attorney
Denver District Attorney's
    Economic Crimes Unit
303 West Colfax Avenue, Suite
    1300
Denver, CO 80204
303-640-5956 (administration)
303-640-3557 (complaints)
TDD/TTY: 303-640-5127
Fax: 303-640-2592
Web site: infodenver.denver.co.us

Chief Deputy District Attorney
Economic Crime Division
El Paso and Teller Counties
    District Attorney's Office
105 East Vermijo, Suite 205
Colorado Springs, CO 80903-2083
719-520-6002
Fax: 719-520-6006

District Attorney
Pueblo County District Attorney's
    Office
201 West 8th Street, Suite 801
Pueblo, CO 81003
719-583-6030
Fax: 719-583-6666

Chief Investigator
Weld County District Attorney's
    Office
P. O. Box 1167
Greeley, CO 80632
970-356-4010
Fax: 970-352-8023

Connecticut

State Offices

Department of Consumer
    Protection
165 Capitol Avenue
Hartford, CT 06106
860-566-2534

Toll free in CT: 1-800-842-2649
Fax: 860-566-1531
Web site: www.state.ct.us/dcp/

Antitrust/Consumer Protection
Office of Attorney General
110 Sherman Street
Hartford, CT 06105
860-808-5400
Fax: 860-808-5593
Web site: www.cslnet.ctstateu.
    edu/attygenl

City Office

Director
Middletown Office of Consumer
    Protection
245 DeKoven Drive
Middletown, CT 06457
860-344-3491
TDD: 860-344-3521
Fax: 860-344-0136

Delaware

State Offices

Director
Consumer Protection Unit
Department of Justice
820 North French Street
Wilmington, DE 19801
Outside DE: 302-577-8600
Fax: 302-577-6499
Toll free in DE: 1-800-220-5424

Deputy Attorney General
Fraud and Consumer Protection
    Unit
Office of Attorney General
820 North French Street
Wilmington, DE 19801
302-577-8800
Toll free in DE: 1-800-220-5424
Fax: 302-577-3090

District of Columbia

Director
Department of Consumer and
  Regulatory Affairs
614 H Street, NW, Room 1120
Washington, DC 20001
202-727-7120
TDD/TTY: 202-727-7842
Fax: 202-727-8073

Florida

State Offices

Director
Department of Agriculture and
  Consumer Services
Division of Consumer Services
407 South Calhoun Street
Mayo Building, 2nd Floor
Tallahassee, FL 32399-0800
Outside FL: 850-488-2221
Toll free in FL: 1-800-435-7352
Fax: 850-487-4177
Web site: www.fl-ag.com

Chief of Multi-State Litigation
Consumer Litigation Section
110 SE 6th Street
Fort Lauderdale, FL 33301
954-712-4600
Fax: 954-712-4706

Assistant Deputy Attorney
  General
Economic Crimes Division
Office of the Attorney General
110 SE 6th Street, 10th Floor
Fort Lauderdale, FL 33301
954-712-4600
Fax: 954-712-4658

County Offices

Broward County Consumer Affairs
  Division

115 South Andrews Avenue
Annex Room A460
Fort Lauderdale, FL 33301
954-765-5350, ext. 232
Fax: 954-765-5309
E-mail: mfandel@co.broward.fl.us
Web site: www.co.broward.fl.us

Consumer Advocate
Metropolitan Dade County
Consumer Protection Division
140 West Flagler Street, Suite 902
Miami, FL 33130
305-375-4222
Fax: 305-375-4120

Chief
Dade County Economic Crime Unit
Office of State Attorney
1350 NW 12th Avenue
5th Floor, Graham Building
Miami, FL 33136-2111
305-547-0671

Manager
Hillsborough County Commerce
  Deptartment
Consumer Protection Unit
P. O. Box 1110
Tampa, FL 33601
813-272-6750
Fax: 813-276-8646
Web site: www.hillsborough
  county.org

Chief
Orange County Consumer Fraud
  Unit
415 North Orange Avenue
P. O. Box 1673
Orlando, FL 32802
407-836-2490
Fax: 407-836-2376
Web site: www.onepgov.net

153

Citizens Intake
Office of the State Attorney
401 N. Dixie Highway, Suite 1100
West Palm Beach, FL 33401
561-355-7108
Toll free: 1-800-353-3859
Fax: 561-355-7192

Director
Palm Beach County Division of
    Consumer Affairs
50 South Military Trail, Suite 201
West Palm Beach, FL 33415
561-233-4820
Toll free: 1-800-930-5124 (Palm
    Beach County only)
Fax: 561-233-4838

Consumer Affairs/Code
    Compliance Manager
Pasco County Consumer Affairs
    Division
7530 Little Road, Suite 140
New Port Richey, FL 34654
813-847-8110 / 8106
Fax: 813-847-8969

Director
Pinellas County Office of
    Consumer Protection
14250 49th Street N., 2nd Floor
Clearwater, FL 34622-0268
813-464-6200
Fax: 813-464-6129

City Offices

Chief of Consumer Affairs
City of Jacksonville Division of
    Consumer Affairs
St. James Building
117 West Duval St., Suite M-100
Jacksonville, FL 32202
904-630-3467
Fax: 904-630-3638

Department Secretary
Lauderhill Consumer Protection
    Board
1176 NW 42nd Way
Lauderhill, FL 33313
954-321-2456 (Lauderhill resi-
    dents only)

Georgia

State Office

Administrator
Governor's Office of Consumer
    Affairs
2 Martin Luther King, Jr. Drive,
    SE, Suite 356
Atlanta, GA 30334
404-656-3790
Toll free in GA (outside Atlanta
    area): 1-800-869-1123
Fax: 404-651-9018

Hawaii

State Offices

Executive Director
Office of Consumer Protection
Department of Commerce and
    Consumer Affairs
235 S. Beretania Street (96813)
Room 801, P. O. Box 3767
Honolulu, HI 96812-3767
808-586-2636
Fax: 808-586-2640

Investigator
Office of Consumer Protection
Department of Commerce and
    Consumer Affairs
75 Aupuni Street
Hilo, HI 96720
808-974-6230
Fax: 808-974-6233

Investigator
Office of Consumer Protection
Department of Commerce and
  Consumer Affairs
54 High Street, P. O. Box 1098
Wailuku, HI 96793
808-984-8244
Fax: 808-984-8245

Idaho

State Office

Deputy Attorney General
Office of the Attorney General
Consumer Protection Unit
650 West State Street
Boise, ID 83720-0010
208-334-2424
Toll free in ID: 1-800-432-3545
TDD/TTY: 208-334-2424
Fax: 208-334-2830
Web site: www.state.id.us/ag/mid
  dle/consumer/consumer.htm

Illinois

Governor's Office of Citizens
  Assistance
222 South College Street
Springfield, IL 62706
217-782-0244
Toll free in IL: 1-800-642-3112
  (handles problems related to
  state government)

State Offices

Chief
Consumer Protection Division
Office of Attorney General
100 West Randolph, 12th Floor
Chicago, IL 60601
312-814-3000
TDD: 312-793-2852
Fax: 312-814-2593

Bureau Chief
Consumer Fraud Bureau
100 West Randolph, 12th Floor
Chicago, IL 60601
312-814-3580
Toll free in IL: 1-800-386-5438
TDD: 312-814-3374
Fax: 312-814-2593

Office of Attorney General
1001 E. Main St.
Carbondale, IL 62901
618-529-6400
Toll free in IL: 1-800-243-0607
  (consumer hotline serving
  southern Illinois)
TDD: 618-457-4421
Fax: 618-457-5509

Regional Offices

Bureau Chief
Office of Attorney General
Department of Consumer Affairs
500 South Second Street
Springfield, IL 62706
217-782-1090
Toll free in IL: 1-800-243-0618
  (handles problems related to
  state government)

County Offices

Supervisor
Consumer Fraud Division–303
Cook County Office of State's
  Attorney
28 North Clark, Suite 400
Chicago, IL 60602
312-345-2400
Fax: 312-345-2401

155

State's Attorney
Madison County Office of State's
 Attorney
157 North Main Street
Suite 402
Edwardsville, IL 62025
618-692-6280
Fax: 618-656-7312

City Offices

Commissioner
Chicago Department of Consumer
 Services
121 North LaSalle Street, Room
 808
Chicago, IL 60602
312-744-4006
TDD: 312-744-9385
Fax: 312-744-9089
Web site: www.ci.chi.il.us

Administrator
Consumer Protection Office
City of Des Plaines
1420 Miner Street
Des Plaines, IL 60016
847-391-5006
Fax: 847-391-5378

Indiana

State Office

Chief Counsel and Director
Consumer Protection Division
Office of Attorney General
Indiana Government Center South
402 West Washington Street, 5th
 Floor
Indianapolis, IN 46204
317-232-6330
Toll free in IN: 1-800-382-5516
Fax: 317-233-4393
E-mail: INATTGN@ATG.IN.US
Web site: www.al.org/hoosierad
 vocate

County Office

Marion County Prosecuting
 Attorney
560 City-County Building
200 East Washington Street
Indianapolis, IN 46204-3363
317-327-3892
TDD/TTY: 317-327-5186
Fax: 317-327-5409
E-mail:
 bphillip@ci.indianapolis.in.us
Web site: www.indygov.org

Iowa

State Office

Assistant Attorney General
Consumer Protection Division
Office of the Attorney General
1300 East Walnut Street, 2nd
 Floor
Des Moines, IA 50319
515-281-5926
Fax: 515-281-6771
E-mail:
 consumer@max.state.ia.us
Web site: www.state.ia.us/govern
 ment/ag/consumer.html

Kansas

State Office

Deputy Attorney General
Consumer Protection Division
Office of Attorney General
301 West 10th
Kansas Judicial Center
Topeka, KS 66612-1597
913-296-3751
Toll free in KS: 1-800-432-2310
Fax: 913-291-3699

County Office

Consumer Fraud Division
Johnson County District Attorney's
    Office
Johnson County Courthouse
100 North Kansas Avenue
Olathe, KS 60061
913-764-8484, ext. 5287
Fax: 913-791-5011

Kentucky

State Offices

Director
Consumer Protection Division
Office of the Attorney General
1024 Capital Center Drive
Frankfort, KY 40601-8204
502-696-5389
Toll free in KY: 1-888-432-9257
Fax: 502-573-8317
Web site: www.law.state.ky.us/cp/
    default.htm
E-mail: webmaster@mail.law.
    state.ky.us

Administrator
Consumer Protection Division
Office of Attorney General
9001 Shelbyville Road, #3
Louisville, KY 40222
502-425-4825
Fax: 502-425-9406

Louisiana

State Office

Chief
Consumer Protection Section
Office of the Attorney General
1 America Place
P. O. Box 94095
Baton Rouge, LA 70804-9095
504-342-9639
Toll free nationwide: 1-800-351-
    4889
Fax: 504-342-9637
Web site: www.laag.com

County Office

Investigator
Consumer Protection Division
Jefferson Parish District
    Attorney's Office
Gretna Courthouse Annex, 5th
    Floor
Gretna, LA 70053
504-365-3334
504-368-1020
Fax: 504-368-4562

Maine

State Offices

Director
Office of Consumer Credit
    Regulation
35 State House Station
Augusta, ME 04333-0035
207-624-8527
Toll free in ME: 1-800-332-8529
Fax: 207-582-7699

Division Chief
Public Protection Division
Office of Attorney General
6 State House Station
Augusta, ME 04333
207-626-8849

157

Maryland

State Offices

Chief
Consumer Protection Division
200 Saint Paul Place, 16th Floor
Baltimore, MD 21202-2021
410-528-8662 (consumer complaint hotline)
410-576-6550 (consumer information)
TDD: 410-576-6372 (MD only)
Fax: 410-576-6566 and 410-576-7040
E-mail:
consumer@oag.state.md.us
Web site: www.oag.state.md.us

Division Manager
Business Licensing & Consumer Service
Motor Vehicle Administration
6601 Ritchie Highway, NE
Glen Burnie, MD 21062
410-768-7248
Fax: 410-768-7489

Director
Western Maryland Branch Office
Consumer Protection Division
Office of the Attorney General
138 East Antietam Street, Suite 210
Hagerstown, MD 21740-5684
301-791-4780

Consumer Affairs Specialist
Eastern Shore Branch Office
Consumer Protection Division
Office of the Attorney General
201 Baptist Street, Suite 30
Salisbury, MD 21801-4976
410-543-6620
Fax: 410-543-6642

County Offices

Administrator
Howard County Office of Consumer Affairs
6751 Columbia Gateway Drive
Columbia, MD 21046
410-313-6420
TDD: 410-313-6401
Fax: 410-313-6424

Acting Director
Montgomery County Office of Consumer Affairs
100 Maryland Avenue, 3rd Floor
Rockville, MD 20850
301-217-7373
Fax: 301-217-7367

Director
Prince George's County Office of Business and Regulatory Affairs
County Administration Building, Suite L1177
Upper Marlboro, MD 20772
301-952-5232
TDD: 301-925-5167
Fax: 301-952-4709

Massachusetts

State Offices

Chief
Consumer Protection and Antitrust Division
Department of the Attorney General
One Ashburton Place
Boston, MA 02108-1698
617-727-8400 (information and referral to local consumer offices that work in conjunction with the Department of the Attorney General)
Fax: 617-727-5765

Assistant Attorney General
Western Massachusetts Consumer
   Protection Division
Office of the Attorney General
436 Dwight Street
Springfield, MA 01103
413-784-1240
Fax: 413-784-1244

Director
Office of Consumer Affairs and
   Business Regulation
One Ashburton Place, Room 1411
Boston, MA 02108
617-727-7780 (info and referral
   only)
TDD/TTY: 617-727-1729
Fax: 617-227-6094
E-mail: ask@consumer.com
Web site: www.consumer.
   com/consumer

County Offices

Director
Consumer Protection Division
Northwestern District Attorney's
   Office
238 Main Street, 4th Floor
Greenfield, MA 01301
413-774-5102
Fax: 413-773-3278

Case Coordinator
Consumer Protection Division
NorthWestern District Attorney's
   Office
1 Court Square
Northampton, MA 01060
413-586-9225
Fax: 413-584-3635

Director
Consumer Council of Worcester
   County
484 Main Street, 2nd Floor

Worcester, MA 01608-1690
508-754-1176
Fax: 508-754-0203

City Offices

Director
Mayor's Office of Consumer
   Affairs and Licensing
Boston City Hall, Room 817
Boston, MA 02201
617-635-4165
Fax: 617-635-4174

Director
Consumer Information Center
Springfield Action Commission
P. O. Box 1449, Main Office
Springfield, MA 01101
413-263-6513 (Hamden and
   Hampshire Counties)
Fax: 413-263-6514

Michigan

State Offices

Assistant in Charge
Consumer Protection Division
Office of the Attorney General
P. O. Box 30212
Lansing, MI 48909
517-373-1140 (complaint infor-
   mation)
517-373-1110
Fax: 517-335-1935

Director
Bureau of Automotive Regulation
Michigan Department of State
Lansing, MI 48918-1200
517-373-4777
Toll free in MI: 1-800-292-4204
Fax: 517-373-0964

159

County Offices

Chief Investigator
Bay County Consumer Protection
    Unit
Bay County Building
515 Center Avenue
Bay City, MI 48707-5994
517-895-4139
Fax: 517-895-4167

Director
Consumer Protection Department
Macomb County
Office of the Prosecuting Attorney
40 North Main Street, 6th Floor
Mt. Clemens, MI 48043
810-469-5350
TDD: 810-466-8714
Fax: 810-469-5609
Web site: www.macomb.lib.
    mi.us/macatt

City Office

Director
City of Detroit Department of
    Consumer Affairs
1600 Cadillac Tower
Detroit, MI 48226
313-224-3508
313-224-6995 (complaints)
Fax: 313-224-2796

Minnesota

State Office

Director
Consumer Services Division
Minnesota Attorney General's
    Office
1400 NCL Tower
445 Minnesota Street
St. Paul, MN 55101
612-296-3353
Toll free: 1-800-657-3787

TDD/TTY: 612-297-7206;
TDD/TTY toll free: 1-800-366-
    4812
Fax: 612-282-5801
Web site: www.ag.state.mn.
    us/consumer
E-mail: consumer.ag@state.mn.us

County Office

Hennepin County Citizen
    Information Hotline
Office of Hennepin County
    Attorney
C-2000 County Government
    Center
Minneapolis, MN 55487
612-348-4528
TDD/TTY: 612-348-5875
Fax: 612-348-9712
Web site: www.co.hennepin.mn.
    us/coatty/hcatty.htm

City Office

Director
Minneapolis Department of
    Regulatory Services
Division of Licenses & Consumer
    Services
City Hall, Room 1C
350 South 5th Street
Minneapolis, MN 55415
612-673-2080
TDD/TTY: 612-673-3300/3360
Fax: 612-673-3399
E-mail:
    opa@ci.minneapolis.mn.us
Web site:
    www.ci.minneapolis.mn.us

Mississippi

State Offices

Director
Bureau of Regulatory Services
Department of Agriculture and
    Commerce
121 North Jefferson Street
P. O. Box 1609
Jackson, MS 39201
601-354-7063
Fax: 601-354-6502

Director
Consumer Protection Division
802 North State Street, 3rd Floor
P. O. Box 22947
Jackson, MS 39225-2947
601-359-4230
Toll free in MS: 1-800-281-4418
Fax: 601-359-4231
Web site: www.ago.state.ms.
    us/consprot.htm

Missouri

State Office

Chief Counsel
Consumer Complaint Unit
Office of the Attorney General
P. O. Box 899
Jefferson City, MO 65102
573-751-3321
Toll free in MO: 1-800-392-8222
TDD/TTY toll free in MO: 1-800-
    729-8668
Fax: 314-751-7948

Montana

State Office

Chief Legal Counsel
Consumer Affairs Unit
Department of Commerce
1424 Ninth Avenue
Box 200501
Helena, MT 59620-0501
406-444-4312
Fax: 406-444-2903

Nebraska

State Office

Assistant Attorney General
Department of Justice
2115 State Capitol
P. O. Box 98920
Lincoln, NE 68509
402-471-2682
Fax: 402-471-3297

Nevada

State Offices

Commissioner of Consumer
    Affairs
Department of Business and
    Industry
1850 East Sahara, Suite 101
Las Vegas, NV 89104
702-486-7355
Toll free: 1-800-326-5202
TDD: 702-486-7901
Fax: 702-486-7371
E-mail: consumer@govmail.
    state.nv.us
Web site: www.state.nv.us/
    fyiconsumer/

Supervisory Compliance
    Investigator
Consumer Affairs Division
Department of Business and
    Industry
4600 Kietzke Lane, Bldg. B,
    Suite 113
Reno, NV 89502
702-688-1800
Toll free in NV: 1-800-326-5202
TDD: 702-486-7901
Fax: 702-688-1803

New Hampshire

State Office

Consumer Protection/Antitrust
    Bureau
New Hampshire Attorney
    General's Office
33 Capitol Street
Concord, NH 03301-6397
603-271-3641
TDD toll free: 1-800-735-2964
Fax: 603-271-2110
Web site: www.state.nh.us/oag/
    cpb.htm

New Jersey

State Offices

Director
New Jersey Consumer Affairs
    Division
124 Halsey Street
Newark, NJ 07102
973-504-6200
Fax: 973-648-3538
TDD: 973-504-6588
E-mail: askconsumeraffairs@oag.
    lps.state.nj.us
Web site: www.state.nj.us/lps/
    ca/home.htm

Deputy Attorney General
New Jersey Division of Law
P. O. Box 45029
124 Halsey Street, 5th Floor
Newark, NJ 07101
973-648-7457
Fax: 201-648-3879
E-mail: lambegai@smtp.lps.
    state.nj.us

County Offices

Director
Atlantic County Consumer Affairs
1333 Atlantic Avenue, 8th Floor
Atlantic City, NJ 08401
609-345-6700
Fax: 609-343-2164

Director
Bergen County Office of Consumer
    Protection
21 Main Street, Room 101-E
Hackensack, NJ 07601-7000
201-646-2650
Fax: 201-489-6095

Director/Superintendent
Burlington County Office of
    Consumer Affairs/Weights and
    Measures
49 Rancocas Road
P. O. Box 6000
Mount Holly, NJ 08060
609-265-5098
Fax: 609-265-5065

Director/Superintendent
Camden County Office of
    Consumer Protection/Weights
    and Measures
Jefferson House
Lakeland Road
Blackwood, NJ 08012
609-374-6161
609-374-6001
Fax: 609-232-0748

Director
Cape May County Consumer
  Affairs
4 Moore Road
Cape May Court House, NJ 08210
609-463-6475
Fax: 609-465-6189

Director
Cumberland County Department
  of Consumer Affairs and
  Weights and Measures
788 East Commerce Street
Bridgeton, NJ 08302
609-453-2203
Fax: 609-453-2206

Senior Contact Person
Essex County Consumer Services
15 South Munn Avenue
3rd Floor
East Orange, NJ 07018
973-678-8071
Fax: 973-674-1209

Director
Gloucester County Department of
  Consumer Protection/Weights
  and Measures
152 North Broad Street
Woodbury, NJ 08096
609-853-3349
609-853-3358
TDD: 609-848-6616
Fax: 609-853-6813

Director
Hudson County Division of
  Consumer Affairs
595 Newark Avenue
Jersey City, NJ 07306
201-795-6295
Fax: 201-795-6462

Director
Hunterdon County Consumer
  Affairs
P. O. Box 283
Lebanon, NJ 08833
908-236-2249

Division Chief
Mercer County Consumer Affairs
640 South Broad St., Room 215,
P. O. Box 8068
Trenton, NJ 08650-0068
609-989-6671
Fax: 609-989-6670

Director
Middlesex County Consumer
  Affairs
10 Corporate Place South
Piscataway, NJ 08854
908-463-6000
Fax: 908-463-6008

Director
Monmouth County Consumer
  Affairs
50 East Main Street
P. O. Box 155
Freehold, NJ 07728-1255
732-431-7900
Fax: 732-845-2037

Director
Ocean County Department of
  Consumer Affairs
P. O. Box 2191
Toms River, NJ 08754-2191
908-929-2105
Toll free in NJ: 1-800-722-0291,
  ext. 2105
Fax: 908-506-5330

163

Director
Passaic County Department of
Consumer Affairs
401 Grand Street, Room 532
Paterson, NJ 07505
973-881-4547
Fax: 973-881-0012

Director
Somerset County Consumer
Affairs
County Administration Building
P. O. Box 3000
Somerville, NJ 08876-1262
908-231-7000, ext. 7400
Fax: 908-707-4127

Director
Union County Consumer Affairs
300 North Avenue East
P. O. Box 186
Westfield, NJ 07091
908-654-9840
Fax: 908-654-3082

City Offices

Administrator
Cinnaminson Consumer Affairs
P. O. Box 2100
1621 Riverton Road
Cinnaminson, NJ 08077
609-829-6000
Fax: 609-829-3361

Director
Livingston Consumer Affairs
357 South Livingston Avenue
Livingston, NJ 07039
973-535-7976
Fax: 973-740-9408

Director
Maywood Consumer Affairs
459 Maywood Avenue
Maywood, NJ 07607

201-845-2900
201-845-5749
Fax: 201-909-0673

Director
Middlesex Borough Consumer
Affairs
1200 Mountain Avenue
Middlesex, NJ 08846
732-356-8090, ext. 250
Fax: 732-356-7954

Director
Mountainside Consumer Affairs
1455 Coles Avenue
Mountainside, NJ 07092
908-232-6600

Director
Consumer Protection
Township of North Bergen
Municipal Building
4233 Kennedy Boulevard
North Bergen, NJ 07047
201-330-7291
Fax: 201-392-8551

Director
Nutley Consumer Affairs
Public Safety Building
228 Chestnut Street
Nutley, NJ 07110
973-284-4936
Fax: 973-284-4906

Investigator
Perth Amboy Consumer Affairs
Office of Social Services
Fayette and Reade Streets
Perth Amboy, NJ 08861
732-826-4300
Fax: 908-826-8069

Director
Plainfield Action Services
510 Watchung Avenue
Plainfield, NJ 07060
908-753-3519
Fax: 908-753-3540

Town Attorney
Secaucus Department of
    Consumer Affairs
Municipal Government Center
Secaucus, NJ 07094
201-330-2019

Director
Township of Union Consumer
    Affairs
Municipal Building
1976 Morris Avenue
Union, NJ 07083
908-851-5477
908-688-2800, ext. 5458
Fax: 908-686-4664

Director
Wayne Township Consumer
    Affairs
475 Valley Road
Wayne, NJ 07470
201-694-1800, ext. 3290

Director
Weehawken Consumer Affairs
400 Park Avenue
Weehawken, NJ 07087
201-319-6005
Fax: 201-319-0112

Director
Woodbridge Consumer Affairs
Municipal Building
One Main Street
Woodbridge, NJ 07095
732-634-4500, ext. 6058
Fax: 732-602-6016

New Mexico

State Office

Consumer Protection Division
Office of Attorney General
P. O. Drawer 1508
Santa Fe, NM 87504
505-827-6060
Toll free in NM: 1-800-678-1508

New York

State Offices

Bureau of Consumer Frauds and
    Protection
Office of Attorney General
State Capitol
Albany, NY 12224
518-474-5481
Toll free in NY: 1-800-771-7755
TDD toll free: 1-800-788-9898
Fax: 518-474-3618
Web site: www.oag.state.ny.us

165

Chairman and Executive Director
New York State Consumer
    Protection Board
5 Empire State Plaza, Suite 2101
Albany, NY 12223-1556
518-474-8583
Toll free in NY: 1-800-697-1220
Fax: 518-474-2474
Web site:
    www.consumer.state.ny.us
E-mail: groatn@consumer.
    state.ny.us

Consumer Frauds and Protection
    Bureau
Office of Attorney General
120 Broadway
New York, NY 10271
212-416-8345
Toll free: 1-800-771-7755
TDD toll free: 1-800-788-9898

Regional Offices

Assistant Attorney General in
    Charge
Binghamton Regional Office
State Office Building
44 Hawley Street, 17th Floor
Binghamton, NY 13901
607-721-8779
Toll free: 1-800-771-7755
Fax: 607-721-8789

Assistant Attorney General in
    Charge
Buffalo Regional Office
Statler Towers
107 Delaware Avenue, 4th Floor
Buffalo, NY 14202
716-853-6271
Fax: 716-847-7170
Toll free: 1-800-771-7755
Fax: 716-853-8414

Assistant Attorney General in
    Charge
Suffolk Regional Office
Office of Attorney General
300 Motor Parkway, Suite 305
Hauppauge, NY 11788
516-231-2400
Fax: 516-435-4757

Assistant Attorney General in
    Charge
Nassau Regional Office
Office of the Attorney General
200 Old Country Road
New York, NY 11501
516-248-3302

Assistant Attorney General in
    Charge
Harlem Regional Office
Office of the Attorney General
State Office Building
163 West 125th Street, 25th Floor

New York, NY 10271-0332
212-961-4475
Fax: 212-961-4003

Assistant Attorney General in
    Charge
Plattsburgh Regional Office
Office of Attorney General
70 Clinton Street
Plattsburgh, NY 12901
518-562-3288
Toll free: 1-800-771-7755
Fax: 518-562-3294

Assistant Attorney General in
    Charge
Poughkeepsie Regional Office
Office of Attorney General
235 Main Street, 3rd Floor
Poughkeepsie, NY 12601
914-485-3900
Toll free: 1-800-771-7755
Fax: 914-452-3303

Assistant Attorney General in
    Charge
Rochester Regional Office
Office of Attorney General
144 Exchange Boulevard
Rochester, NY 14614
716-546-7430
Toll free: 1-800-771-7755
TDD: 716-327-3249
Fax: 716-546-7514

Assistant Attorney General in
    Charge
Syracuse Regional Office
Office of Attorney General
615 Erie Boulevard West,
    Suite 102
Syracuse, NY 13204-2465
315-448-4800
Toll free: 1-800-771-7755
Fax: 315-448-4853

Assistant Attorney General in
   Charge
Utica Regional Office
Office of Attorney General
207 Genesee Street, Room 504
Utica, NY 13501
315-793-2225
Fax: 315-793-2228
Toll free: 1-800-771-7755

Assistant Attorney General in
   Charge
Watertown Regional Office
Office of Attorney General
Dulles State Office Building
317 Washington Street
Watertown, NY 13601
315-785-2444
Fax: 315-785-2294
Toll free: 1-800-771-7755

Assistant Attorney General in
   Charge
Westchester Regional Office
Office of Attorney General
143 Grand Street
White Plains, NY 13501
914-422-8755
Fax: 914-422-8706
Toll free: 1-800-771-7755

County Offices

Director
Albany County Consumer Affairs
Albany County Courthouse
Albany, NY 12207
518-487-5048

Director
Dutchess County Department of
   Consumer Affairs
94-A Peach Road
Poughkeepsie, NY 12601
914-486-2949
Fax: 914-486-2947

Assistant District Attorney
Consumer Fraud Bureau
Erie County District Attorney's
   Office
25 Delaware Avenue
Buffalo, NY 14202
716-858-2424
Fax: 716-858-7425

Commissioner
Nassau County Office of Consumer
   Affairs
160 Old Country Road
Mineola, NY 11501
516-571-2600
Fax: 516-571-3389

District Attorney
Orange County District Attorney's
   Office
255 Main Street
County Government Center
Goshen, NY 10924
914-291-2050
Fax: 914-291-2085

Director
Rockland County Office of
   Consumer Protection
County Office Building
18 New Hempstead Road
New City, NY 10956
914-638-5280
Fax: 914-638-5415

* 167 *

Director
Schenectady County Consumer
    Affairs
64 Kellar Avenue
Schenectady, NY 12307
518-356-7473
Fax: 518-357-8319

Director
Steuben County Department of
    Weights, Measures and
    Consumer Affairs
3 East Pulteney Square
Bath, NY 14810
607-776-9631
TDD: 607-776-9631, ext. 2406

Director
Suffolk County Executive's Office
    of Consumer Affairs
North County Complex, Bldg. 340
Veterans Memorial Highway
Hauppauge, NY 12402
516-853-4600
Fax: 516-853-4825

168

Consumer Affairs Director
Ulster County District Attorney's
    Consumer Fraud Bureau
20 Lucas Avenue
Kingston, NY 12401
914-340-3260

Deputy Director
Westchester County Department
    of Consumer Protection
112 East Post Road, 4th Floor
White Plains, NY 10601
914-285-2155
Fax: 914-285-3115

Chief
Frauds Bureau
Westchester County District
    Attorney's Office

District Attorney's Office
111 Grove Street
White Plains, NY 10601
914-285-3414
Fax: 914-285-3115

City Offices

Citizen Advocate
Office of Citizen Services
Babylon Town Hall
200 E. Sunrise Highway
Lindenhurst, NY 11757
516-957-7474

Town of Colonie Consumer
    Protection
Memorial Town Hall
Newtonville, NY 12128
518-783-2790

Commissioner
Mt. Vernon Office of Consumer
    Protection
City Hall, 11th Floor
Mount Vernon, NY 10550
914-665-2433
Fax: 914-665-2496

Commissioner
New York City Department of
    Consumer Affairs
42 Broadway
New York, NY 10004
212-487-4444 (English)
212-487-4481 (Spanish)
212-487-4488 (Chinese)
718-286-2296 (Korean)
TDD: 212-487-4465
Fax: 212-487-4197
Web site: www.ci.nyc.ny.us/html/
    dca/home.html

Director
Queens Neighborhood Office
New York City Department of
    Consumer Affairs
120-55 Queens Boulevard
Room 301
Kew Gardens, NY 11424
718-286-2990
Fax: 718-286-2997

Schenectady Bureau of Consumer
    Protection
City Hall, Room 204
Jay Street
Schenectady, NY 12305
518-382-5061
Fax: 518-382-5074

Executive Director
New Justice Conflict Resolution
    Services Inc.
1153 West Fayette Street,
    Suite 301
Syracuse, NY 13204
315-471-4676
Fax: 315-475-0769

Director
Yonkers Office of Consumer
    Protection, Weights and
    Measures
87 Nepperhan Avenue
Yonkers, NY 10701
914-377-6807
Fax: 914-377-6601

North Carolina

State Office

Special Deputy Attorney General
Consumer Protection Section
Office of Attorney General
P. O. Box 629
Raleigh, NC 27602
919-716-6000

Fax: 919-716-6050
Web site: www.jus.state.nc.us/
    justice/cpsmain

North Dakota

State Offices

Attorney General
The State Capitol Building
600 East Boulevard Avenue
Bismarck, ND 58505-0040
701-328-2210
TDD: 701-328-3409
Fax: 701-328-2226
Web site: www.state.nd.us/ndag

Director
Consumer Protection and
    Antitrust Division
Office of the Attorney General
600 East Boulevard Avenue
Bismarck, ND 58505-0040
701-328-3404
Toll free in ND: 1-800-472-2600
TDD: 701-328-3409
Fax: 701-328-3535
Web site:
    www.state.nd.us/cpat/cpat.html

County Office

Executive Director
Community Action Agency
1013 North 5th Street
Grand Forks, ND 58203
701-746-5431
Toll free in ND: 1-800-450-1823
Fax: 701-746-0406

169

Ohio

State Offices

Consumer Protection Section
Office of the Attorney General
State Office Tower, 25th Floor
30 East Broad Street
Columbus, OH 43215-3428
614-466-4986 (complaints)
Toll free in OH: 1-800-282-0515
TDD: 614-466-1393
E-mail: consumer@ag.ohio.gov

Office of Consumers' Counsel
77 South High Street, 15th Floor
Columbus, OH 43266-0550
614-466-8574 (outside OH)
Toll free in OH: 1-800-282-9448
E-mail: occ@occ.state.oh.us
Web site: www.state.oh.us/cons/

County Offices

Director
Economic Crime
Franklin County Office of
  Prosecuting Attorney
369 South High Street
Columbus, OH 43215
614-462-3555
Fax: 614-462-6103

Assistant Prosecuting Attorney
Montgomery County Fraud and
  Economic Crimes Division
301 West 3rd Street
Dayton, OH 45402
513-225-4747
Fax: 513-225-3470

Prosecuting Attorney
Portage County Office of
  Prosecuting Attorney
466 South Chestnut Street
Ravenna, OH 44266-3000

170

330-296-4593
Fax: 330-297-3856

Prosecuting Attorney
Summit County Office of
  Prosecuting Attorney
53 University Avenue
Akron, OH 44308-1680
330-643-2800
TDD/TTY: 330-643-8277 (criminal)
Fax: 330-643-2137 (civil)

City Offices

Department of Neighborhood
  Services
Division of Human Services/Office
  of Consumer Services
City Hall, Room 126
801 Plum Street
Cincinnati, OH 45202
513-352-3971
Fax: 513-352-5241

Youngstown Office of Consumer
  Affairs and Weights and
  Measures
City Hall
26 South Phelps Street
Youngstown, OH 44503-1318
330-742-8884
330-742-8885
330-743-1335
Fax: 330-743-1318

Oklahoma

State Offices

Administrator
Department of Consumer Credit
4545 North Lincoln Boulevard,
  Suite 260
Oklahoma City, OK 73105
405-521-3653
Fax: 405-521-6740

Consumer Representative
Office of Attorney General
Consumer Protection Unit
4545 North Lincoln Boulevard,
Suite 260
Oklahoma City, OK 73105
405-521-2029 (consumer hotline)
Fax: 405-528-1867

Oregon

State Office

Attorney in Charge
Financial Fraud Section
Department of Justice
1162 Court Street NE
Salem, OR 97310
503-378-4732
503-378-4320 (hotline)
503-229-5576 (in Portland only)
Fax: 503-378-5017
Web site: www.doj.state.or.us/
FinFraud/welcome3.html

Pennsylvania

State Offices

Director
Bureau of Consumer Protection
Office of the Attorney General
Strawberry Square, 14th Floor
Harrisburg, PA 17120
717-787-9707
Toll free in PA: 1-800-441-2555
Fax: 717-787-1190
Web site: www.attorneygeneral.
gov
E-mail: consumers@attorneygen
eral.gov

Consumer Advocate
Office of Consumer Advocate
Office of the Attorney General

Forum Place, 5th Floor
555 Walnut Street
Harrisburg, PA 17101-1921
717-783-5048 (for utilities only)
Fax: 717-783-7152
E-mail: paoca@ptd.net
Web site: www.oca.state.pa.us

Regional Offices

Deputy Attorney General
Bureau of Consumer Protection
Office of the Attorney General
1251 South Cedar Crest
Boulevard, Suite 309
Allentown, PA 18103
610-821-6690
Fax: 610-821-6529

Senior Deputy Attorney General
Bureau of Consumer Protection
Office of the Attorney General
171 Lovell Avenue, Suite 202
Ebensburg, PA 15931
814-949-7900
Toll free in PA: 1-800-441-2555
Fax: 814-949-7942

Deputy Attorney General
Bureau of Consumer Protection
Office of the Attorney General
919 State Street, Room 203
Erie, PA 16501
814-871-4371
Fax: 814-871-4848

Bureau of Consumer Protection
Office of the Attorney General
132 Kline Village
Harrisburg, PA 17104
717-787-7109
Fax: 717-772-3560

Deputy Attorney General
Bureau of Consumer Protection
Office of the Attorney General
21 South 12th Street, 2nd Floor
Philadelphia, PA 19107
215-560-2414
Toll free in PA: 1-800-441-2555

Deputy Attorney
Bureau of Consumer Protection
Office of the Attorney General
Manor Complex, 6th Floor
564 Forbes Avenue
Pittsburgh, PA 15219
412-565-5135
Toll free in PA: 1-800-441-2555
Fax: 412-565-5475

Deputy Attorney General, Bureau
of Consumer Protection
Office of the Attorney General
Samter Building, Room 214
101 Penn Avenue
Scranton, PA 18503-2025
717-963-4913
Fax: 717-963-3418
Toll free: 1-800-441-2555

172

County Offices

Director
Beaver County Alliance for
Consumer Protection
699 Fifth Street
Beaver, PA 15009-1997
412-728-7267
Fax: 412-728-6762

Director/Chief Sealer
Bucks County Consumer
Protection/Weights and
Measures
50 North Main Street
Doylestown, PA 18901
215-348-7442
Fax: 215-348-4570

Director
Chester County Weights and
Measures/Consumer Affairs
Government Services Center, Suite
390
601 Westtown Road
West Chester, PA 19382-4547
610-344-6150
Toll free in PA: 1-800-692-1100

Director
Cumberland County Consumer
Affairs/Weights and Measures
One Courthouse Square
Carlisle, PA 17013-3330
717-240-6180
Fax: 717-240-6490

Director
Delaware County Office of
Consumer Affairs
Media Courthouse
201 West Front Street
Media, PA 19063
610-891-4865
Fax: 610-566-3947

Montgomery County Office of
Consumer Affairs
Montgomery County Courthouse
P. O. Box 311
Norristown, PA 19404-0311
610-278-3565, 717-963-4913
Toll free: 1-800-441-2555
Fax: 610-278-3556 or 717-963-
3418

City Office

Chief, Economic Crime Unit
Philadelphia District Attorney's
Office
1421 Arch Street
Philadelphia, PA 19102
215-686-8750
Fax: 215-686-8765

Puerto Rico

Department of Consumer Affairs
Minillas Station, P. O. Box 41059
Santurce, PR 00940-1059
787-721-0940
Fax: 787-726-6570
E-mail: Jalicea@Caribe.net

Secretary
Department of Justice
P. O. Box 902192
San Juan, PR 00902
787-721-2900
Fax: 787-725-2475

Rhode Island

State Office

Chief, Consumer Unit
Department of the Attorney
    General
72 Pine Street
Providence, RI 02903
401-274-4400
Toll free in RI: 1-800-852-7776
TDD: 401-453-0410
Fax: 401-277-1331

South Carolina

State Offices

Senior Assistant Attorney General
Office of the Attorney General
P. O. Box 11549
Columbia, SC 29211
803-734-3970
Fax: 803-734-3677
Web site: www.scattorney
    general.org

Administrator/Consumer
    Advocate
Department of Consumer Affairs
2801 Devine Street

P. O. Box 5757
Columbia, SC 29250-5757
803-734-9452
Toll free in SC: 1-800-922-1594
Fax: 803-734-9365
E-mail: scdca@infoave.net
Web site: www.state.sc.us/
    consumer

State Ombudsman
Office of Executive Policy and
    Program
1205 Pendleton Street, Room 308
Columbia, SC 29201
803-734-0457
TDD: 803-734-1147
Fax: 803-734-0546

South Dakota

State Office

Director of Consumer Affairs
Office of the Attorney General
500 East Capitol
State Capitol Building
Pierre, SD 57501-5070
605-773-4400
Toll free in SD: 1-800-300-1986
TDD: 605-773-6585
Fax: 605-773-4106

Tennessee

State Offices

Division of Consumer Affairs
500 James Robertson Parkway
Nashville, TN 37243-0600
615-741-4737
Toll free in TN: 1-800-342-8385
Fax: 615-532-4994
E-mail: mwilliams2@mail.
    state.tn.us
Web site: www.state.tn.us/
    consumer

* 173 *

Deputy Attorney General
Division of Consumer Protection
Office of Attorney General
425 Fifth Avenue North, 2nd Floor
Nashville, TN 37243-0491
615-741-1671
Fax: 615-532-2910

Texas

State Offices

Assistant Attorney General and
    Chief
Consumer Protection Division
Office of Attorney General
P. O. Box 12548
Austin, TX 78711-2548
512-463-2070
Fax: 512-463-8301

Office of Public Insurance Counsel
333 Guadalupe, Suite 3-120
Austin, TX 78701
512-322-4143
Fax: 512-322-4148

Regional Offices

Assistant Attorney General
Consumer Protection Division
    Dallas Regional Office
Office of Attorney General
1600 Pacific Avenue, Suite 1700
Dallas, TX 75201-3513
214-969-5310
Fax: 214-969-7615

Assistant Attorney General
Consumer Protection Lubbock
    Regional Office
Office of Attorney General
916 Main Street, Suite 806
Lubbock, TX 79401-3997
806-747-5238
Fax: 806-747-6307

Assistant Attorney General
Consumer Protection El Paso
    Regional Office
Office of Attorney General
310 North Mesa, Suite 900
El Paso, TX 79901-1301
915-542-4800
Fax: 915-542-1596
E-mail: VJA@OAG.STATE.TX.US

Assistant Attorney General
Consumer Protection Houston
    Regional Office
Office of Attorney General
808 Travis, Suite 812
Houston, TX 77002
713-223-5886, ext. 118
Fax: 713-223-5821
E-mail: JOHN.OWENS@OAG.
    STATE.TX.US

Assistant Attorney General
Consumer Protection McAllen
    Regional Office
Office of Attorney General
3201 North McColl Rd., Suite B
McAllen, TX 78501
956-682-4547
Fax: 956-682-1957

Assistant Attorney General
Consumer Protection San Antonio
    Regional Office
Office of Attorney General
115 East Travis Street, Suite 925
San Antonio, TX 78205-1615
210-224-1007
Fax: 210-225-1075

County Office

Assistant District Attorney and
  Chief
Harris County Consumer Fraud
  Division
Harris County District Attorney's
  Office
201 Fannin, Suite 200
Houston, TX 77002-1901
713-755-5836
Fax: 713-755-5262

City Offices

Director
Department of Environmental and
  Health Services
City Hall
1500 Marilla, Room 7A-North
Dallas, TX 75201
214-670-5216
Fax: 214-670-3863
E-mail: BWEAVER@gwsmtp.ci.
  dallas.tx.us

Interim Director
Economic Development
City Hall
500 Marilla, Room 5C-South
Dallas, TX 75201
214-670-1685
Fax: 214-670-0158

Utah

State Office

Director
Division of Consumer Protection
Department of Commerce
160 East 300 South
Box 146704
Salt Lake City, UT 84114-6704
801-530-6601
Toll free in UT: 1-800-721-7233
Fax: 801-530-6001

Vermont

State Offices

Assistant Attorney General and
  Chief
Public Protection Division
Office of the Attorney General
109 State Street
Montpelier, VT 05609-1001
802-828-5507
Fax: 802-828-2154
E-mail:
  jhasen@ag10.atg.state.vt.us

Supervisor
Consumer Assurance Section
Department of Agriculture, Food
  and Market
116 State Street
Montpelier, VT 05602
802-828-2436
Fax: 802-828-2361

Virgin Islands

Commissioner
Department of Licensing and
  Consumer Affairs
Property and Procurement
  Building
Subbase #1, Room 205
St. Thomas, VI 00802
340-774-3130
Fax: 340-776-0605

Weights and Measures Division
Golden Rock Shopping Center
Christiansted
St. Croix, VI 00820
340-773-2226
Fax: 340-778-8250

175

Administrator's Complex
St. John's, VI 00830
340-693-8036
Fax: 340-776-6992

Virginia

State Offices

Chief
Antitrust and Consumer Litigation
    Section
Office of the Attorney General
900 East Main Street
Richmond, VA 23219
804-786-2116
804-371-2086/2087

Program Manager
Office of Consumer Affairs
Department of Agriculture and
    Consumer Services
Washington Building, Suite 100
P. O. Box 1163
Richmond, VA 23219
804-786-2042
Toll free in VA: 1-800-552-9963
TDD: 804-371-6344
Fax: 804-371-7479

County Offices
Program Manager
Office of Citizen and Consumer
    Affairs
#1 Court House Plaza, Suite 310
2100 Clarendon Boulevard
Arlington, VA 22201
703-358-3260
Fax: 703-358-3295
E-mail:
    GLUCAS@co.arlington.va.us
Web site: www.co.arlington.va.us

176

Director
Fairfax County Department of
    Telecommunications and
    Consumer Services
12000 Government Center
    Parkway, Suite 433
Fairfax, VA 22035
703-222-8435
Fax: 703-222-5921 (mail compa-
    nies only)

City Offices

Administrator
Alexandria Office of Consumer
    Affairs
City Hall, P. O.Box 178
Alexandria, VA 22313
703-838-4350
TDD: 703-838-5056
Fax: 703-838-6426
E-mail: PBARBASH@capacces.org

Coordinator
Division of Consumer Affairs
City Hall
Norfolk, VA 23510
757-664-4888
TDD/TTY: 757-441-1065
Fax: 757-664-4889
Web site: www.city.norfolk.va.us

Director
Consumer Affairs Division
Office of the Commonwealth's
    Attorney
Judicial Center, Building 10B
2305 Judicial Boulevard
Virginia Beach, VA 23456-9050
757-426-5836
Fax: 757-427-8779
Web site: www.virginia-
    beach.va.us/courts/oca/co.htm

Washington

State Offices

Supervisor
Consumer Protection Division
Office of the Attorney General
103 East Holly Street, Suite 308
Bellingham, WA 98225
360-738-6185
Toll free in WA: 1-800-551-4636
Toll free in WA: 1-800-692-5082
 (consumer line tapes)
TDD: 206-464-7293
TDD toll free: 1-800-276-9883
Fax: 360-738-6190
Web site: www.wa.gov/ago

Lead Volunteers
Consumer Protection Division
Office of the Attorney General
500 North Moran Street,
 Suite 1250
Kennewick, WA 99336-2607
509-734-7140
Toll free in WA: 1-800-551-4636
TDD: 206-464-7293
TDD toll free in WA: 1-800-551-
 4636
Fax: 509-734-7290

Supervisor
Consumer Protection Division
Office of the Attorney General
P. O. Box 40118
Olympia, WA 98504-0118
360-753-1808
360-753-6210
Toll free in WA: 1-800-551-4636
TDD: 206-464-7293
TDD toll free in WA: 1-800-276-
 9883

Director of Consumer Services
Consumer Protection Division
Office of the Attorney General
900 Fourth Avenue, Suite 2000
Seattle, WA 98164-1012
206-464-6684
Toll free in WA: 1-800-551-4636
TDD: 206-464-7293
TDD toll free in WA: 1-800-276-
 9883
E-mail: protect@atg.wa.gov
Web site: www.wa.gov/ago

Chief
Consumer Protection Division,
 Spokane
Office of the Attorney General
West 1116 Riverside Avenue
Spokane, WA 99201
509-456-3123
TDD: 206-464-7293
TDD toll free: 1-800-276-9883
Fax: 509-458-3548

Contact Person
Consumer and Business
Office of the Attorney General
1019 Pacific Avenue, 3rd Floor
Tacoma, WA 98402-4411
253-593-2904
Toll free in WA: 1-800-551-4636
TDD: 253-464-7293
TDD toll free: 1-800-276-9883

Supervisor
Consumer Protection Division
Office of the Attorney General
500 West 8th Street, Suite 55
Vancouver, WA 98660
360-690-4751
Toll free in WA: 1-800-551-4636
TDD: 206-464-7293
TDD toll free in WA: 1-800-276-
 9883
Fax: 360-690-4762
Web site: www.wa.gov/ago

177

City Offices

Chief Deputy Prosecuting Attorney
Fraud Division
900 4th Avenue, #1002
Seattle, WA 98164
206-296-9010
Fax: 206-296-9009
E-mail:
    pat.sainsburg@metrokc.gov
Web site:
    www.metrokc.gov/proatty/

Director
Revenue and Consumer Affairs
Seattle Department of Finance
600 4th Avenue, #103
Seattle, WA 98104-1891
206-684-8625
Fax: 206-684-8625
E-mail:
    peggie.scott@ci.seattle.wa.us

Consumer Affairs Supervisor
Revenue and Consumer Affairs
Seattle Department of Finance
805 South Dearborn
Seattle, WA 98134
206-386-1298
206-386-1296
Fax: 206-386-1129
Web site: www.PAN.ci.seattle.wa.
    us/ESD/consumer/default.htm

Consumer Affairs Inspector
Executive Services Department
Revenue and Consumer Affairs
Division of Finance
600 4th Avenue, #103
Seattle, WA 98104-1891
206-233-7837
Fax: 206-684-5170
E-mail: edgonzaga@ci.
    seattle.wa.us
Web site: 199.174.51.22/
    esd/home.htm

West Virginia

State Offices

Deputy Attorney General
Consumer Protection Division
Office of the Attorney General
812 Quarrier Street, 6th Floor
P. O. Box 1789
Charleston, WV 25326-1789
304-558-8986
Toll free in WV: 1-800-368-8808
Fax: 304-558-0184

Director
Division of Weights and Measures
570 MacCorkle Avenue
St. Albans, WV 25177
304 722-0602
Fax: 304-722-0605

City Office

Director
City of Charleston
Department of Consumer
    Protection
P. O. Box 2749
Charleston, WV 25330
304-348-6439
Fax: 304-348-8157

Wisconsin

State Offices

Administrator Division of Trade
    and Consumer Protection
Department of Agriculture, Trade
    and Consumer Protection
2811 Agriculture Drive
P. O. Box 8911
Madison, WI 53708
608-224-4976
Toll free in WI: 1-800-422-7128
Fax: 608-224-4939

Regional Supervisor
Division of Trade and Consumer
  Protection
Department of Agriculture, Trade
  and Consumer Protection
3610 Oakwood Hills Parkway
Eau Claire, WI 54701-7754
715-839-3848
Toll free in WI: 1-800-422-7128
Fax: 715-839-1645

Regional Supervisor
Division of Trade and Consumer
  Protection
Department of Agriculture, Trade
  and Consumer Protection
200 North Jefferson Street,
  Suite 146A
Green Bay, WI 54301
920-448-5110
Toll free in WI: 1-800-422-7128
TDD: 608-224-5058
Fax: 920-448-5118

Regional Supervisor
Consumer Protection Regional
  Office
Department of Agriculture, Trade
  and Consumer Protection
10930 West Potter Road, Suite C
Milwaukee, WI 53226-3450
414-226-1231
Toll free: 1-800-422-7128

County Offices

Assistant District Attorney
Milwaukee County District
  Attorney's Office
Consumer Fraud Unit
821 West State Street, Room 412
Milwaukee, WI 53233-2485
414-278-4585
Fax: 414-223-1955

Consumer Fraud Investigator
Racine County Sheriff's
  Department
717 Wisconsin Avenue
Racine, WI 53403
414-636-3125
Toll free: 1-800-242-4202, ext.
  3125
Fax: 414-637-5279

Wyoming

State Office

Assistant Attorney General
Office of the Attorney General
123 State Capitol Building
Cheyenne, WY 82002
307-777-7874
Fax: 307-777-6869

Source: *1998–99 Consumer's
Resource Handbook,* United States
General Services Administration
Consumer Information Center
http://www.pueblo.gsa.gov/crh/crh
.txt

179

Consumer Advocacy Organizations

Here is a list of organizations that define their missions as consumer assistance, protection, and/or advocacy. The organizations in this list may or may not take action on behalf of individual consumers, but usually provide consumer education materials and advocate for consumer rights in the media and to lawmakers. There is sometimes a charge for consumer education materials.

Alliance Against Fraud in Telemarketing (AAFT)
c/o National Consumers League
1701 K Street, NW, Suite 1200
Washington, DC 20006
202-835-3323
Fax: 202-835-0747

The Alliance, coordinated by the National Consumers League, is a coalition of public interest groups, trade associations, labor unions, businesses, law enforcement agencies, educators, and consumer protection agencies. AAFT members promote efforts to educate the public about the threat of telemarketing and Internet fraud, and offer information about how consumers can protect themselves.

American Association of Retired Persons (AARP)
Consumer Issues Section
601 E Street, NW
Washington, DC 20049
202-434-6030
Fax: 202-434-6466

AARP's Consumer Issues Section advocates on behalf of older consumers, develops and distributes consumer information, and educates the private sector about the specific needs of older consumers. Programs and materials on housing, insurance, funeral practices, eligibility for public benefits, financial security, transportation, and consumer protection issues are offered, with special focus on the needs and problems of older consumers.

American Council on Consumer Interests (ACCI)
240 Stanley Hall
University of Missouri
Columbia, MO 65211
573-882-3817
Fax: 573-884-6571
Web site: acci.ps.missouri.edu
E-mail: acci@showme.
   missouri.edu

Serving the professional needs of consumer educators, researchers and policy-makers, ACCI publications and educational programs foster the production, synthesis, and dissemination of information about consumer interests.

American Council on Science and Health (ACSH)
1995 Broadway, 2nd Floor
New York, NY 10023-7044
212-362-7044
Fax: 212-362-4919

Web site: www.acsh.org
E-mail: acsh@acsh.org

A nonprofit public education group, ACSH's goal is to provide consumers with up-to-date, scientifically sound information on the relationship between human health and a variety of factors, including: chemicals, food, lifestyles, and the environment. Booklets and special reports on a variety of topics are available, as is a quarterly magazine, *Priorities.*

Center for Science in the Public Interest (CSPI)
1875 Connecticut Avenue, NW
Suite 300
Washington, DC 20009
202-332-9110
Fax: 202-265-4954
E-mail: cspi@cspinet.org

A nonprofit membership organization, CSPI conducts research, education, and advocacy on nutrition, health, food safety, and related issues, and publishes the monthly "Nutrition Action Health Letter," as well as other consumer information materials.

Citizen Action
1900 L Street NW
Suite 602
Washington, DC 20036
202-775-1580
Fax: 202-296-4054

Citizen Action works on behalf of its three million members and thirty-four state organizations on health care reform, environment, energy, transportation, and civil rights issues.

Coalition Against Insurance Fraud
1511 K Street, NW, Suite 623
Washington, DC 20005
202-393-7330
Fax: 202-393-7329
Web site: www.Insurance Fraud.org

The Coalition Against Insurance Fraud is a national alliance of consumer groups, government agencies, and insurance companies dedicated to combating all forms of insurance fraud through advocacy and public information. It conducts research, develops public education programs, and publishes a consumer brochure, "How to Avoid Becoming a Victim of Insurance Fraud," which is available on request. It also refers consumers to appropriate agencies to report incidences of insurance fraud.

Community Nutrition Institute (CNI)
910 17th Street, NW
Suite 413
Washington, DC 20006
202-776-0595
Fax: 202-776-0599
E-mail: CNI@digex.net

An advocate for programs and services that enable consumers to enjoy a diet that is adequate, safe, and healthy, CNI also works to increase citizen participation in the state and federal policy and administrative processes to

181

achieve these goals. CNI publishes "Nutrition Week," a newsletter covering nutrition and food safety issues, as well as related legislative and regulatory actions.

Congress Watch
215 Pennsylvania Avenue, SE
Washington, DC 20003
202-546-4996
Fax: 202-547-7392
E-mail:
congresswatch@citizen.org

An arm of Public Citizen, Congress Watch works for consumer-related legislation, regulation, and policies in such areas as trade, health and safety, and campaign finance, and has publications available on these issues.

Consumer Action
717 Market Street, Suite 310
San Francisco, CA 94103
415-777-9635 (consumer complaint hotline, 10 A.M. to 2 P.M., PST)
213-624-8327 (hotline)
Fax: 415-777-5267
TTY: 415-777-9456
E-mail: info@consumer-action.org

Consumer Action assists consumers with marketplace problems. An education and advocacy organization specializing in credit, finance and telecommunications issues, Consumer Action offers a multilingual consumer complaint hotline, free information on its surveys of banks and long-distance telephone companies, and consumer education materials in as many as eight languages.

Consumer Federation of America (CFA)
1424 16th Street, NW
Suite 604
Washington, DC 20036
202-387-6121
Fax: 202-265-7989

Comprised of more than 240 organizations representing a membership exceeding fifty million consumers, CFA is a consumer advocacy and education organization. Issues on which it currently represents consumer interests before Congress and federal regulatory agencies include: telephone service, insurance and financial services, product safety, indoor air pollution, health care, product liability, and utility rates. It develops and distributes studies of various consumer issues, as well as consumer guides in book and pamphlet form. In addition, CFA publishes several newsletters.

Consumers for World Trade (CWT)
2000 L Street, NW
Suite 200
Washington, DC 20036
202-785-4835
Fax: 202-416-1734
Web site: www.cwt.org
E-mail: cwt@cwt.org

A nonprofit organization, CWT supports trade expansion and liberalization to promote economic growth and increase consumer choice and price competition in the marketplace. Various publications are available.

Families USA Foundation
1334 G Street, NW
Suite 300
Washington, DC 20005-3169
202-628-3030
Fax: 202-347-2417
Web site: www.familiesusa.org
E-mail: info@familiesusa.org

A national, nonprofit membership
organization committed to comprehensive reform of health and
long-term care, Families USA
works to educate and mobilize
consumers on health care issues.
In addition to its two grass roots
advocacy networks—asap!, a network of health and long-term care
reform activists, and HealthLink
USA, a nationwide health reform
computer network for public
interest groups—Families USA
develops and distributes reports
and other materials on health and
long-term care issues.

**HALT: An Organization of
Americans for Legal Reform**
1612 K Street, NW
Suite 520
Washington, DC 20006
202-887-8355
Fax: 202-887-9699
Web site: www.halt.org

HALT's mission is to enable
Americans to handle their legal
affairs affordably, equitably, and
simply. HALT publishes a series of
self-help legal manuals, operates
a legal information clearinghouse,
and advocates for legal reforms
which will benefit consumers.

Health Research Group (HRG)
1600 20th Street, NW
Washington, DC 20009
202-588-1000
Web site: www.citizen.org/hrg

A division of Public Citizen, HRG
works for protection against
unsafe foods, drugs, medical
devices, and workplaces, and
advocates for greater consumer
control over personal health decisions. A monthly "Health Letter"
and a monthly letter on prescrip-
tion drugs are available.

Jump$tart Coalition
919 18th Street, NW
Washington, DC 20006
Toll free: 1-888-400-2233
Fax: 202-223-0321

The Coalition's direct objective is
to encourage curriculum enrich-
ment to ensure that basic personal financial management skills
are attained during the K-12
years.

NACAA
1010 Vermont Avenue, NW
Suite 514
Washington, DC 20005
202-347-7395
Fax: 202-347-2563
E-mail: nacaa@erols.com

An association of administrators
of local, state, and federal consumer protection agencies,
NACAA provides training programs, public policy studies and
conferences, professional publications, and other member services.

* 183 *

National Coalition for Consumer Education (NCCE)
295 Main Street, Suite 200
P.O. Box 576
Madison, NJ 07040
973-377-8987
Fax: 973-377-4828
Web site: www.lifesmarts.org
E-mail: ncce@gti.net

NCCE is a national, nonprofit organization, which owns and sponsors LifeSmarts, a game-show style competition open to all teens in the United States in the ninth through the twelfth grade. NCCE develops and provides educational materials and resources to consumer educators through a network of state coordinators, but does not handle requests from individuals.

National Community Reinvestment Coalition (NCRC)
733 15th Street, NW
Suite 540
Washington, DC 20005
202-628-8866
Fax: 202-628-9800
Web site: www.youthlink.net/ncrc

NCRC was founded in 1990 with the goal of ending discriminatory banking practices and increasing the flow of private capital and credit into underserved communities across the country. NCRC has over six hundred members in every state and major city in America, as well as in many smaller cities and rural areas.

National Consumer Law Center (NCLC)
18 Tremont Street
Boston, MA 02108
617-523-8010
Fax: 617-523-7398
Web site: www.consumerlaw.org
E-mail: consumerlaw@nclc.org

NCLC is an advocacy and research organization focusing on the needs of low-income consumers. It represents the interests of consumers in court, as well as before administrative agencies and legislatures. The Center also publishes *Surviving Debt: A Guide for Consumers and the Consumer Credit* and the *Sales Legal Practice Series* consisting of thirteen desk reference manuals for attorneys.

National Consumers League (NCL)
1701 K Street, NW
Suite 1200
Washington, DC 20006
202-835-3323
Fax: 202-835-0747
Web site: www.natlconsumers league.org
E-mail: nclncl@aol.com

Founded in 1899, the NCL is America's pioneer consumer advocacy organization. The league is a nonprofit membership organization working for health, safety, and fairness in the marketplace and workplace. Current principal issue areas include consumer fraud, food and drug safety, fair labor standards, child labor, health care, the environment, financial services, and telecommunications. The league develops and distributes consumer education materials and newsletters.

National Fraud Information Center (NFIC)
P.O. Box 65868
Washington, DC 20035
Toll free: 1-800-876-7060 (9 A.M. to 8 P.M. M-F EST; TDD available)
Fax: 202-835-0767
TDD/TTY: 202-835-0778
Web site: www.fraud.org
E-mail: fraudinfo@psinet.com

NFIC assists consumers with recognizing and filing complaints about telemarketing and Internet fraud. A project of the National Consumers League, the center has a hotline that provides consumers with information to help them avoid becoming victims of fraud, refers consumers to appropriate law enforcement agencies and professional associations, and provides assistance in filing complaints. The center also provides professionals involved in consumer fraud prevention, and enforcement with telecommunications systems and data links to improve fraud regulation, prevention and law enforcement. Spanish-speaking counselors available.

National Institute for Consumer Education (NICE)
Eastern Michigan University
207 Rackham Building
Ypsilanti, MI 48197
313-487-2292

Fax: 313-487-7153
E-mail: nice@online.emich.edu

NICE is a consumer education resource and professional development center for K-12 classroom teachers, as well as business, government, labor, and community educators. NICE conducts training programs, develops teaching guides and resource lists, and manages a national clearinghouse of consumer education materials, including videos, software programs, textbooks, and curriculum guides.

Project OPEN (the Online Public Education Network)
c/o Interactive Services Association
8403 Colesville Road, Suite 865
Silver Spring, MD 20910
301-495-4955
Fax: 301-495-4959
Web site: www.isa.net/project-open
E-mail: project-open@isa.net

Project OPEN is a joint effort of the National Consumers League (NCL), the Interactive Services Association (ISA), and leading on-line/Internet service companies dedicated to helping consumers use the Internet in an informed and responsible way. Publications provide basic information for parents and educators about going on-line and dealing with privacy issues.

Public Citizen, Inc.
1600 20th Street, NW
Washington, DC 20009
202-588-1000

A national, nonprofit membership
organization representing consumer interests through lobbying,
litigation, research, and publications, Public Citizen represents
consumer interests in Congress,
the courts, government agencies,
and the media. Primary current
areas of interest include product
liability, health care delivery, safe
medical devices and medications,
open and ethical government, and
safe and sustainable energy
use.

**Public Voice for Food and Health
Policy**
1012 14th Street, NW
Washington, DC 20005
202-347-5200
E-mail: pvoice@ix.netcom.com

A national research, education,
and advocacy organization, Public
Voice works for food and agriculture policies and practices that
promote a safe, healthy, afford-
able food supply, while protecting
the environment. Public Voice
develops and distributes consumer information materials on
pesticide reduction, nutrition,
labeling, seafood safety, and
inner-city food access.

**United Seniors Health
Cooperative (USHC)**
1313 H Street NW, Suite 500
Washington, DC 20005
Fax: 202-783-0588

Web site: www.ushc-online.org
E-mail: 103134.2627@com
    puserve.com

USHC is a nonprofit, membership
organization that provides consumer tested information to help
seniors achieve good health, inde-
pendence, and financial security.
Publications include books on
long-term care planning, managing health care finances, and
choosing an HMO. Professionals
working with low-income persons
of all ages will find USHC's benefit
screening software valuable for a
quick, comprehensive determination of a person's eligibility for
public benefits and assistance
programs.

**U.S. Public Interest Research
Group (U.S. PIRG)**
218 D Street, SE
Washington, DC 20003-1900
202-546-9707
202-546-2461
Web site: www.pirg.org
E-mail: uspirg@pirg.org

U.S. PIRG is the national lobbying
office for state public interest
research groups. PIRGs are consumer environmental advocacy
groups active in many states
across the country. U.S. PIRG
works on a variety of consumer
and environmental protection
issues, including bank fees, credit
bureau abuses, clean air and
clean water, right to know, campaign finance reform, and various
other issues. U.S. PIRG does not
handle individual consumer complaints directly, but measures

complaint levels to gauge the need
for remedial legislation.

Source: *1998–99 Consumer's
Resource Handbook*, United States
General Services Administration
Consumer Information Center
http://www.pueblo.gsa.gov/crh/
    crh.txt

State Securities Administrators

Each state has its own laws and regulations for securities brokers
and for all types of securities, including: stocks, mutual funds, com-
modities, real estate offerings, uninsured investment products sold
by banks, and others. The officials and agencies listed below
enforce these laws and regulations. Many of these offices can provide you with information to help you make informed investment
decisions. State securities agencies are also responsible for pre-
venting fraud and abuse in the sale of all but the largest securities
offerings.

187

Alabama

Director
Securities Commission
770 Washington Street, Suite 570
Montgomery, AL 36130-4700
334-242-2984
Toll free in AL: 1-800-222-1253
Fax: 334-242-0240
E-mail: alseccone@dsmd.
    dsmd.state.al.us

Alaska

Senior Examiner
Department of Commerce and
    Economic Development
P.O. Box 110807
Juneau, AK 99811-0807
907-465-2521
Fax: 907-465-2549

Arizona

Investigator on Duty
Corporation Commission
Securities Division
1300 West Washington
3rd Floor
Phoenix, AZ 85007
602-542-4242
Fax: 602-594-7470
E-mail: accsec@ccsd.cc.
    state.az.us.
Web site: www.cc.state.az.us

Arkansas

Commissioner
Securities Division
Heritage West Building
201 East Markham, 3rd Floor
Little Rock, AR 72201-1692
501-324-9260
Fax: 501-324-9268
E-mail: arsec@ccon.net

California

Commissioner
Department of Corporations
3700 Wilshire Boulevard
Suite 600
Los Angeles, CA 90010-3001
213-736-2741
Toll free: 1-800-400-0815 (Health
    Plan issues only)
Fax: 213-736-2117
Web site: www.corp.ca.gov

Colorado

Securities Commissioner
Division of Securities
1580 Lincoln
Suite 420
Denver, CO 80203-1506
303-894-2320
Fax: 303-861-2126
TDD: 303-894-7880

Connecticut

Banking Commissioner
Department of Banking
260 Constitution Plaza
Hartford, CT 06103-1800
860-240-8299
Toll free: 1-800-831-7225
Fax: 860-240-8178
Web site: www.state.ct.us

Delaware

Securities Commissioner
Department of Justice
Division of Securities
State Office Building
820 North French Street, 5th
    Floor
Wilmington, DE 19801
302-577-8424
Fax: 302-655-0576
E-mail: pdailey@state.de.us

District of Columbia

Acting Director
Office of Consumer Services
D.C. Public Service Commission
717 14th Street, NW
Washington, DC 20005
202-626-5152
Fax: 202-393-1389
TDD/TTY: 202-638-2428
E-mail: fjames@bellatlantic.net

Florida

Comptroller
Division of Securities
101 East Gaines Street
Tallahassee, FL 32399-0350
850-410-9805
Toll free in FL: 1-800-372-3792
Fax: 850-681-2428

Georgia

Secretary of State
Divison of Securities and Business
    Regulation
Two Martin Luther King, Jr. Drive
West Tower, Suite 802
Atlanta, GA 30334
404-656-3920
Fax: 404-657-8410

Hawaii

Commissioner of Securities
Department of Commerce and
   Consumer Affairs
P.O. Box 40
Honolulu, HI 96810
808-586-2744
808-586-2740 (Securities
   Enforcement Unit)
Fax: 808-586-2733
Web site: www.hawaii.gov/dbedt

Idaho

Bureau Chief
Securities Bureau
P.O. Box 83720
Boise, ID 83720-0031
208-332-8004
Toll free in ID: 1-888-346-3378
Fax: 208-332-8099
E-mail: mscanlan@fin.state.id.us
Web site: www.state.id.us/
   finance/dof.htm

Consumer Credit Supervisor
Department of Finance
P.O. Box 83720
Boise, ID 83720-0031
208-332-8002
Fax: 208-332-8098

Illinois

Director
Illinois Securities Department
Office of Secretary of State
Lincoln Tower, Suite 200
520 South Second Street
Springfield, IL 62701
217-782-2256
Toll free in IL: 1-800-628-7937
Fax: 217-524-9637
Web site: www.sos.state.il.us

Indiana

Securities Commissioner
Office of the Secretary of State,
   Securities Division
302 West Washington
Room E-111
Indianapolis, IN 46204
317-232-6681
Toll free in IN: 1-800-223-8791
Fax: 317-233-3675
Web site: www.ai.org/sos

Iowa

Enforcement Section
Securities Bureau
Lucas State Office Building
2nd Floor
Des Moines, IA 50319
515-281-4441
Fax: 515-281-6467
E-mail: iowasec@max.state.ia.us
Web site: www.state.ia.us/
   government/com/ins/security/
   security.htm

Kansas

Securities Commissioner
Office of the Securities
   Commissioner
618 South Kansas Avenue
Topeka, KS 66603-3804
913-296-3307
Toll free in KS: 1-800-232-9580
Fax: 913-296-6872
E-mail: ksecom@cjnetworks.com
Web site: www.cjnetworks.
   com/~ksecom

Kentucky

Commissioner
Department of Financial
  Institutions
477 Versailles Road
Frankfort, KY 40601-3868
502-573-3390
Toll free: 1-800-223-2579
Fax: 502-573-8787
Web site: www.dfi.state.ky.us

Louisiana

Deputy Commissioner of
  Securities
Office of Financial Institutions
Securities Division
8660 United Plaza Boulevard, 2nd
  Floor
Baton Rouge, LA 70809
504-925-4512

Maine

Securities Administrator
Securities Division
121 State House Station
Augusta, ME 04333
207-624-8551
Fax: 207-624-8590

Maryland

Securities Commissioner
Office of the Attorney General
Division of Securities
200 Saint Paul Place, 20th Floor
Baltimore, MD 21202-2020
410-576-6360
Fax: 410-576-6532
TDD: 410-576-6372
E-mail: securities@oag.state.
  md.us

Massachusetts

Secretary of the Commonwealth
Securities Division
One Ashburton Place
Room 1701
Boston, MA 02108
617-727-3548
Toll free in MA: 1-800-269-5428
Fax: 617-248-0177

Michigan

Director
Corporation Securities and Land
  Development Bureau
P.O. Box 222
Lansing, MI 48909
517-334-6213
Fax: 517-334-6155
Web site: www.cis.state.mi.
  us/corp/

Minnesota

Commissioner of Commerce
Department of Commerce
133 East Seventh Street
St. Paul, MN 55101
612-296-4026
Toll free in MN: 1-800-657-3602
Fax: 612-296-4328
TDD: 612-296-2860

Mississippi

Assistant Secretary of State for
  Business Services
P.O. Box 136 (39205)
202 North Congress Street
Suite 601
Jackson, MS 39201
601-359-6371
Fax: 601-359-2894

Missouri

Commissioner of Securities
P.O. Box 1276
Jefferson City, MO 65102
573-751-4136
Toll free in MO: 1-800-721-7996
Fax: 573-526-3124
Web site: www.mose.sos.
  state.mo.us

Montana

State Auditor & Securities
  Commissioner
Office of the State Auditor
Securities Department
P.O. Box 4009
Helena, MT 59604
406-444-2040
Toll free in MT: 1-800-332-6148
Fax: 406-444-3497

Nebraska

Assistant Director
Department of Banking & Finance
Bureau of Securities
P.O. Box 95006
Lincoln, NE 68509-5006
402-471-2171
E-mail: jackh@bkg.state.ne.us
Web site: www.ndof.org

Nevada

Deputy Secretary of State
Office of the Secretary of State,
  Securities Division
555 East Washington Avenue
Suite 5200
Las Vegas, NV 89101
702-486-2440

Toll free nationwide: 1-800-758-
  6440
Fax: 702-486-2452

New Hampshire

Director of Securities
Bureau of Securities Regulation
Department of State
State House, Room 204
Concord, NH 03301-4989
603-271-1463
Fax: 603-271-7933
TDD/TTY toll free in NH: 1-800-
  735-2964

New Jersey

Bureau Chief, Department of Law
  and Public Safety
Division of Consumer Affairs
Bureau of Securities
P.O. Box 47029
Newark, NJ 07101
201-504-3600
Fax: 201-504-3601

New Mexico

Deputy Director
Regulation & Licensing
  Department
Securities Division
725 St. Michaels Drive
Santa Fe, NM 87505-7605
505-827-7140 (general informa-
  tion)
Fax: 505-984-0617

191

New York

New York State Department of
 Law
Bureau of Investor Protection and
 Securities
Office of the Attorney General
120 Broadway, 23rd Floor
New York, NY 10271
212-416-8200 (securities, stock
 and bonds only)
Fax: 212-416-8816

North Carolina

Secretary of State
Securities Division
300 North Salisbury Street
Raleigh, NC 27603-5909
919-733-3924
Toll free: 1-800-688-4507
 (investor hotline)
Fax: 919-821-0818
Web site: www.state.nc.us/
 secstate/

North Dakota

Office of the Securities
 Commissioner
600 East Boulevard
Bismarck, ND 58505-0510
701-328-4698
Toll free in ND: 1-800-297-5124
Fax: 701-255-3113

Ohio

Commissioner
Division of Securities
77 South High Street
Columbus, OH 43215
614-644-7381
Toll free: 1-800-788-1194
 (investor protection hotline)

Fax: 614-466-3316
Web site: www.securities.
 state.oh.us

Oklahoma

Administrator
Department of Securities
First National Center
120 North Robinson, Suite 860
Oklahoma City, OK 73102
405-280-7700
Fax: 405-280-7742
E-mail: ods.general@oklaoss.
 state.ok.us
Web site: lklaoss.state.ok.us/~osc

Oregon

Administrator
Department of Consumer and
 Business Services
Division of Finance & Corporate
 Securities
350 Winter Street, NE, Room 21
Salem, OR 97310
503-378-4387 (Corporate
 Securities Section)
503-378-4140 (Finance Section)
Fax: 503-947-7862
E-mail: dcbs.dfcsmail@state.or.us
Web site: www.cbs.or.us/
 external/dfcs/index.html

Pennsylvania

Chairman
Securities Commission
Eastgate Office Building
1010 North 7th Street, 2nd Floor
Harrisburg, PA 17102-1410
717-787-8061
Toll free in PA: 1-800-600-0007
Fax: 707-783-5122

Puerto Rico

Commissioner
Office of the Commissioner of
    Financial Institutions
Securities Division
Centro Europa Building, Suite 600
1492 Ponce de Leon Avenue
San Juan, PR 00907-4127
787-723-3131
Fax: 787-723-4042

Assistant Securities Commissioner
Office of the Commissioner of
    Financial Institutions
Securities Division
Centro Europa Building, Suite 600
1492 Ponce de Leon Avenue
San Juan, PR 00907-4127
787-723-8403 (hotline)
787-723-3131
Fax: 787-723-3857

Associate Director Securities
Office of the Commissioner of
    Financial Institutions
Securities Division
Centro Europa Building, Suite 600
1492 Ponce de Leon Avenue
San Juan, PR 00907-4127
Hotline: 787-723-8403
Fax: 787-723-5838

Rhode Island

Associate Director and
    Superintendent of Securities
Department of Business
    Regulation
233 Richmond Street
Suite 232
Providence, RI 02903-4232
401-277-3048
Fax: 401-273-5202
TDD: 401-277-2223

South Carolina

Deputy of Security Commission
Department of State
Securities Division
1000 Assembly Street
Columbia, SC 29201
803-734-9916
Fax: 803-734-2164

South Dakota

Enforcement Director
Division of Securities
118 West Capitol Avenue
Pierre, SD 57501-2017
605-773-4823
Fax: 605-773-5953

Tennessee

Assistant Commissioner
Department of Commerce and
    Insurance
Securities Division
Davy Crockett Tower, Suite 680
500 James Robertson Parkway
Nashville, TN 37243-0485
615-741-2947
Toll free in TN: 1-800-863-9117
Fax: 615-532-8375

Texas

Securities Commissioner
State Securities Board
P.O. Box 13167
Austin, TX 78711-3167
512-305-8300
Fax: 512-305-8310
Web site: www.ssb.state.tx.us

Utah

Director, Securities Division
Department of Commerce
P.O. Box 146760
Salt Lake City, UT 84114-6760
801-530-6600
Toll free in UT: 1-800-721-SAFE
Fax: 801-530-6980
Web site: www.commerce.
　state.ut.us

Vermont

Deputy Commissioner
Department of Banking,
　Insurance and Securities
89 Main Street, Drawer 20
Montpelier, VT 05620-3101
802-828-3420
Fax: 802-828-2896
E-mail: rcortese@bishca.
　state.vt.us
Web site: www.state.vt.us/bis

Virginia

Director
State Corporation Commission
Division of Securities and Retail
　Franchising
P.O. Box 1197
Richmond, VA 23218
804-371-9051
Toll free in VA: 1-800-552-7945
Fax: 804-371-9911
TDD: 804-371-9203
Web site: www.state.va.us/scc

Washington

Administrator
Department of Financial
　Institutions
Securities Division

P.O. Box 9033
Olympia, WA 98507-9033
360-902-8760
Fax: 360-586-5068
TDD: 360-664-8126
Web site: www.wa.gov/dfi/
　securities

West Virginia

Deputy Commissioner of
　Securities
State Auditor's Office, Securities
　Division
State Capitol Building
1900 Kanawha Boulevard East,
　Bldg. 1, Room W-110
Charleston, WV 25305
304-558-2257
Fax: 304-558-4211

Wisconsin

Administrator
Department of Financial
　Institutions
Division of Securities
P.O. Box 1768
Madison, WI 53702-1768
608-266-3432
Toll free in WI: 1-800-47-CHECK
Fax: 608-256-1259
Web site: www.badger.state.
　wi.us/agencies/dfi

Wyoming

Secretary of State & Securities
State Capitol Building
Cheyenne, WY 82002-0020
307-777-7370
Fax: 307-777-5339
TDD: 307-777-5351
Web site: www.soswy.state.wy.us

Source: *1998–99 Consumer's Resource Handbook,* United States General Services Administration Consumer Information Center http://www.pueblo.gsa.gov/crh/ crh.txt

State Utility Commissions

State utility commissions regulate consumer service and rates for gas, electricity, and a variety of other services within your state. These services include rates for telephone calls and moving household goods. In some states, the utility commissions regulate water and transportation rates. Rates for utilities and services provided between states are regulated by the federal government. Many utility commissions handle consumer complaints. Sometimes, if a number of complaints are received about the same utility matter, they will conduct investigations.

Note: I personally have had excellent results complaining through utility commissions. Such commissions know the territory and seem to have a genuine interest in resolving complaints.

195

Alabama

President
Public Service Commission
P.O. Box 991
Montgomery, AL 36101-0991
Toll free in AL: 1-800-392-8050
   (Consumer Services office)
Fax: 334-242-0727 (Consumer
   Services office)

Alaska

Chairman
Alaska Public Utilities Commission
1016 West 6th Avenue
Suite 400
Anchorage, AK 99501-1963
907-276-6222
Toll free in AK: 1-800-390-2782
Fax: 907-276-0160

TDD: 907-276-4533
E-mail: apuc@commerce.state.
   ak.us
Web site: www.state.ak.us

Arizona

Commissioner
Arizona Corporation Commission
1200 West Washington Street
Phoenix, AZ 85007
602-542-4251
Toll free in AZ: 1-800-222-7000
Fax: 602-542-0752
TDD: 602-542-2105
E-mail: rjennings@cc.state.az.us
Website: www.cc.state.az.us

Arkansas

Chairman
Public Service Commission
P.O. Box 400
Little Rock, AR 72203-0400
501-682-1453
Toll free in AR: 1-800-482-1164
(complaints)
Fax: 501-682-5731

California

President
Public Utilities Commission
505 Van Ness Avenue, Room 5218
San Francisco, CA 94102
415-703-2782
Toll free in CA: 1-800-649-7570
(complaints)
Fax: 415-703-2532
TDD: 415-703-2032
Web site: www.cpuc.ca.gov/

Colorado

Chairman
Public Utilities Commission
Logan Tower, Office Level 2
1580 Logan Street
Denver, CO 80203
303-894-2000
Toll free in CO: 1-800-888-0170
Fax: 303-894-2065
TDD: 303-894-2512
E-mail: puconsumer.complaints@
dora.state.co.us
Web site: www.dora.state.
co.us/puc/

Connecticut

Chairman
Department of Public Utility
Control

10 Franklin Square
New Britain, CT 06051
860-827-1553
Toll free in CT: 1-800-382-4586
Fax: 860-827-2613
TDD: 860-827-2837
Web site: www.state.ct.us/dpuc/

Delaware

Commissioner
Public Service Commission
Cannon Building #100
861 Silver Lake Boulevard
Dover, DE 19904
302-739-4247
Toll free in DE: 1-800-282-8574
Fax: 302-739-4849
TDD: 302-739-4333
Web site: www.state.de.us

District of Columbia

Chairperson
Public Service Commission of D.C.
717 14th Street, NW
2nd Floor
Washington, DC 20005
202-626-5120 (Consumer
Services Division)
Fax: 202-638-1785
TDD: 202-638-2428

Florida

Chairman
Public Service Commission
2540 Shumard Oak Boulevard
Tallahassee, FL 32399-0850
850-413-6044
Toll free: 1-800-342-3552
Fax: 850-487-1716
E-mail: contact@psc.state.fl.us
Web site: www.scri.net/psc

Georgia

Commissioner
Public Service Commission
244 Washington Street, SW
Atlanta, GA 30334
404-656-4501
Toll free in GA: 1-800-282-5813
Fax: 404-656-2341
E-mail: dbaker@psc.state.ga.us
Web site: www.psc.state.ga.us

Hawaii

Chairman
Public Utilities Commission
465 South King Street, Room 103
Honolulu, HI 96823
808-468-4644
Fax: 808-586-2066

Idaho

President
Public Utilities Commission
P.O. Box 83720
Boise, ID 83720-0074
208-334-0300
Toll free in ID: 1-800-377-3529
Fax: 208-334-3762
TDD: 208-334-3151
E-mail: ipuc@puc.state.id.us
Web site: www.puc.state.id.us

Illinois

Chairman
Illinois Commerce Commission
527 East Capitol Avenue
P.O. Box 19280
Springfield, IL 62794-9280
217-782-7295
Fax: 217-782-1042
TDD: 217-782-7434
Web site: www.state.il.us/icc

Indiana

Director, Consumer Affairs
Utility Regulatory Commission
302 West Washington Street
Suite E-306
Indianapolis, IN 46204
317-232-2712
Toll free in IN: 1-800-851-4268
Fax: 317-233-6758
TDD: 317-232-8556
E-mail: mleppert@gwnet.isd.
    state.in.us
Web site: www.state.in.us/iurc

Iowa

Chairperson
Iowa Utilities Board
350 Maple Street
Des Moines, IA 50319
515-281-5979
Fax: 515-281-5329

Kansas

Chairman
Kansas Corporation Commission
1500 Southwest Arrowhead Road
Topeka, KS 66604-4027
785-271-3140
Toll free in KS: 1-800-662-0027
Fax: 913-271-3354
E-mail: public.affairs@kcc.
    state.ks.us
Web site: www.kcc.state.ks.us

197

Kentucky

Chairman
Public Service Commission
730 Schenkel Lane
P.O. Box 615
Frankfort, KY 40602
502-564-3940
Toll free in KY: 1-800-772-4636
    (complaints only)
TDD: 1-800-648-6056
Fax: 502-564-3460
Web site: www.state.ky.us/agency/
    psc/pschome.htm

Louisiana

Commissioner
Public Service Commission
P.O. Box 91154
Baton Rouge, LA 70821-9154
504-342-4404
Toll free in LA: 1-800-256-2413
Fax: 504-342-2831
Web site: www.lpsc.org/

Maine

Chairman
Public Utilities Commission
242 State Street
Augusta, ME 04333
207-287-3831
Toll free in ME: 1-800-452-4699
Fax: 207-287-1039
E-mail: maine.puc@state.me.us
Web site: www.state.me.us/mpuc/
TTY toll free relay: 1-800-437-
    1220

Maryland

Chairman
Public Service Commission
6 St. Paul Street
16th Floor
Baltimore, MD 21202-6806
410-767-8000
Toll free in MD: 1-800-492-0474
Fax: 410-333-6495
TDD toll free in MD: 1-800-735-
    2258
E-mail: mpsc@psc.state.md.us
Web site: www.psc.state.
    md.us/psc/

Massachusetts

Chairman
Department of
    Telecommunications & Energy
100 Cambridge Street
12th Floor
Boston, MA 02202
617-305-3500
Fax: 617-723-8812
TDD toll free: 1-800-323-3298
E-mail: holly.lechtur@state.ma.us
Web site: www.state.ma.us/
    dpu/index.htm

Michigan

Chairperson
Public Service Commission
6545 Mercantile Way, Suite 7
P.O. Box 30221
Lansing, MI 48909
517-334-6445
Toll free in MI: 1-800-292-9555
Fax: 517-882-5002
TDD toll free in MI: 1-800-649-
    3777
Web site: www.ermisweb.
    state.mi.us/mpsc

Minnesota

Manager, Consumer Affairs Office
Public Utilities Commission
121 7th Place East
Suite 350
St. Paul, MN 55101-2147
612-296-7124
Toll free in MN: 1-800-657-3782
Fax: 612-297-7073
TDD: 612-297-1200
E-mail: deborah@pucgate.puc.
    state.mn.us
Web site: www.state.mn.us/
    ebranch/puc/

Mississippi

Chairman
Public Service Commission
P.O. Box 1174
Jackson, MS 39215
601-961-5430
Toll free in MS: 1-800-356-6430
Fax: 601-961-5469
Web site: www.mslawyer.com/
    mpsc/mpsc.html

Missouri

Chairman
Public Service Commission
P.O. Box 360
Jefferson City, MO 65102
573-751-9300
Toll free in MO: 1-800-392-4211
Fax: 573-526-7341
TDD toll free in MO: 1-800-735-
    2966
Web site:
    www.ecodev.state.mo.us/psc/

Montana

Chair
Public Service Commission
1701 Prospect Avenue
P.O. Box 202601
Helena, MT 59620-2601
Toll free in MT: 1-800-646-6150
Fax: 406-444-7618
TDD: 406-444-6199
Web site: www.psc.mt.gov

Nebraska

Chairman
Public Service Commission
300 The Atrium, 1200 N Street
P.O. Box 94927 (68509-4917)
Lincoln, NE 68509
402-471-3101
Toll free in NE: 1-800-526-0017
Fax: 402-471-0254
TDD: 402-471-0213
E-mail: celton@navix.net
Web site: www.nol.org/
    home/NPSC

Nevada

Chairman
Public Utilities Commission
555 East Washington Avenue
Room 4500
Las Vegas, NV 89101
702-486-2600
Fax: 702-486-2595
Web site: www.state.nv.us/puc

199

New Hampshire

Chairman
Public Utilities Commission
8 Old Suncook Road
Building No. 1
Concord, NH 03301
603-271-2431
Toll free in NH: 1-800-852-3793
Fax: 603-271-3878
TDD toll free in NH: 1-800-735-2964
Web site: www.puc.state.nh.us

New Jersey

President
Board of Public Utilities
Two Gateway Center
Newark, NJ 07102
973-648-2823
Toll free in NJ: 1-800-624-0241
Web site: www.njin.net/njbpu/index.html

New Mexico

Chairman
New Mexico Public Utility
     Commission
Marian Hall
224 East Palace Avenue
Santa Fe, NM 87501-2013
505-827-6940
Toll free in NM: 1-800-663-9782
Fax: 505-827-6973
TDD: 505-827-6911
Web site: www.puc.state.nm.us

New York

Chairman
Public Service Commission
3 Empire State Plaza
Albany, NY 12223

518-474-2530
Toll free in NY: 1-800-342-3377
     (complaints—gas, electric, tele-
     phone)
Toll free in NY: 1-800-342-3330
     (complaints—cable)
Toll free in NY: 1-800-335-2120
     (PSC Opinion Line)
Toll free in NY: 1-888-ASKPSC-1
     (to get information)
Fax: 518-474-7146
TDD toll free in NY: 1-800-662-1220
Web site: www.dps.state.ny.us

North Carolina

Chairman
Utilities Commission
P.O. Box 29510
Raleigh, NC 27626-0510
919-733-9277 (consumer com-
     plaints)
Fax: 919-733-7300
Web site: www.ncuc.commerce.
     state.nc.us/

North Dakota

President
Public Service Commission
600 East Boulevard
12th Floor
Bismarck, ND 58505-0480
701-328-2400
Fax: 701-328-2410
TDD in ND: 1-800-366-6888
E-mail: msmail.sab@oracle.
     psc.state.nd.us
Web site: www.psc.state.nd.us

Ohio

Chairman
Public Utilities Commission
180 East Broad Street
Columbus, OH 43215-3793
614-466-3292
Fax: 614-466-7366
Toll free in OH: 1-800-686-7826
TDD: 614-466-8180
TDD toll free in OH: 1-800-686-1570
Web site: www.puc.ohio.gov/

Oklahoma

Chairman
Oklahoma Corporation
    Commission
Jim Thorpe Office Building
2101 North Lincoln Boulevard
Oklahoma City, OK 73105
405-522-2211
Toll free in OK: 1-800-521-8154
Fax: 405-521-2087
TDD: 405-521-3513
Web site: www.occ.state.ok.us

Oregon

Chairman
Public Utility Commission
550 Capitol Street, NE
Salem, OR 97310-1380
503-378-6611
Toll free in OR: 1-800-522-2404
    (consumer services only)
Fax: 503-378-5505
TDD toll free in OR: 1-800-553-9600
Web site: www.puc.state.or.us

Pennsylvania

Chairman
Public Utility Commission
P.O. Box 3265
Harrisburg, PA 17105
717-783-7349
Toll free in PA: 1-800-782-1110
Fax: 717-787-5813
TDD toll free: 1-800-782-1110
Web site: www.puc.paonline.com

Puerto Rico

Chairman
Public Service Commission
P.O. Box 190870
San Juan, PR 00919-0817
787-756-1425

Rhode Island

Chairman
Public Utilities Commission
100 Orange Street
Providence, RI 02903
Toll free in RI: 1-800-341-1000
Fax: 401-277-2883
TDD: 401-277-3500
Web site: www.ripuc.org

South Carolina

Chairman
Public Service Commission
P.O. Drawer 11649
Columbia, SC 29211
803-737-5100
Toll free in SC: 1-800-922-1531
Fax: 803-737-5199
TDD toll free in SC: 1-800-735-2905
Web site: www.psc.state.sc.us

South Dakota

Consumer Affairs Division
Public Utilities Commission
500 East Capitol Avenue
Pierre, SD 57501-5070
605-773-3201
Toll free: 1-800-332-1782
Fax: 605-773-3809
Web site: www.state.sd.us/
    state/executive/puc/puc.htm

Tennessee

Chairman
Tennessee Regulatory Authority
460 James Robertson Parkway
Nashville, TN 37243-0505
615-741-2904
Fax: 615-741-8953
TDD toll free in TN: 1-800-342-
    8359
E-mail: lgreeer@mail.state.tn.us
Web site: www.state.tn.us/tra

Texas

Chairman
Public Utility Commission
1701 North Congress Avenue
P.O. Box 13326
Austin, TX 78711-3326
512-936-7000
Toll free: 1-800-PUC-TIPS (782-
    8477)
Fax: 512-936-7003
TYY: 512-936-7136
E-mail: customer@puc.state.tx.us
Web site: www.puc.state.texas.
    gov/index.htm

Utah

Chairman
Public Service Commission
160 East 300 South
Salt Lake City, UT 84111
801-530-6716
Fax: 801-530-6796
Toll free in UT: 1-800-874-0904
TDD: 801-530-6706
E-mail: sfmecham@state.ut.us

Vermont

Chairman
Vermont Public Service Board
112 State Street
Montpelier, VT 05620-2701
802-828-2358
Fax: 802-828-3351
TDD toll free in VT: 1-800-253-
    0191
E-mail: clerk@psb.state.vt.us
Web site: www.state.vt.us/psb

Virgin Islands

Chairman
Public Services Commission
P.O. Box 861
St. Thomas, VI 00804
809-774-4750, ext. 2304
Fax: 809-776-4028

Virginia

Chairman
State Corporation Commission
P.O. Box 1197
Richmond, VA 23218
804-371-9141 (general info.)
Toll free in VA: 1-800-552-7945
Fax: 804-371-9211
TDD: 804-371-9206
Web site: www.state.va.us/scc

Washington

Chairman
Utilities and Transportation
    Commission
1300 South Evergreen Park Dr.,
    SW
Olympia, WA 98504
360-664-1173
Toll free in WA: 1-800-562-6150
Fax: 360-586-1150
TTY: 360-586-8203
Web site: www.wutc.wa.gov/

West Virginia

Chairman
Public Service Commission
201 Brooks Street
Charleston, WV 25323
Toll free in WV: 1-800-344-5113
Fax: 304-340-0325
TDD: 304-340-0300
Web site: www.state.wv.us/psc

Wisconsin

Consumer Affairs Program
    Director
Public Service Commission

610 North Whitney Way (53705)
P.O. Box 7854
Madison, WI 53707-7854
608-266-2001
Toll free: 1-800-225-7729
Fax: 608-266-3957
TDD: 608-267-1479
E-mail: lawrej@psc.state.wi.us
Web site: badger.state.wi.us/
    agencies/psc/

Wyoming

Chairman
Public Service Commission
2515 Warren Avenue
Suite 300
Cheyenne, WY 82002
307-777-7427
Toll free in WY: 1-800-877-9965
Fax: 307-777-5700
TTY: 307-777-7247
E-mail: sellen@missc.state.wy.us
Web site: psc.state.wy.us

* 203 *

Source: *1998–99 Consumer's
Resource Handbook*, United States
General Services Administration
Consumer Information Center
http://www.pueblo.gsa.gov/crh/
    crh.txt

Call for Action Locations

Call for Action, Inc. is a 35-year-old international nonprofit network of consumer hotlines, which operates in conjunction with broadcast partners to educate and assist consumers and small businesses with consumer problems. Listed below are hotlines in major markets staffed with trained volunteers who offer advice and mediate complaints at no cost to consumers. If there's no local listing, use the Bethesda location listed first below. This is an effective method of dealing with many consumer complaints because businesses usually detest negative media exposure. I have seen many complaints handled expeditiously via this service.

Call for Action, Inc.
5272 River Road, Suite 300
Bethesda, MD 20816
301-657-7490
Fax: 301-657-2914
Web site: www.callforaction.org
TDD/TTY: 301-657-9462

WTAJ-TV Call for Action
Altoona, PA
814-944-9336

WBZ-TV & Radio Call for Action
Boston, MA
617-787-7070

WIVB-TV Call for Action
Buffalo, NY
716-879-4900

WJW-TV Call for Action
Cleveland, OH
216-578-0700

WJR Radio/WXYZ-TV Call for
  Action
Detroit, MI
810-827-3362

WINK-TV Call for Action
Fort Myers, FL
941-334-4357

KCTV-5 Call for Action
Kansas City, MO
913-831-1919

WABC Radio Call for Action
New York, NY
212-268-5626

KYW-TV & Newsradio Call for
  Action
Philadelphia, PA
215-238-4500

KDKA Radio Call for Action
Pittsburgh, PA
412-333-9370

KTVI-TV Call for Action
St. Louis, MO
314-282-2222

KCBS Radio Call for Action
San Francisco, CA
415-478-3300

WTVG-TV Call for Action
Toledo, OH
419-534-3838

WTOP Newsradio Call for Action
Washington, DC
301-652-4357

Source: *1998–99 Consumer's
Resource Handbook*, United States
General Services Administration
Consumer Information Center
http://www.pueblo.gsa.gov/crh/
  crh.txt

Better Business Bureaus

Better Business Bureaus (BBBs) are nonprofit organizations supported primarily by local business members. The focus of BBB activities is to promote an ethical marketplace by encouraging honest advertising and selling practices, and by providing alternative dispute resolution.

BBBs offer a variety of consumer services. For example, they provide consumer education materials, answer consumer questions, provide information about a business (particularly about the existence of unanswered or unsettled complaints against the business or other marketplace problems), help resolve buyer/seller complaints against a business (including mediation and arbitration services), and provide information about charities and other organizations that are seeking public donations.

BBBs usually request that a complaint be submitted in writing so that an accurate record of the dispute exists. The BBB will then take up the complaint with the company involved. If the complaint cannot be satisfactorily resolved through communication with the business, the BBB may offer an alternative dispute settlement process, such as mediation or arbitration.

If you need help with a consumer question or complaint, call your local BBB to ask about its services. The Council of Better Business Bureaus, the umbrella organization for the BBBs, can assist with complaints about the truthfulness and accuracy of national advertising claims (including children's advertising) provide reports on national soliciting charities, and help to settle disputes with automobile manufacturers through the BBB AUTO LINE program.

205

Council

Council of Better Business
   Bureaus, Inc.
4200 Wilson Boulevard
Arlington, VA 22203
703-276-0100
Fax: 703-525-8277
Web site: www.bbb.org

Bureaus

Alabama

1210 South 20th Street
P.O. Box 55268 (35255-5268)
Birmingham, AL 35205
205-558-2222
Toll free: 1-800-834-5274 (in AL)
Fax: 205-538-2239
Web site: www.birmingham.
   bbb.org

1528 Peachtree Lane, Suite 1
Cullman, AL 35057
205-558-2222
Toll free: 1-800-824-5274 (in AL)
Fax: 205-538-2239

118 Woodburn
Dothan, AL 36305
334-794-0492
Toll free: 1-800-824-5274 (in AL)
Fax: 334-794-0659

205 South Seminary Street,
 Suite 114
Florence, AL 35630
205-740-8223

107 Lincoln Street, N.E.
P.O. Box 36804
Huntsville, AL 35801
205-533-1640
Fax: 205-533-1177
Web site: www.huntsville.bbb.org

100 North Royal Street
P.O. Box 2008 (36652-2008)
Mobile, AL 36602-3295
334-433-5494
Fax: 334-438-3191
Web site: www.mobile.bbb.org

Alaska

2805 Bering Street, Suite 5
P.O. Box 93550
Anchorage, AK 99503-3819
907-562-0704
Fax: 907-562-4061
Web site: www.anchorage.bbb.org

P.O. Box 74675
Fairbanks, AK 99707
907-451-0222
Fax: 907-451-0228

Arizona

4428 North 12th Street
Phoenix, AZ 85014-4585
900-225-5222
602-264-1721
Web site: www.phoenix.bbb.org

3620 North 1st Avenue, Suite 136
Tucson, AZ 85719
520-888-5353
Fax: 520-888-6262
Web site: www.tucson.bbb.org

Arkansas

1415 South University
Little Rock, AR 72204-2605
501-664-7274
Fax: 501-664-0024
Web site: www.arkansas.bbb.org

California

705 18th Street
P.O. Box 1311 (93302-1311)
Bakersfield, CA 93301
805-322-2074
Fax: 805-322-8318
Web site: www.bakersfield.
 bbb.org

315 North LaCadena
P.O. Box 970 (92324-0814)
Colton, CA 92324
900-225-5222
Fax: 909-825-6246
Web site: www.la.bbb.org

6101 Ball Road, Suite 309
Cypress, CA 90630-3966
900-225-5222
909-426-0813
Fax: 714-527-3208
Web site: www.la.bbb.org

2519 West Shaw, #106
Fresno, CA 93711
209-222-8111
Fax: 209-228-6518
Web site: www.fresno.bbb.org

3727 West Sixth Street, Suite 607
Los Angeles, CA 90020
900-225-5222
909-426-0813
Fax: 213-251-9984
Web site: www.la.bbb.org

510 16th Street, Suite 550
Oakland, CA 94612-1584
510-238-1000
Fax: 510-238-1018
Web site: www.oakland.bbb.org

400 S Street
Sacramento, CA 95814-6997
916-443-6843
Fax: 916-443-0376
Web site: www.sacramento.
  bbb.org

5050 Murphy Canyon Road, Suite
  110
San Diego, CA 92123
619-496-2131
Fax: 619-496-2141
Web site: www.sandiego.bbb.org

1530 Meridian Avenue, Suite 100
San Jose, CA 95125
408-445-3000
Fax: 408-265-4528
Web site: www.sanjose.bbb.org

400 South El Camino Real, Suite
  350
P.O. Box 294
San Mateo, CA 94401-0294
650-696-1240
Fax: 650-696-1250

213 Santa Barbara Street
P.O. Box 129 (93102-0129)
Santa Barbara, CA 93102
805-963-8657
Fax: 805-963-8556
Web site: www.santabarbara.
  bbb.org

11 South San Joaquin Street, Suite
  803
Stockton, CA 95202-3202
209-948-4880
Fax: 209-465-6302
Web site: www.stockton.bbb.org

Colorado

3022 North El Paso (80907-5454)
P.O. Box 7970
Colorado Springs, CO 80933-7970
719-636-1155
Fax: 719-636-5078
Web site: www.coloradosprings.
  bbb.org

1780 South Bellaire, Suite 700
Denver, CO 80222-4350
303-758-2100
Fax: 303-758-8321
Web site: www.denver.bbb.org

1730 South College Avenue
Suite 303
Fort Collins, CO 80525-1073
970-484-1348
Toll free: 1-800-571-0371 (in CO)
Fax: 970-221-1239
Web site: www.rockymnt.bbb.org

119 West 6th Street, Suite 203
Pueblo, CO 81003-3119
719-542-6464
Fax: 719-542-5229
Web site: www.pueblo.bbb.org

Connecticut

Parkside Building
821 North Main Street Ext.
Wallingford, CT 06492-2420
Fax: 203-269-3124/203-269-2700
Web site: www.connecticut.
  bbb.org

Delaware

1010 Concord Avenue, Suite 101
Wilmington, DE 19808-5532
302-594-9200
Fax: 302-594-1052
Web site: www.wilmington.
  bbb.org

District of Columbia

1012 14th Street, N.W., 9th Floor
Washington, DC 20005-3406
202-393-8000
Fax: 202-393-1198
Web site: www.dc.bbb.org

Florida

5830 142nd Avenue North, Suite B
  (34620)
P.O. Box 7950
Clearwater, FL 33758-7950
813-535-5522 (Pinellas County)
Toll free: 1-800-525-1447 (in FL)
Fax: 813-530-5863
Web site: www.clearwater.bbb.org

7820 Arlington Expressway, #147
Jacksonville, FL 32211
904-721-2288
Fax: 904-721-7373
Web site: www.jacksonville.
  bbb.org

921 East Gadsden (32501)
P.O. Box 1511
Pensacola, FL 32597-1511
850-429-0222
Fax: 850-429-0006
Web site: www.pensacola.bbb.org

1950 S.E. Port Street Lucie
  Boulevard, Suite 211
Port St. Lucie, FL 34952-5579
561-870-2010
Fax: 561-337-2083

580 Village Boulevard, Suite 340
West Palm Beach, FL 33409-1904
561-686-2200
Fax: 561-686-2775
Web site: www.westpalm.bbb.org

1011 North Wymore Road, Suite
  204
Winter Park, FL 32789-1736
407-621-3300
Toll free: 1-800-275-6614 (in FL)
Fax: 407-629-5167
Web site: www.orlando.bbb.org

Georgia

101 1/2 South Jackson, Suite 2
P.O. Box 808 (31702)
Albany, GA 31701
912-883-0744
Fax: 912-438-8222

P.O. Box 2707
Atlanta, GA 30301
404-688-4910
Fax: 404-688-8901
Web site: www.atlanta.bbb.org

301 7th Street (30901)
P.O. Box 2087
Augusta, GA 30903-2085
706-722-1574
Fax: 706-724-0969
Web site: www.augusta-
ga.bbb.org

208 13th Street
P.O. Box 2587 (31902-2587)
Columbus, GA 31901-2137
706-324-0712
Fax: 706-324-2181
Web site: www.columbus-
ga.bbb.org

277 Martin Luther King, Jr.
Boulevard, Suite 102
Macon, GA 31201-3476
912-742-7999
Fax: 912-742-8191
Web site: www.macon.bbb.org

6606 Abercorn Street, Suite 108-C
Savannah, GA 31405
912-354-7521 (9 am-1 pm, M-Th)
Fax: 912-354-5068
Web site: www.savannah.bbb.org

Hawaii

First Hawaiian Tower
1132 Bishop Street, 15th Floor
Honolulu, HI 98613-2822
808-536-6956
Fax: 808-523-2335
Web site: www.hawaii.bbb.org

Idaho

1333 West Jefferson
Boise, ID 83702-5320
208-342-4649
Fax: 208-342-5116
Web site: www.boise.bbb.org

1575 South Boulevard
Idaho Falls, ID 83404-5926
208-523-9754
Fax: 208-524-6190
Web site: www.idahofalls.bbb.org

Illinois

330 North Wabash Avenue, Suite
2006
Chicago, IL 60611
312-832-0500
Fax: 312-832-9985
Web site: www.chicago.bbb.org

3024 West Lake, Suite 200
Peoria, IL 61615-3770
309-688-3741
309-688-9496 (auto line)
Fax: 309-681-7290
Web site: www.peoria.bbb.org

810 East State Street, 3rd Floor
Rockford, IL 61104-1101
815-963-2222
Fax: 815-963-0329
Web site: www.chicago.bbb.org

Indiana

722 West Bristol Street, Suite H-2
P.O. Box 405 (46514-2988)
Elkhart, IN 46515-0405
219-262-8996
Fax: 219-266-2026
Web site: www.elkhart.bbb.org

4004 Morgan Avenue, Suite 201
Evansville, IN 47715-2265
812-473-0202
Fax: 812-473-3080
Web site: www.evansville.bbb.org

1203 Webster Street
Fort Wayne, IN 46802-3493
219-423-4433
Fax: 219-423-3301
Web site: www.fortwayne.bbb.org

22 East Washington Street, Suite 200
Victoria Center
Indianapolis, IN 46204-3584
317-488-2222
Fax: 317-488-2224
Web site: www.indianapolis.
   bbb.org

6111 Harrison Street, Suite 101
Merriville, IN 46410
219-980-1511
219-769-8053
Toll free: 1-800-637-2118 (in IN)
Fax: 219-554-2123
Web site: www.gary.bbb.org

207 Dixie Way North, Suite 130
South Bend, IN 46637-3360
219-277-9121
Fax: 219-273-6666

Iowa

852 Middle Road, Suite 290
Bettendorf, IA 52722-4100
319-355-6344
Fax: 319-355-0306

505 5th Avenue, Suite 950
Des Moines, IA 50309-2375
515-243-8137
Toll free: 1-800-202-1600 (in IA)
Fax: 515-243-2227
Web site: www.desmoines.bbb.org

505 6th Street, Suite 417
Sioux City, IA 51101
712-252-4501
Fax: 712-252-0285
Web site: www.siouxcity.bbb.org

Kansas

501 Southeast Jefferson, Suite 24
Topeka, KS 66607-1190
785-232-0454
Fax: 785-232-9677
Web site: www.topeka.bbb.org

328 Laura
P.O. Box 11707 (67201)
Wichita, KS 67211
316-263-3146
Fax: 316-263-3063
TDD/TTY toll free in KS: 1-800-
   856-2417
Web site: www.wichita.bbb.org

Kentucky

410 West Vine Street, Suite 340
Lexington, KY 40507-1629
606-259-1008
Toll free: 1-800-866-6668 (in KY)
Fax: 606-259-1639
Web site: www.lexington.bbb.org

844 South Fourth Street
Louisville, KY 40203-2186
502-583-6546
Toll free: 1-800-388-2222 (in KY)
Fax: 502-589-9490
Web site: www.louisville.bbb.org

Louisiana

1605 Murray Street, Suite 117
Alexandria, LA 71301-6875
318-473-4494
Fax: 318-473-8906
Web site: www.alexandria.bbb.org

2055 Wooddale Boulevard
Baton Rouge, LA 70806-1546
504-926-3010
Fax: 504-924-8040
Web site: www.batonrouge.
   bbb.org

3008 Park Avenue, Suite 204
Houma, LA 70364
504-868-3456
Toll free: 1-800-259-9766 (in LA)
Fax: 504-876-7664

100 Huggins Road
Lafayette, LA 70506
318-981-3497
Fax: 318-981-7559
Web site: www.lafayette.bbb.org

3941-L Ryan Street (70605)
P.O. Box 7314
Lake Charles, LA 70606-7314
318-478-6253
Fax: 318-474-8981
Web site: www.lakecharles.
   bbb.org

141 Desiard Street, Suite 808
Monroe, LA 71201-7380
318-387-4600
Fax: 318-361-0461
Web site: www.monroe.bbb.org

1539 Jackson Avenue, Suite 400
New Orleans, LA 70130-5843
504-581-6222
Fax: 504-524-9110
Web site: www.neworleans.
   bbb.org

3612 Youree Drive
Shreveport, LA 71105
318-861-6417
Toll free: 1-800-372-4222 (in LA)
Fax: 318-861-6426
Web site: www.shreveport.bbb.org

Maine

812 Stevens Avenue
Portland, ME 04013-2648
207-878-2715
Fax: 207-797-5818

Maryland

2100 Huntingdon Avenue
Baltimore, MD 21211-3215
900-225-5222
Fax: 410-347-3936
Web site: www.baltimore.bbb.org

Massachusetts

20 Park Plaza, Suite 820
Boston, MA 02116-4344
617-426-9000
Fax: 617-426-7813
Web site: www.bosbbb.org

293 Bridge Street, Suite 320
Springfield, MA 01103-1402
413-734-3114
Fax: 413-734-2006
Web site: www.springfield-
   ma.bbb.org

32 Franklin Street
P.O. Box 16555 (01601-6555)
Worcester, MA 01608-1900
508-755-2548
Fax: 508-754-4158
Web site: www.worcester.bbb.org

Michigan

40 Pearl, N.W., Suite 354
Grand Rapids, MI 49503
616-774-8236
Fax: 616-774-2014
Web site: www.grandrapids.
bbb.org

30555 Southfield Road, Suite 200
Southfield, MI 48076-7751
248-644-9100
Fax: 248-644-5026
Web site: www.detroit.bbb.org

Minnesota

2706 Gannon Road
St. Paul, MN 55116-2600
651-699-1111
Toll free: 1-800-646-6222
Fax: 651-699-7665
Web site: www.mnd.bbb.org
Serves both MN and ND.

Mississippi

4500 155 North, Suite 287
(39211)
P.O. Box 12745
Jackson, MS 39236-2745
601-987-8282
Toll free: 1-800-987-8280 (in MS)
Fax: 601-987-8285
Web site: www.mississippi.
bbb.org

Missouri

306 East 12th Street
Suite 1024
Kansas City, MO 64106-2418
816-421-7800
Fax: 816-472-5442
website: www.kansascity.bbb.org

205 Park Central East, Suite 509
Springfield, MO 65806-1326
417-862-4222
Fax: 417-869-5544
Web site: www.springfield-
mo.bbb.org

12 Sunnen Drive, Suite 121
St. Louis, MO 63143
314-645-3300
Fax: 314-645-2666
Web site: www.stlouis.bbb.org

Nebraska

3633 O Street, Suite 1
Lincoln, NE 68510-1670
402-476-5855
Fax: 402-476-8221
Web site: www.lincoln.bbb.org

2237 North 91st Plaza
Omaha, NE 68134-6022
402-391-7612
Fax: 402-391-7535
Web site: www.omaha.bbb.org or
www.omahafreenet.org/bbb/

Nevada

P.O. Box 44108 (89116-2108)
Las Vegas, NV 89116-2108
702-320-4500
Fax: 702-320-4560
Web site: www.lasvegas.bbb.org

991 Bible Way (89502)
P.O. Box 21269
Reno, NV 89515-1269
702-322-0657
Toll free: 1-888-350-4222
Fax: 702-322-8163
Web site: www.reno.bbb.org

New Hampshire

410 South Main Street, Suite 3
Concord, NH 03301-3483
603-224-1991
Fax: 603-228-9035
Web site: www.concord.bbb.org

New Jersey

400 Lanidex Plaza
Parsippany, NJ 07054-2797
973-581-1313
Fax: 973-581-7022
Web site: www.parsippany.
  bbb.org

1721 Route 37 East
Toms River, NJ 08753-8239
732-270-5577
Fax: 732-270-6739

1700 Whitehorse-Hamilton
  Square, Suite D-5
Trenton, NJ 08690-3596
609-588-0808
Fax: 609-588-0546
Web site: www.trenton.bbb.org

16 Maple Avenue, P.O. Box 303
Westmont, NJ 08108-0303
609-854-8467
Fax: 609-854-1130
Web site: www.westmont.bbb.org

New Mexico

2625 Pennsylvania, N.E., Suite
  2050
Albuquerque, NM 87110-3657
505-346-0110
Toll free: 1-800-873-2224 (in NM)
Fax: 505-346-2696
Web site: www.albuquerque.
  bbb.org

308 North Locke
Farmington, NM 87401-5855
505-326-6501
Fax: 505-327-7731
Web site: www.farmington.bbb.org

201 North Church, Suite 330
Las Cruces, NM 88001-3548
505-524-3130
Fax: 505-524-9624

New York

346 Delaware Avenue
Buffalo, NY 14202-1899
716-856-7180
Fax: 716-856-7287
Web site: www.buffalo.bbb.org

266 Main Street
Farmingdale, NY 11735-2618
900-225-5222
212-533-6200
Web site: www.newyork.bbb.org

257 Park Avenue South
New York, NY 10010-7384
900-225-5222
212-533-6200
Fax: 212-477-4912
Web site: www.newyork.bbb.org

Learbury Centre
401 North Salina Street
Syracuse, NY 13203
900-225-5222
Fax: 315-479-5754
Web site: www.syracuse.bbb.org

30 Glenn Street
White Plains, NY 10603-3213
900-225-5222
212-533-6200
Web site: www.newyork.bbb.org

213

North Carolina

1200 BB&T Building
Asheville, NC 28801-3418
704-253-2392
Fax: 704-252-5039
Web site: www.asheville.bbb.org

5200 Park Road, Suite 202
Charlotte, NC 28209-3650
704-527-0012
Fax: 704-525-7624
Web site: www.charlotte.bbb.org

3608 West Friendly Avenue
Greensboro, NC 27410-4895
336-852-4240
Fax: 336-852-7540
Web site: www.greensboro.bbb.org

3125 Poplarwood Court, Suite 308
Raleigh, NC 27604-1080
919-872-9240
Fax: 919-954-0622
Web site: www.raleigh.bbb.org

P.O. Box 69
Sherrils Ford, NC 28673-0069
828-478-5622
Fax: 828-478-5462

500 West 5th Street, Suite 202
Winston-Salem, NC 27101-2728
336-725-8384
Fax: 336-777-3727
Web site: www.winstonsalem.
    bbb.org

Ohio

222 West Market Street
Akron, OH 44303-2111
330-253-4590
Fax: 330-253-6249
Web site: www.akron.bbb.org

1434 Cleveland Avenue, N.W.
    (44703)
P.O. Box 8017
Canton, OH 44711-8017
330-454-9401
Toll free: 1-800-362-0494 (in OH
    and WV)
Fax: 330-456-8957
Web site: www.canton.bbb.org

898 Walnut Street
Cincinnati, OH 45202-2097
513-421-3015
Fax: 513-621-0907
Web site: www.cincinnati.bbb.org

2217 East 9th Street, Suite 200
Cleveland, OH 44115-1299
216-241-7678
Fax: 216-861-6365
Web site: www.cleveland.bbb.org

1335 Dublin Road, #30-A
Columbus, OH 43215-1000
614-486-6336
Fax: 614-486-6631
Web site: www.columbus-
    oh.bbb.org

40 West Fourth Street, Suite 1250
Dayton, OH 45402-1830
937-222-5825
Toll free: 1-800-776-5301 (local
    area only)
Fax: 973-222-3338
Web site: www.dayton.bbb.org

219 North McDonel (45801)
P.O. Box 269
Lima, OH 45802-0269
419-223-7010
Fax: 419-229-2029
Web site: www.wcohio.bbb.org

3103 Executive Pkwy., Suite 200
Toledo, OH 43606-1310
419-531-3116
Toll free: 1-800-743-4222 (north-
west OH and southeast MI)
Fax: 419-578-6001
Web site: www.toledo.bbb.org

25 Market Street
P.O. Box 1495
Youngstown, OH 44501-1495
330-744-3111
Fax: 330-744-7336
Web site: www.youngstown.
bbb.org

Oklahoma

17 South Dewey Avenue
Oklahoma City, OK 73102-2400
405-239-6081
Fax: 405-235-5891
Web site: www.oklahomacity.
bbb.org

6711 South Yale, Suite 230
Tulsa, OK 74136-3327
918-492-1266
Fax: 918-492-1276
Web site: www.tulsa.bbb.org

Oregon

333 S.W. Fifth Avenue, Suite 300
Portland, OR 97204
503-226-3981
Fax: 503-226-8200
Web site: www.portland.bbb.org

Pennsylvania

528 North New Street
Bethlehem, PA 18018-5789
610-866-8780
Fax: 610-868-8668

29 East King Street, Suite 322
Lancaster, PA 17602-2852
900-225-5222, 215-448-3870
Fax: 717-291-3241
Web site: www.easternpa.bbb.org

1608 Walnut Street, Suite 6
Philadelphia, PA 19103
900-225-5222, 215-893-3870
Fax: 215-893-9312
Web site: www.easternpa.bbb.org

300 6th Avenue, Suite 100-UL
Pittsburgh, PA 15222-2511
412-456-2700
Fax: 412-456-2739
Web site: www.pittsburgh.bbb.org

The Connell Building, Suite 407
129 North Washington Avenue
(18503-2204)
P.O. Box 993
Scranton, PA 18501-0993
717-342-9129
Fax: 717-342-1282
Web site: www.scranton.bbb.org

Puerto Rico

P.O. Box 363488
San Juan, PR 00936-3488
787-756-5400 (8:30 am-4:30 pm)
Fax: 787-758-0095
Web site: www.sanjuan.bbb.org

Rhode Island

120 Lavan Street
Warwick, RI 02888-1071
401-785-1212
Fax: 401-785-3061
Web site:
www.rhodeisland.bbb.org

South Carolina

2330 Devine Street (29205)
P.O. Box 8326
Columbia, SC 29202-8326
803-254-2525
Fax: 803-779-3117
Web site: www.columbia.bbb.org

307-B Falls Street
Greenville, SC 29601-2829
864-242-5052
Fax: 864-271-9802
Web site: www.greenville.bbb.org

1601 North Oak Street, Suite 101
Myrtle Beach, SC 29577-1601
843-626-6881
Fax: 843-626-7455
Web site: www.myrtlebeach.
    bbb.org

Tennessee

P.O. Box 1178 TCA
Blountville, TN 37617-1178
423-325-6616
Fax: 423-325-6621
Web site: www.knoxville.bbb.org

1010 Market Street, Suite 200
Chattanooga, TN 37402-2614
423-266-6144
Fax: 423-267-1924
Web site:
    www.chattanooga.bbb.org

2633 Kingston Pike, Suite 2
    (37919)
P.O. Box 10327
Knoxville, TN 37939-0327
423-522-2552
Fax: 423-637-8042
Web site: www.knoxville.bbb.org

6525 Quail Hollow, Suite 410
    (38120), P.O. Box 17036
Memphis, TN 38187-0036
901-759-1300
Fax: 901-757-2997
Web site: www.memphis.bbb.org

414 Union Street, Suite 1830
P.O. Box 198436
Nashville, TN 37219-8436
615-242-4BBB
Fax: 615-254-8356
Web site: www.nashville.bbb.org

Texas

3300 South 14th Street, Suite 307
Abilene, TX 79605-5052
915-691-1533
Fax: 915-691-0309
Web site: www.abilene.bbb.org

724 South Polk (79101)
P.O. Box 1905
Amarillo, TX 79105-1905
806-379-6222
Fax: 806-379-8206
Web site: www.amarillo.bbb.org

2101 South IH35, Suite 302
Austin, TX 78741-3854
512-445-2911
Fax: 512-445-2096
Web site: www.centraltx.bbb.org

P.O. Box 2988
Beaumont, TX 77701-2988
409-835-5348
Fax: 409-838-6858
Web site: www.beaumont.bbb.org

P.O. Box 3868
Bryan, TX 77802-4413
409-260-2222
Fax: 409-846-0276
Web site: www.bryan.bbb.org

216 Park Avenue
Corpus Christi, TX 78401
512-887-4949
Fax: 512-887-4931
Web site:
  www.corpuschristi.bbb.org

2001 Bryan Street, Suite 850
Dallas, TX 75201-3093
900-225-5222
214-740-0348
Fax: 214-740-0321
Web site: www.dallas.bbb.org

Northwest Plaza, Suite 1101
El Paso, TX 79901
915-577-0191
Fax: 915-577-0209
Web site: www.elpaso.bbb.org

1612 Summit Avenue, Suite 260
Fort Worth, TX 76102-5978
817-332-7585
Fax: 817-882-0566
Web site: www.fortworth.bbb.org

5225 Katy Freeway, Suite 500
Houston, TX 77007
900-225-5222, 713-867-4946
713-867-4944 (Spanish)
Fax: 713-867-4947
Web site: www.houston.bbb.org

916 Main Street, Suite 800
Lubbock, TX 79401-3410
806-763-0459
Fax: 806-744-9748
Web site: www.lubbock.bbb.org

10100 County Road, 118 West
P.O. Box 60206
Midland, TX 79711-0206
915-563-1880
Fax: 915-561-9435
Web site: www.midland.bbb.org

3121 Executive Drive (76904)
P.O. Box 3366
San Angelo, TX 76902-3366
915-949-2989
Fax: 915-949-3514
Web site: www.sanangelo.bbb.org

1800 Northeast Loop, 410, Suite
  400
San Antonio, TX 78217-5296
210-828-9441
Fax: 210-828-3101
Web site:
  www.sanantonio.bbb.org

3600 Old Bullard Road, #103-A
  (75701)
P.O. Box 6652
Tyler, TX 75711-6652
903-581-5704
Toll free: 1-800-443-0131 (in TX)
Fax: 903-534-8644
Web site: www.tyler.bbb.org

2210 Washington Avenue
Waco, TX 76701-1019
254-755-7772
Fax: 254-755-7774
Web site: www.waco.bbb.org

609 International Boulevard
  (78596)
P.O. Box 69
Weslaco, TX 78599-0069
956-968-3678
Fax: 956-968-7638
Web site: www.weslaco.bbb.org

4245 Kemp Boulevard, Suite 900
Wichita Falls, TX 76308-2830
817-691-1172
Toll free: 1-800-388-1778
Fax: 817-691-1174
Web site: www.wichitafalls.
  bbb.org

* 217 *

Utah

1588 South Main Street
Salt Lake City, UT 84115-5382
801-487-4656
Fax: 801-485-9397
Web site: www.saltlakecity.
    bbb.org

Vermont

(Contact Boston office)
Toll free: 1-800-4BBB-811 (802-
    Vermont only)
Web site: www.bosbbb.org

Virginia

586 Virginian Drive
Norfolk, VA 23505
757-531-1300
Fax: 757-531-1388
Web site: www.norfolk.bbb.org

701 East Franklin, Suite 712
Richmond, VA 23219
804-648-0016
Fax: 804-648-3115
Web site: www.richmond.bbb.org

31 West Campbell Avenue
Roanoke, VA 24011-1301
540-342-3455
Fax: 540-345-2289
Web site: www.roanoke.bbb.org

Washington

1401 North Union, #105
Kennewick, WA 99336-3819
509-783-0892
Fax: 509-783-2893

4800 South 188th Street, Suite
    222 (98188)
P.O. Box 68926
Sea Tac, WA 98168-0926
206-431-2222
Fax: 206-431-2211
Web site: www.seatac.bbb.org

508 West 6th Avenue, Suite 401
Spokane, WA 99204-2730
509-455-4200
Fax: 509-838-1079
Web site: www.spokane.bbb.org

32 North 3rd Street, Suite 410
P.O. Box 1584
Yakima, WA 98901
509-248-1326
Fax: 509-248-8026
Web site: www.yakima.bbb.org

Wisconsin

740 North Plankinton Avenue
Milwaukee, WI 53203-2478
414-273-1600
Toll free: 1-800-213-1002 (in WI)
Fax: 414-224-0081
Web site: www.wisconsin.bbb.org

Source: *1998–99 Consumer's
Resource Handbook*, United States
General Services Administration
Consumer Information Center
http://www.pueblo.gsa.gov/crh/
    crh.txt

The World's Best Bargain in Consumer Information

These publications are *free* if you have web access. If not, you can still order most of them for spare change. They're from the Consumer Information Center, a part of the federal government's General Services Administration. The web address is http://www.pueblo.gsa.gov. The mailing address is Consumer Information Center, Pueblo, Colorado 81009. I have listed a few that will be of special interest to readers of this book.

Money

At-Home Shopping Rights. How to deal with late deliveries, unordered merchandise, billing errors, and much more when making purchases by mail or phone order. 5 pp. (1994. OCA) 373E. 50¢.

Buying Time: The Facts about Pre-Paid Phone Cards. How to buy long distance telephone services in advance. 2 pp. (1997. FTC) 340E. 50¢.

Doing Your Taxes. Explains what tax forms to use, how to fill them out, where to send your return, and how to get free help. Lists the most common errors to watch for. 12 pp. (1995. TREA) 576E. Free.

Getting What You Pay For: Weights & Measures Tips for Consumers. Get the best buys on items sold by weight or measure (gasoline, groceries, firewood, etc.). Tells who to contact with problems or questions. 21 pp. (1993. DOC) 342E. 50¢.

Making Sense of Savings. How to compare the various types of bank accounts available.

Describes the different services and fees, and suggests questions to ask about interest rates and service charges. 12 pp. (1994. FRB) 343E. 50¢.

Swindlers Are Calling. Eight things you should know about telemarketing fraud, nine tipoffs that a caller could be a crook, and ten ways to avoid becoming a victim. 4 pp. (1990. CFTC/FTC) 346F. 50¢.

What You Should Know about Buying Life Insurance. Describes various types of life insurance with tips on choosing a company and agent and for making sure a policy meets your needs. 23 pp. (1995. HHS) 582F. Free.

Year 2000, Your Bank, and You. What's going to happen to your money on midnight January 1, 2000? Get the facts on what your bank is doing to prepare and how you can protect yourself with this guide. (1998. FDIC) 613F. Free.

219

Credit

Choosing & Using Credit Cards. Credit cards vary widely in their charges and how fees are calculated. Learn how to compare costs for the best deal. 5 pp. (1993. FTC) 345E. 50¢.

Consumer Handbook to Credit Protection Laws. Explains how consumer credit laws can help you apply for credit, keep up good credit standing, and complain about an unfair deal. 44 pp. (1993. FRB) 347F. 50¢.

Credit & Divorce. Compares the benefits and disadvantages of individual, joint, and "user" accounts. Steps to take if you divorce or separate. 2 pp. (1998. FTC) 348F. 50¢.

Fair Credit Reporting. How to find the credit bureau that has your report, how to dispute information, and who can get a copy of your report. 8 pp. (1997. FTC) 349F. 50¢.

Fair Debt Collection. Describes what debt collectors may and may not do if you owe money. How and where to complain if you are harassed, threatened, or abused. 2 pp. (1996. FTC) 350F. 50¢.

How to Dispute Credit Report Errors. Gives tips on correcting errors, registering a dispute, and adding information to your file. 2 pp. (1998. FTC) 351F. 50¢.

Shop . . . The Card You Pick Can Save You Money. Use the helpful chart of major credit card issuers to select the best card for you by comparing annual percentage rates, fees, and

other features. 18 pp. (1996. FRB) 353F. 50¢.

What Savvy Consumers Need to Know about Debit Cards. Explains how debit cards work and what to do if your debit card is lost or stolen. Includes ten tips on how to protect your card and a special form to keep track of card numbers. 7 pp. (1997. USDA) 583F. Free.

Saving and Investing

66 Ways to Save Money. Practical ways to cut everyday costs on transportation, insurance, banking, credit, housing, utilities, food, and more. 4 pp. (1995. HHS) 354F. 50¢.

Introduction to Mutual Funds. Explains what they are, how to compare them, what to consider before investing, and how to avoid common pitfalls. 15 pp. (1994. SEC) 356F. 50¢.

Invest Wisely. Basic tips to help you select a brokerage firm and representative, and to make and monitor an investment. Identifies questions to ask and warning signs to look for in order to avoid problems. 15 pp. (1994. SEC) 357F. 50¢.

Investment Swindles: How They Work & How to Avoid Them. Protect against illegal, but legitimate-sounding, telemarketing and direct mail offers. 22 pp. (1994. CFTC) 584F. Free.

Investors' Bill of Rights. Tips to help you make informed investment decisions. 7 pp. (1998. CFTC/USPS) 585F. Free.

Cars

Buying a New Car. Discusses pricing terms, financing options, and various contracts. Includes a worksheet to help you bargain. 2 pp. (1998. FTC) 302F. 50¢.

Buying a Used Car. Learn about your limited rights when buying a car from a dealer or private owner and about the "Buyer's Guide" sticker required by law on all used cars sold by a dealer. Also provides tips on what to watch out for when shopping for used cars. 16 pp. (1998. FTC) 303F. 50¢.

How to Get a Great Deal on a New Car. Step-by-step instructions for a proven negotiation technique that you can use to save money on your next car. 4 pp. (1996. USDA) 307F. 50¢.

Keys to Vehicle Leasing. Explains the difference between leasing and buying a car. Sample form shows required information on a lease agreement, as well as your rights and responsibilities. 6 pp. (1997. FRB) 308F. 50¢.

Travel

Fly-Rights. Advice for travelers on getting the best fares, what to do when faced with lost tickets and baggage, canceled or overbooked flights, and much more. 58 pp. (1994. DOT) 129F. $1.75.

Using Credit & Charge Cards Overseas. Explains how your credit is protected and how to get cash. Also discusses currency conversion and fees, tips on shopping, renting a car, making lodging and travel reservations, and airline travel. 16 pp. (1995. DOC) 367E. 50¢.

Some More Free Publications of Interest to Consumers

The Federal Trade Commission offers a variety of useful consumer-oriented publications. But a large number of their publications are written for businesses or banks, so picking what you want takes some effort. Luckily, I've done that for you. Here is a list of consumer-oriented publications available at http://www.ftc.gov

Advertising

Project Mailbox II: Wanted: The Bandit in Your Mailbox Campaign

Advertising and Marketing on the Internet: The Rules of the Road

When Yellow Pages Invoices Are Bogus

Automobiles

Auction Guides: Not So Hot Properties

Auto Service Contracts

Buying a New Car

Buying a Used Car Alert

Buying a Used Car

Car Ads: Reading between the Lines

Gas-Saving Products

Keys to Vehicle Leasing

Look before You Lease Alert

The Low-Down on High Octane Gasoline

223

Index!

Index